"Just like a cup of strong coffee, you can count on Tessa's book *Coffee Shop Devos* to perk up your day and rejuvenate your daily walk with God. These invigorating devotions will challenge you to go deeper with Christ, offering that espresso shot of faith you need every single day. It's a must-read!"

—Michelle Medlock Adams, bestselling author,
Get Your Spirit On! Devotions for Cheerleaders

"Tessa Emily Hall's *Coffee Shop Devos* is brewed to perfection! May we taste and see that the Lord is good as we seek Him each day and savor the flavors of the lessons found within the pages of this beautiful guide to God's Word."

—Emma Danzey Burnham, worship artist,
Polished Living Ministries

"*Coffee Shop Devos* is everything young ladies need to hear. From life truths to encouragements to examples from her own life, Tessa relates to these girls on a level that they understand and in a language that they understand: *coffee!*"

—Rayleigh Gray, associate editor and web manager,
Pursue Magazine

"Tessa's latest book is both relatable and relevant. She takes the reader beyond the surface of Scripture to deeper topics in an engaging yet readable style. I highly recommend this book to all the teens in my life."

—Bekah Hamrick Martin, author, *The Bare Naked Truth*

"Cheers to a fantastic devotional for teen girls! Relatable, honest, current, upbeat, and upfront, *Coffee Shop Devos* hits on the issues, concerns, and hearts of teen girls while offering simple yet thought-provoking prompts to grow your faith and live a life even more satisfying than the richest of mochas."

—Laura L. Smith, bestselling author

coffee shop DEVOS

coffee shop DEVOS

DAILY DEVOTIONAL
PICK-ME-UPS for TEEN GIRLS

TESSA EMILY HALL

BETHANYHOUSE
a division of Baker Publishing Group
Minneapolis, Minnesota

Published by Bethany House Publishers
11400 Hampshire Avenue South
Bloomington, Minnesota 55438
www.bethanyhouse.com

Bethany House Publishers is a division of
Baker Publishing Group, Grand Rapids, Michigan

Printed in the United States of America

ISBN 978-0-7642-3105-6

Library of Congress Cataloging-In-Publication Control Number: 2018935314

Cover design by Emily Weigel

Author is represented by Cyle Young of Hartline Literary Agency.

18 19 20 21 22 23 24   7 6 5 4 3 2 1

Dedicated to my cousins,
Bella, Ashton, Ava, and Emily.
As you're entering your teen years,
I pray you'll discover the fulfillment
that comes from pursuing
a lasting relationship with Jesus.

MENU

COFFEE RECIPES

Introduction

Steaming lattes. Foam that reaches to the rim of the mug. Aroma of coffee permeating the atmosphere. Buzz of chatter and croon of laid-back music.

There's something comforting and rejuvenating about spending time in a coffee shop—especially when it's with a friend. I often leave these coffee conversations inspired and equipped to tackle the rest of the day.

Doesn't sound too different than our morning times with Jesus, does it?

Our friendship with Him satisfies our yearning to be understood and accepted.

Our conversations with Him encourage us to be who He created us to be and inspire us to embrace our potential.

The peace, joy, and love we receive from having an intimate relationship with God give us the spiritual "caffeine" we need to conquer the remainder of the day.

Even if you've yet to experience the benefits that come from pursuing a relationship with Jesus, I hope you'll find the answer to your heart's longing for connection in this book. Because when I was a teen—which wasn't too many years ago—I searched for someone who could understand me. A female who had recently been in my shoes, experienced what I'd experienced, and could answer some of my toughest questions.

So pretend as though we're sitting across the table at a coffee shop. (What are you sipping on? A drink made from one of my coffee recipes in this book, perhaps?) No judgments or criticisms are exchanged; only meaningful conversation.

In the Menu portion of the Contents, choose your preferred devo flavor based on your current need. Then, allow me to share my heart about that topic based on Scripture. Each short devotional gives you the opportunity to reflect, pray, and apply it to your own life. You'll then have the opportunity to continue the conversation on social media using the hashtag #CoffeeShopDevos. (And yes, a selfie taken with your coffee or preferred beverage is more than welcome!)

These devos invite you into a conversation with Jesus—then they'll grow into a group conversation among your friends online. All in hopes that you'll discover for yourself the side effects that come from having a daily addiction to spiritual caffeine.

Because, let's face it: It's not fun to walk through the struggles of being a teen on your own.

So whip up one of the drinks from my coffee recipes in this book, then choose your devo flavor. I'll be waiting! (Sipping on my favorite hazelnut latte, of course.)

Tessa

Mocha

Inspiration for the Soul

Midnight Mocha

What could be better than the two rich indulgences—dark coffee and dark chocolate—*combined*? When I make mochas, it means it's time to relax and read a book, or work on my latest writing project.

If I could stir inspiration and creativity together in a mug, the result would be this midnight mocha.

INGREDIENTS

- 2 shots espresso (or 1/2 cup strong dark roast blend coffee)
- 2 tablespoons unsweetened dark cocoa
- 2 tablespoons sugar
- 1 cup whole milk

INSTRUCTIONS

1. Brew dark roast blend espresso (or coffee). If brewing coffee, add 1 tablespoon of dark cocoa to the coffee grounds.
2. Stir remaining dark cocoa and sugar into espresso (or coffee) and mix well.
3. Steam milk until frothy.
4. Pour milk into espresso (or coffee), using spoon to hold back froth.
5. Cap off mocha with layer of froth.
6. Optional garnish: whipped cream and a sprinkle of cocoa powder.

Bitter Cappuccino

Scripture to sip on

Trust in the Lord with all your heart;
do not depend on your own understanding.
Seek his will in all you do,
and he will show you which path to take.

Proverbs 3:5–6

LET'S CHAT ABOUT IT...

I have a hilarious family picture that was taken when I was ten. We were at a restaurant on a cruise, and every family member was smiling—except me. I was *not* happy.

Why?

A cappuccino.

Yep. A cappuccino—or rather, lack thereof—had the ability to ruin the perfect family photo.

I loved it when my parents let me sip their coffee. Cappuccinos were my favorite. When I saw it listed on the menu, I asked permission to order one. My parents told me I was too young and wouldn't like it anyway. Not getting my way made me grouchy—so when the photo was taken, I apparently didn't smile.

The next day, I begged my parents for a cappuccino. Again. They caved and ordered one, knowing I would learn a lesson. I took one sip—that was all I could handle. Where was the foam? The sugary milk? It left a bitter taste. Nothing like the kind I was familiar with.

Endless begging resulted in receiving exactly what I wanted, but I realized it wasn't what I wanted after all.

How many times do we insist on an answer to a prayer? Instead of begging, let's bring our requests to God, then trust His sovereignty with the end result. After all, He knows what's best for us.

And getting something He didn't have planned for us just might leave a bitter taste in our mouths.

LET'S THINK ABOUT IT...

Do you bring your requests to God and trust in His perfect will and timing?

....

....

....

....

LET'S PRAY ABOUT IT...

Lord, help me to learn how to place my prayer requests in your hands and trust you for the end result. Amen.

TODAY'S DARE

Keep a running list of your prayer requests. Later, you can look back and see how God answered your prayers—even if they weren't answered the way you had originally hoped.

A SHOT OF INSPIRATION

Father, if you are willing, please take this cup of suffering away from me. Yet I want your will to be done, not mine.

Luke 22:42

Join the convo! Inspired by today's chat? Share what you learned! Snap a photo of this book (or the drink you're sipping on), and spark a discussion on social media by answering this question:

Have you ever waited for God to answer a prayer, but now you're grateful it wasn't answered the way you'd originally hoped?

Be sure to use the hashtag #CoffeeShopDevos!

Above the Noise

Scripture to sip on

Quiet down before God,
be prayerful before him.

Psalm 37:7 MSG

LET'S CHAT ABOUT IT...

When I was a teen, there was a season when my schedule was *packed:* School. Homework. Cheer practice. Theater practice. Gymnastics. Church. Repeat. With so many activities, it's no wonder God is often squeezed out of the 24-hour frame! But I don't think there's a Scripture that says, "Seek God first . . . *only* if you have enough time." If we want to live the life He's called us to live, He must have first place in our lives.

Christ longs to have a relationship with us. An intimate relationship is only built when two can devote time and attention to each other. He longs for us to break away from the noise and draw close to His whisper.

I don't know about you, but I don't want to squeeze God into my life. I want Him to become my *entire* life. Not only because He deserves it, but because I want to remain in the center of His will. How will I know what that is if I don't seek Him first daily?

God's whisper of love breathes purpose into our lives and guides our steps. His whisper becomes louder than the other voices that clamor for our attention—but only when we first step away from the noise. Quiet ourselves before God.

And listen.

LET'S THINK ABOUT IT...

How can you draw away from the noise and build a relationship with Jesus?

LET'S PRAY ABOUT IT...

Lord, forgive me for getting so caught up in the hustle and bustle of life that I forget to spend time with you. Help me to hear your still, small voice. Amen.

TODAY'S DARE

I don't think it's a coincidence that the song "In Your Arms" by Meredith Andrews played on my radio as I started to write this devotion! These lyrics emphasize the importance of quieting yourself before God so you can hear Him. Listen to this song, then be silent and try to hear God's still, small voice.

A SHOT OF INSPIRATION

The problem is not that God hasn't spoken but that we haven't listened.

Max Lucado

Join the convo! Inspired by today's chat? Share what you learned! Snap a photo of this book (or the drink you're sipping on), and spark a discussion on social media by answering this question:

What's your advice to people who might struggle to find time to spend with God daily due to their busy schedules?

Be sure to use the hashtag #CoffeeShopDevos!

Half Caf, Half Decaf

I know all the things you do, that you are neither hot nor cold. I wish that you were one or the other! But since you are like lukewarm water, neither hot nor cold, I will spit you out of my mouth!

Revelation 3:15–16

LET'S CHAT ABOUT IT...

I'm picky when it comes to my coffee. I don't settle for a cup of brew that's weak. So, most mornings I use my Moka Express coffee maker. This requires more beans than the standard coffee maker does. I have to use both a decaf blend and a caffeinated blend to make my coffee; otherwise, I'd be jittery all day!

I have to admit—decaffeinated coffee isn't the same as a regular brew. Sure, it might have a similar taste, smell, and appearance. But give a cup to a coffee lover, and he or she will know it's not the real thing, even after one sip.

It might be okay to blend my coffee, but when it comes to being a Christian, I can't have a little of the world and a little of Jesus. It's an impossible mix. I will either be all for Jesus, or all for the world.

Let's be *caffeinated* Christians and chase after God with our whole hearts and in every aspect of our lives. Let's make it our goal to become so close to Christ that people can't help but notice something special and different in us. Even if they've only tasted "one sip." ;)

LET'S THINK ABOUT IT...

Do you think others can tell, based on the way you live your life, that you are a "caffeinated Christian"?

LET'S PRAY ABOUT IT...

Lord, I want to be a caffeinated Christian and live my life sold out for you in every area. You paid a huge sacrifice so I could enjoy a life fully committed to you. Amen.

TODAY'S DARE

The Bible is filled with analogies that illustrate lukewarm Christianity. Look up these Scriptures.

Revelation 3:15–17
1 John 2:15–16
Matthew 12:30
Matthew 5:13
James 3:10–12
1 John 3:10

A SHOT OF INSPIRATION

What a heartbreak it would be to live an "almost" Christian life, then "almost" get into heaven.

Greg Laurie

Join the convo! Inspired by today's chat? Share what you learned! Snap a photo of this book (or the drink you're sipping on), and spark a discussion on social media by answering this question:

What do you think it means to be "in the world but not of the world"? (See John 17:16.)

Be sure to use the hashtag #CoffeeShopDevos!

Spiritual Maturity

Scripture to sip on

Don't let anyone think less of you because you are young. Be an example to all believers in what you say, in the way you live, in your love, your faith, and your purity.

1 Timothy 4:12

LET'S CHAT ABOUT IT...

I'm the youngest of three girls in my family, as well as thirteen cousins. Because of that, any time I'm around my family, I think I'll always feel young, even when I'm old.

This bothered me when I was a teen. I didn't like the way my family treated me like a kid, despite the fact that I felt even older than my age. I wanted to prove to others that I was mature and wasn't just a kid. But I soon realized I didn't have to prove anything to them; instead, I could put this verse into action and be an example for them in the way I lived.

Maturity isn't measured by how intelligent you are or how many accomplishments you've achieved. It's measured by your walk with Christ. The way you love others and keep yourself from being influenced by the sin of the world.

As you develop in spiritual maturity, don't be surprised if your peers and family members begin to admire you for the example you set. They'll become attracted to you because of the way you shine for Him.

Then, if a stranger assumes you're older than you are, you can receive it as a compliment to your maturity in Christ!

LET'S THINK ABOUT IT...

How can you mature in your walk with Christ and set an example for others?

LET'S PRAY ABOUT IT...

Lord, show me how I can mature in you. I want people of all ages to see your light shine through me so I can set an example for them. Amen.

TODAY'S DARE

Do a favor for someone today. You can offer to go to the grocery store for your parents, take out the trash for your elderly neighbor, or help your sibling with their homework. Doing this will be an expression of God's love and an example of your spiritual maturity!

A SHOT OF INSPIRATION

Maturity in the Christian life is measured by only one test: how much closer to His character have we become?

Elyse Fitzpatrick

Join the convo! Inspired by today's chat? Share what you learned! Snap a photo of this book (or the drink you're sipping on), and spark a discussion on social media by answering this question:

Share about a time when you were treated differently because of your age.

Be sure to use the hashtag #CoffeeShopDevos!

It's Just a Season

Scripture to sip on

For everything there is a season,
a time for every activity under heaven.

Ecclesiastes 3:1

LET'S CHAT ABOUT IT...

Sixth grade was tough. The friends I had in elementary school separated into cliques and suddenly had a fascination with makeup, boys, and drama. Me? I didn't want to leave my childhood. During this year, the enemy attempted to make me believe something was wrong with me. I was "weird" because I was different from my peers.

When I came home from school one day, my mom presented me with a journal. The cover was inscribed with Ecclesiastes 3:1. The truth of this verse spoke straight to my heart. Mom told me that even though the year seemed endless, sixth grade was only a season. God could bring beauty even out of this cold season of my life.

I've clung to this verse since then. When I walk through a cold season, I remind myself it won't last forever. God sees the bigger picture and never leaves my side.

When we trudge through the dead of winter—when the cold is bitter and the sunlight seems far from reach—it can be tempting to lose hope and doubt the cold will ever cease. These are the times when we must remind ourselves that even when the seasons change, God remains the same, and His plan exceeds the pain we face.

Soon, the winter will end. Sunshine will replace the murky clouds. And blossoming flowers will replace the bitter memories of winter.

LET'S THINK ABOUT IT...

If you're walking through a cold season, what might God be trying to teach you?

_____

_____

_____

LET'S PRAY ABOUT IT...

Lord, thank you for never changing, even when my life is con-stantly in a state of change. I trust you see the big picture of my life. Amen.

TODAY'S DARE

The journal that my mom gave me served as my first prayer journal. Do you have one? If not, take a trip to your local Christian bookstore and find one.

A SHOT OF INSPIRATION

The Bible teaches that true joy is formed in the midst of the difficult seasons of life.

Francis Chan

Join the convo! Inspired by today's chat? Share what you learned! Snap a photo of this book (or the drink you're sipping on), and spark a discussion on social media by answering this question:

If you've experienced a cold season in the past, what truths did you learn, and how did it shape you into who you are today?

Be sure to use the hashtag #CoffeeShopDevos!

Adoration or Obligation?

Scripture to sip on

So now we can rejoice in our wonderful new relationship with God
because our Lord Jesus Christ has made us friends of God.

Romans 5:11

LET'S CHAT ABOUT IT...

Regardless of whether you're in a relationship or not, pretend for a
moment that you have a boyfriend. He doesn't love you, though. He's
dating you because his parents told him to.

This "boyfriend" takes you out Friday nights. He dresses his best
and frequently buys you gifts . . . but only because he feels like he's
required to. He's only playing the part.

Doesn't sound like an appealing relationship, does it? And yet, this
is exactly how Christians sometimes act in our relationship with God.

Have you ever dragged yourself to church simply because your parents
expected you to attend? I used to. And when I would read the Bible my
eyes sometimes skimmed the pages, but my mind would be elsewhere.

God doesn't want us to go through the motions if our hearts aren't
in it. Going to church, praying, and reading the Bible are activities
that can grow our faith, yes—but they're also activities that can show
our adoration to God. They mean much more to Him when we do
these things not because we feel like we're supposed to, but because
we love Him that much.

Besides, Jesus died for me and took what should've been my place
on the cross out of adoration. So why would I expect to give Him
anything less than my whole heart?

LET'S THINK ABOUT IT...

Do you follow Jesus out of adoration or obligation?

LET'S PRAY ABOUT IT...

Lord, thank you for loving me out of adoration rather than obligation, and help me to do the same for you. Amen.

TODAY'S DARE

What can you do to express your love for Jesus? You could spend an extra thirty minutes with Him rather than watch your favorite TV show. Or maybe you'd like to write a song for Him on the guitar. Make sure the task is done out of a place of adoration rather than obligation.

A SHOT OF INSPIRATION

Believers in Christ owe nothing to God in payment for salvation . . . but they do owe God a life of undivided devotion and service.

Billy Graham

Join the convo! Inspired by today's chat? Share what you learned! Snap a photo of this book (or the drink you're sipping on), and spark a discussion on social media by answering this question:

In your opinion, what's the difference between "relationship" and "religion" in Christianity?

Be sure to use the hashtag #CoffeeShopDevos!

Your Life's Journey

Scripture to sip on

A person may plan his own journey,
but the Lord directs his steps.

Proverbs 16:9 GW

LET'S CHAT ABOUT IT...

As I write, today's the last day of this year. Right now, people are setting new goals, writing down their vision for the next twelve months, and brainstorming their word for the year.

I've never been one to create strict resolutions for the new year. Sure, I don't mind setting goals, but ultimately, I know God may lead me down a different path than the one I had in mind.

As a teen, the future may look unclear. But rest assured, you can trust the one who has already mapped out the path before you.

It can be scary not to know what's on the road ahead. At times I've questioned the path God has led me down and wondered what it'd be like to venture on my own. But I'm terrified of the disaster that could result.

As I begin this new year, I'm clinging to His hand and allowing Him to guide my steps. The road ahead might look unclear, but I have a personal travel agent. I'm not responsible for planning this trip.

And besides, it's exhilarating to journey down a path mapped out specifically for me!

LET'S THINK ABOUT IT...

How can you seek God's direction?

LET'S PRAY ABOUT IT...

Lord, give me wisdom for every decision, and show me the next step clearly. Amen.

TODAY'S DARE

Do you think God is calling you to pursue a certain profession or area of ministry? If so, write down this vision and pray about it, but keep in mind that God's plans for your life might turn out differently than you had expected.

A SHOT OF INSPIRATION

> Those who follow the right path fear the Lord;
> those who take the wrong path despise him.
>
> Proverbs 14:2

Join the convo! Inspired by today's chat? Share what you learned! Snap a photo of this book (or the drink you're sipping on), and spark a discussion on social media by answering this question:

Is there a time when God led you down a path that was different than the one you had planned?

Be sure to use the hashtag #CoffeeShopDevos!

He Holds the Pen

You saw me before I was born.
   Every day of my life was recorded in your book.
Every moment was laid out
   before a single day had passed.

                              Psalm 139:16

LET'S CHAT ABOUT IT...

As a writer, I have a tendency to view my life though the lens of an author.

Writers know that in order to bring about growth and change in a character's life, we need to give them obstacles. In the moment, the character might grow weary and wonder if they'll ever get beyond the challenges. But this conflict will bring them closer to reaching their happy ending.

I remind myself of this when I face obstacles in my own life. Challenges that test my limits. Instead of fretting, I trust in the Author of my life. He holds the pen.

When I begin to write a new book, I craft my characters in a way that will help them to fulfill their purpose in the story. Likewise, God created me with a purpose. My personality wasn't a mistake. My appearance wasn't simply a result of random genes. My design was carefully crafted in the Creator's mind.

He gave detailed attention to your "characterization" as well. God knew He had to create you in a way that would suit your story. So rather than resenting the way He made us or shying away from the challenges we face, let's trust the authorship of our Creator.

He is, after all, the Author of life itself!

LET'S THINK ABOUT IT...

Is it difficult for you to trust that God created you with a purpose and has already written your life story?

_____

_____

_____

_____

LET'S PRAY ABOUT IT...

Lord, help me trust your authorship and embrace the challenges in my life because I know they can bring me closer to the future you have in store for me. Amen.

TODAY'S DARE

Consider writing in a diary or a calendar to record your days and capture memories and events. Later, you'll be encouraged as you witness God's perfect authorship throughout your life story.

A SHOT OF INSPIRATION

"For I know the plans I have for you," says the Lord. "They are plans for good and not for disaster, to give you a future and a hope."

Jeremiah 29:11

Join the convo! Inspired by today's chat? Share what you learned! Snap a photo of this book (or the drink you're sipping on), and spark a discussion on social media by answering this question:

Is there a challenge you've faced in the past that prepared you for your future?

Be sure to use the hashtag #CoffeeShopDevos!

Best Insurance Ever

Scripture to sip on

Well then, since God's grace has set us free from the law, does that mean we can go on sinning? Of course not!

Romans 6:15

LET'S CHAT ABOUT IT...

Pretend your parents are giving you a new car that's been insured by The Best Insurance Agency Ever, or TBIAE for short. This covers everything—crashes, fender benders, tire blowouts, etc. You take the new keys and jump in the car. A thrill rushes through you as you exercise your newfound freedom.

You pull out onto the road, and a thought crosses your mind: "What's the point in driving safely when I'm covered by TBIAE?" So you take advantage of this new insurance coverage by speeding through a red light, and *bam*—your car is totaled.

The initial thrill fades as you examine the damage. Thankfully, there were no injuries, but your car certainly took a beating. TBIAE might cover the wreck, but there's one thing it *can't* insure you from.

And that is the punishment and loss of trust from your parents.

Now, let's apply this analogy to our relationship with Jesus.

Thanks to our personal insurance policy, Jesus' death on cross— the death that paid the price of our penalty—we've gained a newfound freedom. However, He didn't sacrifice himself for us so we could remain in our sin. We're not perfect, so of course we'll make mistakes. When we sin, we can find forgiveness at the feet of Jesus.

Even though He's paid the price of our punishment, that doesn't mean we won't have to live with the damage caused by our sinful decisions.

I don't know about you, but I'd prefer not to abuse this new freedom by seeking thrills. It'd be silly to purposely wreck a new car.

Even if it *was* covered by The Best Insurance Agency Ever.

LET'S THINK ABOUT IT...

Have you taken advantage of your insured grace by living carelessly for a thrill? What were the consequences?

LET'S PRAY ABOUT IT...

Lord, forgive me for abusing the "insurance" for my sins that you paid such a high price for me to enjoy. Thank you for your forgiveness and the freedom found in walking with you. Amen.

TODAY'S DARE

With your parents' permission, watch *The Passion of the Christ* with your family or a friend.

A SHOT OF INSPIRATION

That is the way we should live, because God's grace that can save everyone has come. It teaches us not to live against God nor to do the evil things the world wants to do. Instead, that grace teaches us to live in the present age in a wise and right way and in a way that shows we serve God.

Titus 2:11–12 NCV

Join the convo! Inspired by today's chat? Share what you learned! Snap a photo of this book (or the drink you're sipping on), and spark a discussion on social media by answering this question:

What do grace and freedom mean to you?

Be sure to use the hashtag #CoffeeShopDevos!

Too Dirty for a Shower

"Come now, let's settle this,"
   says the Lord.
"Though your sins are like scarlet,
   I will make them as white as snow.
Though they are red like crimson,
   I will make them as white as wool."

Isaiah 1:18

LET'S CHAT ABOUT IT...

Think back to a time when you spent all day outside—walking, hiking, or riding a bike. When you came home, did you avoid taking a shower because you were too dirty? I'd hope not! That would go against the purpose of taking a shower. We use soap and water to wash away our filth.

The same principle can apply to God's grace.

His grace is our "spiritual soap," and its purpose is to wash away our sins. We can't go a day without getting dirty. God knows this. That's why He provided His son to serve as atonement for our sins.

Avoiding God's forgiveness because you're afraid of sinning again is like avoiding a shower because you know you'll get dirty again tomorrow. The enemy's intention is for us to remain in our filth; Jesus' intention is to make us as pure as snow.

We don't have to remain in the filth of yesterday. Jesus didn't die for the spiritually clean; He died for those who reek with sin. What's the purpose of His blood if not to wash away our yesterday?

When we sin, let's go to Christ with a repentant heart and ask for His cleansing. Trust me—if you've gone for days without rinsing off your dirt, I'm sure Jesus would be more than happy to offer His spiritual soap.

LET'S THINK ABOUT IT...

Have you ever felt too sinful and condemned to ask for God's forgiveness?

....

....

....

....

LET'S PRAY ABOUT IT...

Lord, forgive me for the sins I've committed. Thank you that your forgiveness has the power to make me new. Amen.

TODAY'S DARE

If you have a hard time with moving on from past mistakes—and you've already sought Jesus' forgiveness—here's an idea: Throw them in the trash. Literally. Write the sins you recall on paper. Then, blot them out with a permanent marker, tear them up, and throw them away. Jesus has already blotted out your transgressions as well and He remembers them no more (see Isaiah 43:25).

A SHOT OF INSPIRATION

This means that anyone who belongs to Christ has become a new person. The old life is gone; a new life has begun!

2 Corinthians 5:17

Join the convo! Inspired by today's chat? Share what you learned! Snap a photo of this book (or the drink you're sipping on), and spark a discussion on social media by answering this question:

Why did Jesus die for us even though He knew we'd continue to live in sin?

Be sure to use the hashtag #CoffeeShopDevos!

WANTED: Lost Dog

Scripture to sip on

Take delight in the Lord,
and he will give you your heart's desires.

Psalm 37:4

LET'S CHAT ABOUT IT...

When I was in first grade, I created and hung "WANTED: Lost Dog" signs around my neighborhood.

The funny thing is, I didn't have a lost dog. My first dog had passed away a year earlier, and when I asked my parents for a new one, they continually said no.

So I did what any seven-year-old would do and took matters into my own hands. My thoughts probably went along the lines of this: Surely someone would find one of these handmade signs—complete with a hand-drawn pencil drawing of a dog—and bring me a dog that was lost.

But when that didn't work, Mom told me to confide in God about my desire for a dog. So every night, I asked Him to send me a dog.

Guess what happened.

Before my sister and I went to school one day, we heard rustling in the bushes outside. We thought it was a bird—so you can imagine our surprise when we spotted a puppy, shaking behind the bushes. After we tracked down the owners of the lost dog, we were told they were from out of town and had been visiting one of our neighbors. They had already found a new dog to replace their lost puppy.

We could keep him as our own.

God heard my prayers. He cared for a seven-year-old's desire for a puppy.

I believe He hears your prayers, too. He cares for your needs and desires. So during the time you spend with God, pour your heart out to Him in prayer. He hears you.

And don't be surprised if He brings you exactly what you had prayed for!

LET'S THINK ABOUT IT...

Do you confide in God with the small desires of your heart?

LET'S PRAY ABOUT IT...

Lord, thank you for caring about every aspect of my life. Help me to learn how to come to you in prayer for all things. Amen.

TODAY'S DARE

Start a prayer chain! With a group of your friends, make a list of requests that each of you agree to pray about.

A SHOT OF INSPIRATION

Confess your sins to each other and pray for each other so that you may be healed. The earnest prayer of a righteous person has great power and produces wonderful results.

James 5:16

Join the convo! Inspired by today's chat? Share what you learned! Snap a photo of this book (or the drink you're sipping on), and spark a discussion on social media by answering this question:

Share about a time when you received exactly what you had prayed for.

Be sure to use the hashtag #CoffeeShopDevos!

Power of a Flame

You are the light of the world—like a city on a hilltop that cannot be hidden. No one lights a lamp and then puts it under a basket. Instead, a lamp is placed on a stand, where it gives light to everyone in the house. In the same way, let your good deeds shine out for all to see, so that everyone will praise your heavenly Father.

Matthew 5:14–16

LET'S CHAT ABOUT IT...

The power of a flame is scary when you think about it. When the candle is contained, it looks safe. But what happens if it accidentally tips over? How do I know that the flame won't leap out and catch fire to the surroundings?

These worrisome thoughts especially barrage my mind during Christmas candlelight services at my church. Yet at the same time, it's mesmerizing to watch as one tiny flame can light the candles of a whole congregation.

What a great analogy, don't you think?

As Christians, we can either stay safe and contained—or we can spark flames in those around us. Our love can cause a chain reaction of light. This will only happen if we take the leap to ignite the flame of one person. That one tiny act of love could result in the ignition of multiple flames to come.

Let's keep this in mind the next time we're given the opportunity to share the gospel. Even if it's only one person we approach, let's leap out of our comfort zone and ignite them with Christ's love. There's no telling how much light could result from just one simple spark! If we all would do this, we would soon light up the world with God's love.

Let's never underestimate the power of a flame.

LET'S THINK ABOUT IT...

How can you ignite the flame in the lives of those around you?

LET'S PRAY ABOUT IT...

Lord, I don't want the flame within me to stay safe and contained; instead, I want to ignite a fire in the lives of others. Amen.

TODAY'S DARE

What small thing can you do for someone today that will show Christ's love? Here are some ideas:

- Ask a friend if she has any prayer needs.
- Spend time getting to know a classmate.
- Take your younger sibling out for ice cream.

A SHOT OF INSPIRATION

I have this theory that if one person will go out of their way to show compassion, then it will start a chain reaction of the same.

Rachel Joy Scott

Join the convo! Inspired by today's chat? Share what you learned! Snap a photo of this book (or the drink you're sipping on), and spark a discussion on social media by answering this question:

Can you recall a time when someone sparked a chain reaction of light by reaching out to you?

Be sure to use the hashtag #CoffeeShopDevos!

Fruit That Lasts

Scripture to sip on

When you follow the desires of your sinful nature, the results are very clear: sexual immorality, impurity, lustful pleasures, idolatry, sorcery, hostility, quarreling, jealousy, outbursts of anger, selfish ambition, dissension, division, envy, drunkenness, wild parties, and other sins like these. Let me tell you again, as I have before, that anyone living that sort of life will not inherit the Kingdom of God.

But the Holy Spirit produces this kind of fruit in our lives: love, joy, peace, patience, kindness, goodness, faithfulness, gentleness, and self-control. There is no law against these things!

Galatians 5:19–23

LET'S CHAT ABOUT IT…

I'll never forget about the time when fruit flies swarmed for days in my family's kitchen. Unfortunately, they were originally attracted to our kitchen because of a rotten banana. If only we hadn't let the banana go bad, then we wouldn't have had to deal with the flies!

The act of chasing after the desires of our sinful nature can be a lot like this rotten fruit. It only attracts flies and brings forth a rotten stench. And these flies, like the kind that hung around our kitchen for days, are the stubborn kind that multiply and refuse to leave.

On the other hand, when we follow the desires of our spiritual nature, this produces the best kind of fruit. The kind that is nourishing, refreshing, and most important, it *doesn't* attract a swarm of fruit flies. It brings forth a pleasing aroma rather than a rotten stench.

Resisting the tug of our sinful nature can be difficult. Our flesh will tempt us to make decisions that'll only result in rotten fruit.

That's why we need help from the Holy Spirit. We can do this by finding strength in Him for our weaknesses, filling ourselves with His Word, and building ourselves up in prayer. It's only then that we will bear fruit that will last.

And best of all, we won't have to worry about attracting a single fly.

LET'S THINK ABOUT IT...

What desires of the flesh do you struggle with the most?

....

....

....

....

LET'S PRAY ABOUT IT...

Lord, it's through the help of the Holy Spirit that I can resist the tug of my sinful nature. Help me to find strength in you so I can produce lasting fruit. Amen.

TODAY'S DARE

Is there a fruit of the Spirit that could be more evident in your life (for example, patience)? If so, find a Scripture that dives deeper into this area.

A SHOT OF INSPIRATION

Love, joy, peace, patience, kindness, goodness, faithfulness, gentleness, and self-control. To these I commit my day.

Max Lucado

Join the convo! Inspired by today's chat? Share what you learned! Snap a photo of this book (or the drink you're sipping on), and spark a discussion on social media by answering this question:

Is there someone in your life who seems to bear the fruits of the Spirit in his/her daily life?

Be sure to use the hashtag #CoffeeShopDevos!

Potter's Hand

The Lord gave another message to Jeremiah. He said, "Go down to the potter's shop, and I will speak to you there." So I did as he told me and found the potter working at his wheel. But the jar he was making did not turn out as he had hoped, so he crushed it into a lump of clay again and started over.

Jeremiah 18:1–4

LET'S CHAT ABOUT IT...

Isn't it cool how potters can sculpt a block of clay into a piece of artwork? I've always been intrigued by the process. It's mesmerizing to watch a potter mold a lump of clay until it becomes what they had envisioned. Yet the clay will only become a masterpiece through pressure and hard work.

In this Scripture, the potter's jar he'd been working on didn't turn out as he had hoped. But he didn't throw the pottery away; instead, he used the same lump of clay to sculpt it into his original vision.

God can do the same with our mistakes as well. When we feel as though we've gone too far, we can come to Jesus in repentance and begin again. As we seek Him first, He molds us and shapes our futures into the original plan He had in mind.

Let's strive to live out God's original purpose for our lives. It's only then—when we mature in our relationship with Him—that our lives will become a piece of art molded by God's own hands.

LET'S THINK ABOUT IT...

How can you strive to live in the center of God's will for your life every day?

LET'S PRAY ABOUT IT...

Lord, help me to live my life according to your original vision. I want to grow in you so that I can stay in the center of your will. Amen.

TODAY'S DARE

Read Jeremiah 18. In your journal, answer these questions:

- In what ways did Israel rebel, and how did God piece the Israelites back together?
- Have you witnessed God's mercy in your life or in the lives of others?

A SHOT OF INSPIRATION

> The faithful love of the Lord never ends!
>> His mercies never cease.
> Great is his faithfulness;
>> his mercies begin afresh each morning.
>>> Lamentations 3:22–23

Join the convo! Inspired by today's chat? Share what you learned! Snap a photo of this book (or the drink you're sipping on), and spark a discussion on social media by answering this question:

When we know we've messed up, what can we do to allow ourselves to be molded and reshaped back into God's original design?

Be sure to use the hashtag #CoffeeShopDevos!

Treasures for Eternity

Don't store up treasures here on earth, where moths eat them and rust destroys them, and where thieves break in and steal. Store your treasures in heaven, where moths and rust cannot destroy, and thieves do not break in and steal. Wherever your treasure is, there the desires of your heart will also be.

Matthew 6:19–21

LET'S CHAT ABOUT IT...

A sermon I once heard when I was in children's church has always stuck with me. The pastor spoke on heaven, and he told us we couldn't bring anything from earth with us—not our clothes, toys, houses, etc. The concept still blows my mind. On earth, people strive every day to attain *more*. More money. Clothes. Achievements. Popularity. But how much will all of this be worth in eternity?

Not a thing! The only thing that'll last into eternity is the spiritual treasures: Joy. Peace. Love. Intimacy with our Father.

Humans were born with a natural desire for fulfillment. Unfortunately, we're guilty of trying to fill this spiritual craving with earthly treasures. Yet nothing of earth is of true value. I'd much prefer to spend my life working to seek spiritual treasures, blessings that exceed the natural and satisfy my longings.

Even though I can't carry my material gain with me into eternity, there is one thing that will remain standing.

And that is my relationship with Christ.

LET'S THINK ABOUT IT...

How much time do you spend seeking earthly treasures compared to spiritual treasures?

LET'S PRAY ABOUT IT...

Lord, help me to spend my life working to build eternal treasures rather than earthly treasures. Amen.

TODAY'S DARE

Listen to the song "Lose My Soul" by Toby Mac.

A SHOT OF INSPIRATION

And what do you benefit if you gain the whole world but lose your own soul?

Mark 8:36

Join the convo! Inspired by today's chat? Share what you learned! Snap a photo of this book (or the drink you're sipping on), and spark a discussion on social media by answering this question:

Why do you think even Christians spend so much time and effort profiting our earthly life rather than our eternal life?

Be sure to use the hashtag #CoffeeShopDevos!

Faithful Steward

To those who use well what they are given, even more will be given,
and they will have an abundance. But from those who do nothing,
even what little they have will be taken away.

Matthew 25:29

LET'S CHAT ABOUT IT...

Growing up, I didn't comprehend the value of money. My needs were
always taken care of, so I never thought about it. It wasn't until I grew
older and had to make my own money that I understood the importance.

The same can be said with my time as well: As a kid, it felt as
though time crawled. Now I understand how short life is, and how
every second is a second that I'll never get back.

Time and money are resources God has gifted to us, among others.
We're held responsible for the way we treat these gifts—whether we
spend them wisely or abuse them. How do we abuse these resources?
By wasting them, not considering their value, and being irresponsible.

Think back to the Garden of Eden. God put Adam in charge of
the garden, but what did he do? He abused his role as manager by
disobeying God's command. Look at the destruction Adam caused
simply because he was irresponsible!

According to this Scripture, God will reward us with "abundance"
if we prove to be faithful with our resources. With that in mind, responsibility sounds like a small price to pay, don't you think?

LET'S THINK ABOUT IT...

In what areas of your life could you prove to be more faithful and
responsible?

LET'S PRAY ABOUT IT...

Lord, thank you for trusting me with gifts. Help me to take ownership over them and prove to be a faithful manager for you. Amen.

TODAY'S DARE

Read about the parable of the talents in Matthew 25:14–30. Why do you think God gives us more responsibility when we prove our faithfulness in small areas?

A SHOT OF INSPIRATION

Now, a person who is put in charge as a manager must be faithful.

1 Corinthians 4:2

Join the convo! Inspired by today's chat? Share what you learned! Snap a photo of this book (or the drink you're sipping on), and spark a discussion on social media by answering this question:

What does it look like to be responsible with the resources God has gifted us with?

Be sure to use the hashtag #CoffeeShopDevos!

Proof of Your Values

"Your love for one another will prove to the world that you are my disciples."

John 13:35

LET'S CHAT ABOUT IT...

If someone were to look at my bank account to see where my money goes, they'd notice that I value both books and coffee. I went shopping for clothes the other day for the first time in four months, but I visit a coffee shop at *least* two times a week, and I never hesitate to add a new book to my bookshelf.

If someone could see where you invest your time and money, what would they assume you value? Maybe they'd draw the conclusion that you're a Christian if you purchase Christian merchandise.

Now, let me ask you this: If someone were to take away your belongings and could only learn who you are based on the impression you make, would they still know where your heart lies?

Our interests—the areas where we choose to spend our time and money—might help to explain where our passions lie. But this doesn't define who we are. Anyone can buy Christian merchandise and call themselves a Christian, but it won't mean anything unless their love for God shines through every other aspect of that person's life.

My goal as a Christian should be exactly that: to express my love for God in every encounter I have with others. That way, even if someone were to take away my material blessings, the heart I have for Him would remain evident.

LET'S THINK ABOUT IT...

How can you express your love for God to everyone you come in contact with?

....

....

....

....

LET'S PRAY ABOUT IT...

Lord, help me show that I value being your disciple—not based solely on my church attendance, but by the way I treat others. Amen.

TODAY'S DARE

In every conversation you have today, even if it's with a stranger, ask the Holy Spirit to help you show them that you are a Christian based on your kindness and love.

A SHOT OF INSPIRATION

Through our service to others, God wants to influence our world for Him.

Vonette Bright

Join the convo! Inspired by today's chat? Share what you learned! Snap a photo of this book (or the drink you're sipping on), and spark a discussion on social media by answering this question:

Why do you think some Christians neglect to express their love of God in their speech and actions toward others?

Be sure to use the hashtag #CoffeeShopDevos!

Undeserved Favor

Scripture to sip on

God saved you by his grace when you believed. And you can't take credit for this; it is a gift from God. Salvation is not a reward for the good things we have done, so none of us can boast about it.

Ephesians 2:8–9

LET'S CHAT ABOUT IT...

Do you know someone who always seems to have good things happen to them? Maybe they make straight As and all the teachers love them. Perhaps it seems like everything they touch turns to gold and God's favor shines on them. Having favor can explain several events; however, His favor isn't reserved only for a handful of His children. According to this Scripture, it's available to us all.

Undeserved favor is the evidence of God's love toward us and His goodness in our lives. It's the love Jesus poured out for us on the cross and the grace He extends to us daily. It's simply having the opportunity to refer to ourselves as daughters of the Most High, and it's because of the royalty in our blood that we can receive this undeserved favor.

So rather than shuffling through life, let's walk with our heads held high and live as though we are blessed and loved by God—because we are. Let's train ourselves to stay mindful of the many ways He pours out His love and favor on us daily.

As we do this, not only will we discover more evidence of God's favor, but we'll also realize that one thing exceeds any blessings we may receive in the natural world. And that is the undeserved reward of our salvation.

LET'S THINK ABOUT IT...

Have you found yourself pursuing God in effort to attain His blessings and favor?

LET'S PRAY ABOUT IT...

Lord, thank you for pouring out your undeserved favor on my life. I know the greatest gift doesn't lie in these blessings, but it's found in pursuing a life-giving relationship with you. Amen.

TODAY'S DARE

Read about Joseph and the coat of many colors in Genesis 37–39. Why do you think Joseph had more favor with God than his brothers did?

A SHOT OF INSPIRATION

> May God be merciful and bless us.
> May his face smile with favor on us.
> Psalm 67:1

Join the convo! Inspired by today's chat? Share what you learned! Snap a photo of this book (or the drink you're sipping on), and spark a discussion on social media by answering this question:

Share one example of what God's undeserved favor looks like in your life.

Be sure to use the hashtag #CoffeeShopDevos!

Latte

*Comfort
in Trials*

Almond Hazelnut Latte

When my friends and family come over, this is my favorite latte to whip up for them. There's something comforting about sipping on a frothy latte that helps to spark conversation with our loved ones. The soothing warmth and nutty undertones make this the perfect latte to sip on during chilly mornings.

INGREDIENTS

- 2 shots espresso (or 1/2 cup strong coffee)
- 2 tablespoons hazelnut syrup
- 1/4 teaspoon almond extract
- 1/2 cup unsweetened almond milk

INSTRUCTIONS

1. Brew espresso (or coffee).
2. Stir hazelnut syrup and almond extract into espresso (or coffee).
3. Steam milk until frothy.
4. Pour milk into espresso (or coffee), using spoon to hold back froth.
5. Cap off latte with layer of froth.
6. Optional garnish: whipped cream and extra hazelnut syrup.

Stumbling Block or Stepping-Stone?

Scripture to sip on

You intended to harm me, but God intended it for good to accomplish what is now being done, the saving of many lives.

Genesis 50:20 NIV

LET'S CHAT ABOUT IT...

"It's permanent." Those were the words spoken by my doctor after he diagnosed me with Type 1 Diabetes. When I was released from the hospital, it was like coming home with a newborn baby. My days became a 24/7 math problem, and if I didn't solve this endless equation correctly, my life was at stake.

I had two choices: allow the new diagnosis to keep me down by becoming angry at God—or let it become a stepping-stone. I could allow it to thrust me even further in my relationship with God, as well as in my ministry.

Sometimes the obstacles thrown our way are the enemy's attempts to turn us away from God. He wants us to blame God for the difficulties in our lives because if we do, our walk with Christ will become stagnant.

When a stumbling block comes our way, let's thank God for another opportunity to build our faith. Let's use the difficulty as a stepping-stone, trusting He can bring something good out of it.

I thought having diabetes could only serve as a hindrance in my life. But when this obstacle knocked me down, I fell to my knees. It is there where God lifted me up, giving me strength to rise higher. By doing so, He transformed this stumbling block into a stepping-stone.

LET'S THINK ABOUT IT...

How has your attitude toward trials affected your walk with Christ?

LET'S PRAY ABOUT IT...

Lord, show me how I can use stumbling blocks as stepping-stones so I can thrust forward into a closer relationship with you. Amen.

TODAY'S DARE

Make a list of ways God could bring good out of your current hardships.

A SHOT OF INSPIRATION

The most remarkable thing about suffering is that God can use it for our good.

Billy Graham

Join the conva! Inspired by today's chat? Share what you learned! Snap a photo of this book (or the drink you're sipping on), and spark a discussion on social media by answering this question:

How has God turned previous stumbling blocks in your life into stepping-stones?

Be sure to use the hashtag #CoffeeShopDevos!

Trash Transformed

Scripture to sip on

And we know that God causes everything to work together for the good of those who love God and are called according to his purpose for them.

Romans 8:28

LET'S CHAT ABOUT IT...

Growing up, I knew better than to throw away recyclable objects such as bottle caps, coffee creamer containers, and water bottles. My mom was an art teacher and found several uses for what I considered to be trash. When I see an empty paper towel roll, I don't think about the potential it has to be transformed into a masterpiece. But Mom, on the other hand? A dozen craft possibilities reel through her mind.

Through the eyes of an artist, junk is deemed valuable. With the touch of a paintbrush, trash is transformed into a piece of art.

In the same way, when we view the trials in our life, we might see waste. How could they contribute anything of value? But where we see trash, God sees potential. The Master Artist, with His tender touch, can rework our suffering into a pattern of good.

So instead of attempting to throw away the "trash" in our lives and deem it as worthless, let's bring it to our Father. He'll use His paintbrush to transform our junk into works of art.

He is, after all, pretty experienced in the area of creating a masterpiece out of nothingness!

LET'S THINK ABOUT IT...

What would you consider to be trash in your life?

LET'S PRAY ABOUT IT...

Lord, you can use my circumstances to create something beautiful. I place in your hands the filth of my life and ask that you transform the trash into works of art. Amen.

TODAY'S DARE

Create a transformation masterpiece! Find something you would normally throw away, such as an empty water bottle, a soda can, or an empty paper towel roll.

Then get creative! Find a DIY craft project online you can create with your items and consider inviting your siblings or friends to help you work on the project. As you do, remember God can transform what once were pieces of trash into a worthwhile masterpiece.

A SHOT OF INSPIRATION

If God can make a billion galaxies, can't he make good out of our bad and sense out of our faltering lives? Of course he can. He is God.

Max Lucado

Join the convo! Inspired by today's chat? Share what you learned! Snap a photo of this book (or the drink you're sipping on), and spark a discussion on social media by answering this question:

How has God transformed your suffering and/or sins into something beautiful?

Be sure to use the hashtag #CoffeeShopDevos!

Arms Wide Open

No power in the sky above or in the earth below—indeed, nothing in all creation will ever be able to separate us from the love of God that is revealed in Christ Jesus our Lord.

Romans 8:39

LET'S CHAT ABOUT IT...

One day in middle school, a friend told me she didn't believe God loved her. "Why would I have to suffer if He did?" Nothing I said could convince her of God's love.

We live in a fallen world, so we're going to experience trouble. But it's not a sign of His neglect. He doesn't abandon His children; in fact, He's right there with us. Hurting with us. Holding our hands. Offering comfort and strength. It's our decision whether or not we'll turn to Him and accept His love.

If you, too, struggle with the idea that God loves you—or that your circumstances are a result of His neglect—remember: Jesus came to this earth for you *personally*. He became flesh so He could experience the worst of the worst of the human condition. He took our place on the cross so we could experience this personal, loving relationship with Him. *That's* how much He loves us! So much that He spread His arms out wide on the cross and died a cruel death.

The next time you feel unloved, think of His arms held open for you. The nails that pierced His hands, the crown of thorns He bore. It was His overabundance of love that compelled Him to suffer. "A heartless God" becomes an oxymoron when compared to the image of Jesus' death on the cross.

So go ahead—fall into Jesus' embrace. His hands, the ones that were pierced for you, are held open as He patiently waits for you to accept this invitation of love.

LET'S THINK ABOUT IT...

Have you believed trials were a sign of neglect from God?

LET'S PRAY ABOUT IT...

Jesus, thank you for the love you poured out for me on the cross. Help me to fall into your embrace when I experience hardships. Amen.

TODAY'S DARE

When I was a teenager, I saw a music video on YouTube that illustrated Jesus' love. It's stuck with me to this day. Search for "The Bridge Trailer Music Video" which is played to the song "All for Love" by Hillsong. As you watch, reflect on the love God freely offered you when He gave up His Son.

A SHOT OF INSPIRATION

I asked Jesus, "How much do you love me?" Jesus replied, "This much." And he stretched his arms on the cross, and died.

Unknown

Join the convo! Inspired by today's chat? Share what you learned! Snap a photo of this book (or the drink you're sipping on), and spark a discussion on social media by answering this question:

How can trials compel us to draw closer to our Savior?

Be sure to use the hashtag #CoffeeShopDevos!

Pressure Points

Scripture to sip on

Dear brothers and sisters, when troubles of any kind come your way, consider it an opportunity for great joy. For you know that when your faith is tested, your endurance has a chance to grow.

James 1:2–3

LET'S CHAT ABOUT IT...

I have a love-hate relationship with working out. I love the way I feel afterwards, but I'm not a fan of the painful moments. So what compels me to continue?

The fact that those pressure points will eventually lead to defined muscles. It's during the moments of pushing myself until I'm out of breath that my endurance develops.

Isn't it odd how new growth often arises from uncomfortable challenges? I'm not talking only about working out. I'm referring to life in general. Maybe you're experiencing pressure at home or school, with siblings or your friends. Or maybe your pressure points stem from a greater source of pain, such as the death of a loved one.

Life can often push us until we feel as though we've reached a point of breaking. But it's during those times—when we feel tempted to call it quits, as if we've run out of breath emotionally—that we should draw strength from Christ. He gives us the supernatural ability to persevere. The trials can serve as growth opportunities.

So the next time you feel as though you can't carry on, grasp God's hand. Not only will He carry you through, He'll use the challenge to thrust you into a future only He can see.

LET'S THINK ABOUT IT...

Are there positive changes that could result from the difficulties you face?

LET'S PRAY ABOUT IT...

Lord, help me to allow trials to advance me into a new level in my walk with you and bring growth opportunities. Amen.

TODAY'S DARE

Focus on building your spiritual muscles today. How? By working out with the Word. Challenge yourself to read at least one chapter in your Bible today, or set your timer for 30 minutes and spend that time soaking in Scripture.

A SHOT OF INSPIRATION

Don't let your trials blow you down; let them lift you up.

Woodrow Kroll

Join the convo! Inspired by today's chat? Share what you learned! Snap a photo of this book (or the drink you're sipping on), and spark a discussion on social media by answering this question:

Is there a trial you've faced that gave you the opportunity to rise to a new level?

Be sure to use the hashtag #CoffeeShopDevos!

Just Like a Palm Tree

Scripture to sip on

But the godly will flourish like palm trees
and grow strong like the cedars of Lebanon.

Psalm 92:12

LET'S CHAT ABOUT IT...

I traveled to California for the first time last week to serve on the faculty at a writers' conference. Even though I was already familiar with palm trees because of my visits to Florida and the coast of South Carolina, my home state, I found the palm trees in California mesmerizing. The roads were lined with endless rows of them. These trees were 60 feet tall and had stood strong in all kinds of weather.

When hurricanes hit the coast and wipe away homes, businesses, and cars, palm trees can still be found firm in their foundation.

I'd love to be like those palm trees—so strong that the storms of life have no power over me.

But you know what? This Scripture says we *can* flourish like palm trees. We, too, can grow tall and strong—spiritually speaking, of course—and withstand storms of life. When our roots grow deep in Christ, nothing can shake our faith.

God invites us to build an immovable foundation. One that will keep us steadfast throughout storms. Then, when they blow over, we'll still be found standing our ground—safe and secure.

Just like a palm tree.

LET'S THINK ABOUT IT...

How can you make more time to grow in godliness so you can "flourish like palm trees"?

LET'S PRAY ABOUT IT...

Lord, a relationship with you provides the strong foundation I need to flourish throughout all kinds of weather. Help me to grow in you daily so I can remain steadfast. Amen.

TODAY'S DARE

Take time today to flip through the Psalms and find passages that can speak hope to you and your current situation. Then, write these verses on index cards and read over them daily so your faith can grow deep and strong in these areas.

A SHOT OF INSPIRATION

Disaster strikes like a cyclone and the wicked are whirled away. But the good man has a strong anchor.

Proverbs 10:25 TLB

Join the convo! Inspired by today's chat? Share what you learned! Snap a photo of this book (or the drink you're sipping on), and spark a discussion on social media by answering this question:

Do you have advice for those who might find it difficult to cultivate an immovable relationship with Christ?

Be sure to use the hashtag #CoffeeShopDevos!

Spiritually Sustained

Whom have I in heaven but you?
I desire you more than anything on earth.
My health may fail, and my spirit may grow weak,
but God remains the strength of my heart;
he is mine forever.

Psalm 73:25–26

LET'S CHAT ABOUT IT...

As I mentioned before, I was diagnosed with Type 1 Diabetes at twenty years old. When I came home from the hospital after my diagnosis, it was like coming home with a newborn baby—*minus* the joy. This "baby" required 24/7 attention and changed nearly every aspect of my life. At times I became angry and fell into self-pity. But you know what? The wrong reaction made it worse. So I made a decision: I would use the diagnosis as an opportunity to draw closer to God.

Nothing can take away my salvation in Christ. Oftentimes the only way to discover that our true fulfillment lies in Him is to be stripped of earthly security: Health. Perfect circumstances. Riches. It's when we're emptied of earthly treasures that we experience the true treasure of cultivating a rich relationship with Christ.

Sure, we can take medicine when we're sick. But only God has the ability to give us renewed life deep inside. He wants us to desire Him more than anything—even more than we crave perfect circumstances.

Even if my earthly healing never comes, I've found everlasting joy and peace that far outweighs the pain of this diagnosis. I can now say with joy, as the psalmist did, "He is mine forever."

Yes, even in the midst of suffering.

LET'S THINK ABOUT IT...

If your earthly belongings and security were taken away, could you say your fulfillment rests in Christ?

....

....

....

....

LET'S PRAY ABOUT IT...

Lord, give me the desire to want you above all else. Even if I have nothing on this earth, everything I need is found in my relationship with you. Amen.

TODAY'S DARE

Read the book of Job—on your own or with your friends, parents, or a mentor. Then discuss (or write in your prayer journal) your response to the following questions:

- How did Job react to his suffering?
- Where did he turn?
- How did God reward Job for his attitude?

A SHOT OF INSPIRATION

Don't be afraid, for I am with you.
Don't be discouraged, for I am your God.
I will strengthen you and help you.
I will hold you up with my victorious right hand.

Isaiah 41:10

Join the convo! Inspired by today's chat? Share what you learned! Snap a photo of this book (or the drink you're sipping on), and spark a discussion on social media by answering this question:

Is there a trial you've walked through that helped you rely on God more and drew you closer to Him?

Be sure to use the hashtag #CoffeeShopDevos!

Suffering Like Christ

Scripture to sip on

Yet what we suffer now is nothing compared to the glory he will reveal to us later.

Romans 8:18

LET'S CHAT ABOUT IT...

The other day, I attended a birthday party for my uncle, David, who turned seventy. Both of his grown kids shared about the positive impact he's made on their lives. One of his children said he's never heard his dad say a curse word. The other said he never becomes impatient, even in stressful situations. Others also confirmed his amazing ability to remain peaceful throughout his life. To sum up the things people said about him, Uncle David resembles Christ to everyone.

Crazy thing is, you'd be shocked to learn about the storms he's had to endure. Three strokes caused him to lose most of his vision and part of his memory, as well as his speech. Yet he was determined not to allow his new disabilities to hinder his ministry to the homeless.

This is just one example of the storms he's had to endure. Fortunately, God has completely turned things around for him. Because of Uncle David's devotion to following Christ and serving others—even while facing his own personal challenges—he's been blessed in many ways, and I'm sure there are far more blessings waiting for him in eternity.

It doesn't always seem fair that we have to suffer. Yet this suffering is nothing compared to what awaits us on the other side. Until then, it's our job to remain faithful, leave behind a legacy of love, and maintain a Christlike attitude.

Then, when we reach heaven, we'll be welcomed with these loving words from Christ: "Well done, my good and faithful servant" (Matthew 25:23).

LET'S THINK ABOUT IT...

How can you maintain a Christlike attitude during trials?

LET'S PRAY ABOUT IT...

Lord, help me to remain faithful to you and develop a Christlike attitude. Thank you for the blessings you have in store for those who follow you and endure. Amen.

TODAY'S DARE

The next time you're in a difficult situation and are tempted to become angry, ask yourself, *How would Jesus react?* Then ask God to give you the strength you need to respond the way Jesus would.

A SHOT OF INSPIRATION

Jesus Christ did not suffer so that you would not suffer. He suffered so that when you suffer, you'll become more like him. The gospel does not promise you better life circumstances; it promises you a better life.

Timothy Keller

Join the convo! Inspired by today's chat? Share what you learned! Snap a photo of this book (or the drink you're sipping on), and spark a discussion on social media by answering this question:

Do you have an "Uncle David" in your life? Tell others about the positive impact this person has made on your life.

Be sure to use the hashtag #CoffeeShopDevos!

Safe in His Shelter

Scripture to sip on

The Lord is my light and the one who saves me.
So why should I fear anyone?
The Lord protects my life.
So why should I be afraid? . . .
During danger he will keep me safe in his shelter.
He will hide me in his Holy Tent,
or he will keep me safe on a high mountain.

Psalm 27:1, 5 NCV

LET'S CHAT ABOUT IT...

I've never been a fan of thunderstorms. They're fine on occasion—but my heart beats a little faster when the storm heightens. When the thunder crashes and buckets of rain threaten to overflow the pond in my backyard. When the howling wind sends trees wavering and the storm causes lights inside my house to flicker.

Why should I be afraid, though? It's not like my house wasn't built on a solid foundation. It'd make sense for me to be anxious if I didn't have a secure building to keep me sheltered. But a simple summer thunderstorm isn't strong enough to destroy my shelter.

I often react to certain life events with the same anxiety. When I turn on the news, I hear about new threats to my physical safety. But why should I fear when I remain in the shelter of God? It's only when I choose to step outside of His presence that I become prone to the darkness and random danger that lurks in this world.

The next time a storm comes our way, let's allow the fierce weather to draw us closer "inside" and into God's presence. Let's stay inside, where it's cozy, comfortable, and secure.

Because even when the storm is crashing around us, it's in our father's embrace that we find peace in the midst of the raging thunder.

LET'S THINK ABOUT IT...

When trials of life threaten to steal your peace, where do you seek security?

_____

_____

_____

_____

LET'S PRAY ABOUT IT...

Lord, help me to remain in the shelter of your presence. Thank you for the rest and peace you provide in the midst of storms. Amen.

TODAY'S DARE

Listen to "Eye of the Storm" by Ryan Stevenson.

A SHOT OF INSPIRATION

In a storm there is no shelter like the wings of God.
Thomas Brooks

Join the convo! Inspired by today's chat? Share what you learned! Snap a photo of this book (or the drink you're sipping on), and spark a discussion on social media by answering this question:

What benefits have resulted from staying close to God and seeking His shelter, even during the storms of your life?

Be sure to use the hashtag #CoffeeShopDevos!

Carried Through

These trials will show that your faith is genuine. It is being tested as fire tests and purifies gold—though your faith is far more precious than mere gold. So when your faith remains strong through many trials, it will bring you much praise and glory and honor on the day when Jesus Christ is revealed to the whole world.

1 Peter 1:7

LET'S CHAT ABOUT IT...

I had food poisoning for the first time last week. It crept up at night and stole every ounce of sleep. The stomach pain was unbearable. After a sleepless night, I spent all day on the couch, fighting nausea and dreaming of sleep. (Pun intended!) Even though it was miserable, do you know what helped even more than the herbal teas and soup?

Listening to worship music as I attempted to take a nap. Watching sermons on TV. Talking to God.

These things didn't necessarily help my body feel better, but they lifted my spirits and gave me a rest that surpassed how I felt in the natural. God's presence breathed fresh strength into me, helped me persevere, and reminded me I wasn't alone.

Why does it sometimes take trials and tests to remind us to be still in God's presence?

He wants us to understand how good He is, despite the difficulties. He wants us to personally grasp the greatness of His love—so great that earthly troubles are puny and powerless in comparison.

Food poisoning is an example of suffering on a small scale, but God's goodness is the same despite the measure of difficulty. Trials and tests can stretch our faith, but Jesus will always carry us through.

Yes, even during those dark nights of food poisoning!

LET'S THINK ABOUT IT...

How can you draw closer to God during suffering?

ET'S PRAY ABOUT IT...

Lord, thank you for carrying me through every season. Help me to learn how I can grow spiritually during trials and tests. Amen.

TODAY'S DARE

Start a prayer journal. Prayer journals are a great way to keep a record of how your faith is strengthened during both good and bad times. Then, after a trial ends, you can look back and reflect on how God carried you through.

A SHOT OF INSPIRATION

God blesses those who patiently endure testing and temptation. Afterward they will receive the crown of life that God has promised to those who love him.

James 1:12

Join the convo! Inspired by today's chat? Share what you learned! Snap a photo of this book (or the drink you're sipping on), and spark a discussion on social media by answering this question:

What specific quality of God's character have you seen manifested in your life as a result of a trial or test?

Be sure to use the hashtag #CoffeeShopDevos!

Longing for Perfection

Scripture to sip on

"He will wipe every tear from their eyes, and there will be no more death or sorrow or crying or pain. All these things are gone forever."

Revelation 21:4

LET'S CHAT ABOUT IT...

I'm not a fan of conflict—whether it's in relationships or general life circumstances. I'd imagine you'd prefer a perfect life, too, but unfortunately, that's unattainable in this world. Why is it that we long for a conflict-free life even though it's impossible?

I believe God made us that way on purpose! The longing we have for perfection will never be satisfied until we reach heaven. Yet even though we'll never achieve perfection or live in total peace, we can still have a foretaste of this even while we're here.

Jesus paid a huge sacrifice so He could live inside of us. His death made a way for us to have a taste of heaven on earth. That deep longing for peace you have? It can be found in His perfect presence. We can experience His presence when we cultivate a relationship with Christ and feed on His Word.

So even though we'll never experience perfect circumstances, we can still use this hunger for perfection to launch us into the presence of God, the presence of the only perfect and peaceful One who has ever walked this earth: Jesus Christ.

LET'S THINK ABOUT IT...

Do you have a longing for peace and perfection that remains unsatisfied?

LET'S PRAY ABOUT IT...

Lord, thank you for the hope of heaven. I want my longing for peace and perfection to compel me to know you more. Amen.

TODAY'S DARE

Listen to the song "I Can Only Imagine" by MercyMe.

A SHOT OF INSPIRATION

If we find ourselves with a desire that nothing in this world can satisfy, the most probable explanation is that we were made for another world.

C. S. Lewis

Join the convo! Inspired by today's chat? Share what you learned! Snap a photo of this book (or the drink you're sipping on), and spark a discussion on social media by answering this question:

Share about a time you attempted to find perfection and/or peace on earth.

Be sure to use the hashtag #CoffeeShopDevos!

Punished by Circumstances?

My dear children, I am writing this to you so that you will not sin. But if anyone does sin, we have an advocate who pleads our case before the Father. He is Jesus Christ, the one who is truly righteous. He himself is the sacrifice that atones for our sins—and not only our sins but the sins of all the world.

1 John 2:1–2

LET'S CHAT ABOUT IT...

Have you wondered if your hardships are punishment brought on by God? I have. Especially when I read stories in the Bible about how God inflicted punishment on people who disobeyed Him. I look at my circumstances and wonder, *If God punished them, does that mean He punishes me, too?* But those accounts are from the Old Testament. Most of the time, God didn't punish until *after* He had tried to get His people's attention several times.

In the New Testament, when Jesus stepped onto the scene, things shifted. Grace and love were poured out on the cross so we could receive forgiveness for our sins *without* having to partake in the making of sacrifices. His blood provided atonement for our sins. We needed this so we could remain holy and righteous before God after we receive Jesus into our hearts.

Because of that sacrifice, we are dressed in a robe of righteousness. Cleansed. Made new. Not held back by who we were in the past.

God sent His son because He's a God of mercy and love. This doesn't mean we're free from His discipline or from consequences that may arise from making sinful decisions. However, we are free from experiencing the blow of His anger as a result of our sins.

It was never His original intention, in the Garden of Eden, to punish His children. The enemy is the one to blame for introducing sin into the world.

We can now find forgiveness at the feet of Jesus. Our negative circumstances are not God's anger disguised as trials.

Jesus paid our debt; because of that, we are free from the bondage of sin.

LET'S THINK ABOUT IT...

What's the difference between experiencing consequences brought on by making wrong decisions and being "punished by circumstances"?

LET'S PRAY ABOUT IT...

Jesus, thank you for bearing the punishment I deserve. Help me to follow you so I'll remain in the center of your will. Amen.

TODAY'S DARE

Take a moment to reflect on Jesus' death on the cross by reading John 19, Mark 15, and Luke 23. As you do, try to grasp the measure of the price He paid for you.

A SHOT OF INSPIRATION

But Christ has rescued us from the curse pronounced by the law. When he was hung on the cross, he took upon himself the curse for our wrongdoing.

Galatians 3:13

Join the convo! Inspired by today's chat? Share what you learned! Snap a photo of this book (or the drink you're sipping on), and spark a discussion on social media by answering this question:

What's the difference between condemnation and conviction?

Be sure to use the hashtag #CoffeeShopDevos!

Purpose in Waiting

But those who wait on the Lord
Shall renew their strength;
They shall mount up with wings like eagles,
They shall run and not be weary,
They shall walk and not faint.

Isaiah 40:31 NKJV

LET'S CHAT ABOUT IT...

When I was fifteen, I attended a youth camp and heard a sermon on the topic of waiting on the Lord. The speaker said, "We don't have to wait on God. Doing that implies we're ahead of Him and He's behind us!" I then became confused about the term "waiting on God," which is mentioned multiple times throughout Scripture.

As I matured in my walk with Christ, I experienced waiting seasons. Times when I had to wait for suffering to pass. Healing to come. Answers to prayers to be manifested. I was often tempted to beg God to answer my prayers in *my* timing. But I learned it's not up to me to control the timing.

When we "wait on God," it's not as though we're waiting for Him to get on the ball. We're practicing patience. We can become active waiters when we use the season to pursue a relationship with Him and build character within us. To wait is to have faith in His perfect will and timing, even if circumstances don't play out as we would have them.

Now I understand the point the speaker was trying to make during the youth camp. When we wait, it's not like we're twiddling our thumbs, waiting for God to hurry and act. Instead, we use the time to strive to grow closer to Him until He becomes the ultimate desire of our hearts. We know God has His best in mind for His children.

Even if it means we have to wait just a little bit longer.

LET'S THINK ABOUT IT...

How can you make the most of your waiting seasons?

....

....

....

....

LET'S PRAY ABOUT IT...

Lord, I trust in your perfect will and timing for my life. The prize of finding you in the midst of waiting will be worth it. Amen.

TODAY'S DARE

Make a list of things you're waiting for (such as an answer to a prayer). Keep this list handy. As you lift the prayer requests up to God, watch and see how He answers your prayers in His perfect will and timing.

A SHOT OF INSPIRATION

Joseph waited 13 years. Abraham waited 25 years. Moses waited 40 years. Jesus waited 30 years. If God is making you wait, you're in good company.

Unknown

Join the convo! Inspired by today's chat? Share what you learned! Snap a photo of this book (or the drink you're sipping on), and spark a discussion on social media by answering this question:

Share about a time when you had to wait for an answer to a prayer.

Be sure to use the hashtag #CoffeeShopDevos!

Tornadoes of Change

Scripture to sip on

From the ends of the earth,
I cry to you for help
when my heart is overwhelmed.
Lead me to the towering rock of safety,
for you are my safe refuge.

Psalm 61:2–3

LET'S CHAT ABOUT IT...

My grandpa passed away last week from cancer. His diagnosis crept out of nowhere a month ago and snatched away his life, which left my family in shock—especially since he maintained optimal health throughout his lifetime. This didn't seem fair. We weren't prepared to say good-bye.

Even so, when he passed, I received texts from friends asking me how my family was holding up. And you know what? Even though we're experiencing aftershock, the pain isn't crushing us. My grandma, his wife, said her faith has given her the strength to press on.

Nothing in this life—including our loved ones—will remain. Changes will rip apart our earthly comfort and security.

The only One who is immovable and unchanging is Christ.

His goodness, faithfulness, and steadfast love will never end. He is the solid rock we stand on that doesn't shift like sand. During these trials, we have the opportunity to test His strength. He's strong enough to carry our pain. He's our refuge, our place of safety when tornadoes of change sweep away what we once held dear.

When we build our faith on Christ, we'll have Him as a rock to stand on when harsh winds shake our reality. Seasons will come and go, but the ground beneath our feet will provide the rock-solid stability we need to remain sane throughout the pain.

LET'S THINK ABOUT IT...

In what ways can you strengthen your faith so you'll have a rock to stand on when changes arrive?

LET'S PRAY ABOUT IT...

Lord, thank you for providing the stability and security I need during tornadoes of change. Show me how to build a strong foundation. Amen.

TODAY'S DARE

As I wrote this devotion, the song "Christ the Rock" by Kim Walker Smith came on my Pandora music station. Listen to the song and reflect on the lyrics in your prayer journal. How can you remind yourself of this truth during times of trial and change?

A SHOT OF INSPIRATION

> The Lord is my rock, my fortress, and my savior;
>   my God is my rock, in whom I find protection.
> He is my shield, the power that saves me,
>   and my place of safety.
>
> Psalm 18:2

Join the convo! Inspired by today's chat? Share what you learned! Snap a photo of this book (or the drink you're sipping on), and spark a discussion on social media by answering this question:

Have you experienced a hardship that enabled you to test the rock-solid stability of your foundation in Christ?

Be sure to use the hashtag #CoffeeShopDevos!

Beyond the Wilderness

Scripture to sip on

And if the Lord is pleased with us, he will bring us safely into that land and give it to us. It is a rich land flowing with milk and honey.

Numbers 14:8

LET'S CHAT ABOUT IT...

Do you remember when you were little and car trips seemed unending? When I was a kid, I'd constantly ask my parents, "Are we there yet?" as if my whining would help us reach our destination faster. I didn't know how to relax and trust them.

The Israelites reacted the same way when Moses led them on the journey to the Promised Land in the book of Exodus. They could've reached their destination in eleven *days* instead of forty *years* if it wasn't for the circles of confusion they created due to their whining, self-pity, and lack of faith.

There have been many times when I, too, have been tempted to lose faith and hope. Times when the "Promised Land" felt miles away. Yet when I see situations through a negative lens, I tend to forget the ways God has proved His faithfulness in my past. I become blinded by the murky clouds of negativity.

In the wilderness, let's focus on the light of God's goodness that beams through the clouds of hopelessness. Let's cling to His hand as He guides us, step by step.

Who knows? Our faith might be the very thing that will carry us beyond the wilderness and into our land of promise.

LET'S THINK ABOUT IT...

Are you sometimes tempted to view your current season through a lens of doubt rather than faith?

LET'S PRAY ABOUT IT...

Lord, thank you for how you've proven your goodness and faithfulness to me. Help me to remember those times as I walk through seasons of wilderness. Amen.

TODAY'S DARE

Read Exodus 15:22–25 and 17:1–7.

A SHOT OF INSPIRATION

Faith isn't a feeling. It's a choice to trust God even when the road ahead seems uncertain.

Dave Willis

Join the convo! Inspired by today's chat? Share what you learned! Snap a photo of this book (or the drink you're sipping on), and spark a discussion on social media by answering this question:

When the Israelites were in the wilderness, God performed miracles that increased their faith (momentarily, at least). Do you have any "miracle moments" in your own life that you could share with others?

Be sure to use the hashtag #CoffeeShopDevos!

Powerless Pity

Are any of you suffering hardships? You should pray. Are any of you happy? You should sing praises.

James 5:13

LET'S CHAT ABOUT IT...

Social media can be dangerous. Not only because of the potential it has to leak private information, but because of the temptation it presents us to vent about our lives.

Perhaps you've witnessed these virtual pity parties—or maybe you're guilty of hosting one yourself! Social media is a great tool to spark discussion and engage with others; however, it can cause harm when we use it to seek pity from our friends.

Of course, these pity parties can occur outside of our screens as well. My mom compares these pity parties to a hammer: When others have pity on us and pat us on the back in a gesture of comfort, they're actually hammering us down and zapping our strength. I'm guilty of seeking pity from others, too. But I've learned that when I'm hammered down, I can't rise to my fullest potential. When I'm hammered, I don't have the courage or strength to rise above my circumstances. Pity zaps my strength and keeps me in the scum of trials.

When we face hardships, let's be determined not to make the situation more difficult by seeking pity. Let's instead draw comfort from God, which will give us the power to rise above the filth of our trials.

Next time I'm tempted to host a pity party, I'm going to resist the temptation to open my laptop or unlock my iPhone and turn to God instead. I don't need powerless pity offered by others; I need the victorious power that can only be offered by the Holy Spirit!

LET'S THINK ABOUT IT...

Compare and contrast how you feel after you turn to others for pity versus how you feel after you turn to God for comfort and strength.

LET'S PRAY ABOUT IT...

Lord, when I suffer, help me to seek comfort from you rather than pity from others, and show me when it's okay to receive counsel and encouragement from others. Amen.

TODAY'S DARE

The next time you're tempted to seek pity from others, write in your prayer journal instead.

A SHOT OF INSPIRATION

You can be pitiful or powerful . . . you cannot be both.

Joyce Meyer

Join the convo! Inspired by today's chat? Share what you learned! Snap a photo of this book (or the drink you're sipping on), and spark a discussion on social media by answering this question:

What's the difference between seeking pity and seeking advice? Where do we draw the line between the two?

Be sure to use the hashtag #CoffeeShopDevos!

Redemption Stories

Stay alert! Watch out for your great enemy, the devil. He prowls around like a roaring lion, looking for someone to devour. Stand firm against him, and be strong in your faith. Remember that your family of believers all over the world is going through the same kind of suffering you are.

1 Peter 5:8–9

LET'S CHAT ABOUT IT...

Don't you love movies that feature a lost girl who is rescued from the enemy by her hero? I think we're drawn to stories of rescue or redemption because it's woven into our DNA. That's the story of the gospel, isn't it? God sent His son, Jesus, to save *us*—His bride. He died so we could be set free.

But that doesn't mean the enemy won't try to attack us.

His intention is to wreak havoc and ruin our relationship with God. The good news is, we have a hero who fights for us. Our Savior has already defeated the powers of darkness.

So how can we live in victory? By building ourselves up in the Word, prayer, and praise. Christ within us will fight the battles on our behalf—but only when we seek His help and do our part in growing in our spiritual walk daily.

You know what I especially love about those stories? Not only does the hero get the girl, but the enemy is almost always destroyed in the end. Read the book of Revelation and you'll notice God has written the same ending for His children as well.

Jesus rescues His bride. The devil is defeated, once and for all.

And it'll be the most beautiful redemption story ever told.

LET'S THINK ABOUT IT...

How can you incorporate more prayer, praise, and study of the Word into your schedule?

_____

_____

_____

LET'S PRAY ABOUT IT...

Lord, strengthen me so I won't fall prey to the enemy's tactics. Thank you for fighting my battles. Amen.

TODAY'S DARE

When Jesus was confronted by the enemy in Matthew 4:1–11, He spoke the Word to destroy the enemy's attempts at defeat. If you're facing a battle—such as depression, fear, insecurity, etc.—find Scriptures that speak life into that situation. Confess these verses out loud, and praise God for the victory!

A SHOT OF INSPIRATION

So humble yourselves before God. Resist the devil, and he will flee from you.

James 4:7

Join the convo! Inspired by today's chat? Share what you learned! Snap a photo of this book (or the drink you're sipping on), and spark a discussion on social media by answering this question:

Is there a spiritual battle you've faced in the past? How did you find victory?

Be sure to use the hashtag #CoffeeShopDevos!

Downpours of Disappointments

Scripture to sip on

When you go through deep waters,
I will be with you.
When you go through rivers of difficulty,
you will not drown.

Isaiah 43:2

LET'S CHAT ABOUT IT...

I recently returned from a writing conference that took place near my favorite town—Asheville, North Carolina. Since it's spring, I anticipated sunshine, blue skies, and the perfect "walk in the park" weather. Instead, I was welcomed with murky skies, and rainfall made several appearances throughout the week.

Unfortunately, I think we've all experienced this kind of disappointment. Not necessarily the kind that comes from bad weather, but the disappointment that blocks our joy when bad circumstances come our way. When we receive news that shatters our hopes of "sunshine." When it seems as though heavy clouds follow us throughout the day, and we need to constantly carry an umbrella to guard us from pain.

When this happens, we need to remember that rain is only temporary. And even when it does rain, the sunshine remains bright behind the clouds. No trial is big enough to block the light of Christ.

On the last evening of the conference—when the attendees were weary of fighting bad weather—the rain cleared up. Peace settled over the campus.

And murky clouds left behind a rainbow in their midst.

God sent a reminder that rain never comes in vain. The pain and disappointments of life can give way to something new. Something beautiful.

A promise that God is always with us, even during the heaviest of rainfalls.

LET'S THINK ABOUT IT...

How can you train your eyes to focus on the light, the Son, even during the grayest of days?

LET'S PRAY ABOUT IT...

Lord, when I experience a dreary day or season, remind me to keep my eyes focused on the Son. Thank you for the beauty that will result from the rainfalls. Amen.

TODAY'S DARE

Have you ever heard the advice "Dance in the rain"? Today, find a way to do just that.
Here are some ideas:

- Try a new dessert recipe.
- Find a DIY project to create.
- Get a manicure with a friend.

A SHOT OF INSPIRATION

No matter what storm you face, you need to know that God loves you. He has not abandoned you.

Franklin Graham

Join the convo! Inspired by today's chat? Share what you learned! Snap a photo of this book (or the drink you're sipping on), and spark a discussion on social media by answering this question:

What kind of beauty has risen from the previous rainfalls in your life?

Be sure to use the hashtag #CoffeeShopDevos!

Training to Run

We also have joy with our troubles, because we know that these troubles produce patience. And patience produces character, and character produces hope.

Romans 5:3–4 NCV

LET'S CHAT ABOUT IT...

When an elite runner prepares for a race, the training she experiences beforehand is extensive. She spends countless hours with a trainer, someone who challenges her, motivates her, and tests her limits. This person encourages the runner when she hesitates and challenges her to persevere by reminding her of the prize.

As Christians we, too, are called to run a race. Yet we can't run if we don't first spend necessary time in preparation—conditioning our muscles and building endurance. These seasons of pruning may sometimes come in the form of tribulation. But Jesus, our trainer, sticks with us. His encouragement gives us confidence. These challenges stretch our faith and build character.

Only God knows the race we've been called to run. His preparation will equip us to perform the best.

The next time you feel too weak, find your strength in Christ. Use trials to build your patience, character, and hope.

Remember, you're developing muscles and endurance that will carry you far. These training seasons might seem endless, but they'll be well worth it when you take off, running the race God has called you to run for His glory.

LET'S THINK ABOUT IT...

As you draw nearer to Christ during the training seasons, how is your character developed and faith strengthened?

....

....

....

LET'S PRAY ABOUT IT...

Lord, as I face earthly hardships and "training seasons," help me produce a Christlike character and build muscles that will prepare me for a future that only you can see. Amen.

TODAY'S DARE

Make it a priority today to exercise physically. You can go on a prayer walk, listen to upbeat Christian music as you take a run, or enjoy playing a sport with your family or friends. As you build muscles physically, remember that God will help you become strong spiritually so you can be prepared to run your race for Him.

A SHOT OF INSPIRATION

Don't you realize that in a race everyone runs, but only one person gets the prize? So run to win!

1 Corinthians 9:24

Join the convo! Inspired by today's chat? Share what you learned! Snap a photo of this book (or the drink you're sipping on), and spark a discussion on social media by answering this question:

Have you experienced a "training season" in your life? How was your character built and faith strengthened during this time?

Be sure to use the hashtag #CoffeeShopDevos!

Coffee

Motivation for
the Journey

Caramel-Kissed Coffee

On those mornings when you're rushing to get ready for school, you might not have time to make a fancy coffee shop drink. But rather than making a cup of the plain, classic coffee, why not add a touch of caramel to sweeten it up a bit?

INGREDIENTS

- 1 cup coffee
- 1 tablespoon caramel syrup
- 1/4 cup half-and-half

INSTRUCTIONS

1. Brew coffee.
2. Stir caramel syrup into coffee.
3. Pour half-and-half into coffee and stir.

Heavenly Trophy

Scripture to sip on

Whatever work you do, do your best.

Ecclesiastes 9:10 NCV

LET'S CHAT ABOUT IT...

I was part of a competition cheerleading squad in middle school. The extensive practices we had weekly wore me out. There were times when I'd beg my mom to let me stay home from practice. I'm glad she didn't let me; otherwise, I wouldn't have learned the value of dedication.

In competitive cheerleading, every member of the squad has to give one hundred percent effort. If one cheerleader fails to follow through, the entire routine could be thrown out of balance. Every cheerleader must remain humble enough to work together and adhere to the coach's vision. As a competition approaches, the squad might grow weary from practices—so what gives them the motivation to continue? The possibility of winning a first place trophy. It is a competition, after all!

You may be in the school band, run track, or compete on another sports team at school. I'm sure you, too, have learned how to persevere under pressure, remain humble enough to accept criticism, and work with others, all while keeping the end reward in mind.

These are great lessons to apply to our Christian walk, don't you think?

We're all called to contribute to the body of Christ. It's a team effort, and every member must dedicate their entire effort so we can fulfill God's vision for the church.

So let's not grow weary and instead bring our A game in every area of our lives. Trust me: The trophies we receive on earth are nothing compared to the rewards that await us in heaven!

LET'S THINK ABOUT IT...

Are you one hundred percent dedicated in your work and role in the body of Christ?

....

....

....

LET'S PRAY ABOUT IT...

Lord, help me to give my best effort in every area of my life and to further the body of Christ. Thank you for the heavenly reward that awaits me. Amen.

TODAY'S DARE

Each week, write a new goal that will challenge you to grow in an area of your talent or skill. (For instance, if you're a musician, make it your goal to practice for an extra hour this week.)

A SHOT OF INSPIRATION

Therefore, since we are surrounded by such a huge crowd of witnesses to the life of faith, let us strip off every weight that slows us down, especially the sin that so easily trips us up. And let us run with endurance the race God has set before us.

Hebrews 12:1

Join the convo! Inspired by today's chat? Share what you learned! Snap a photo of this book (or the drink you're sipping on), and spark a discussion on social media by answering this question:

What lessons have you learned from playing or watching sports that you can apply to your walk with Christ?

Be sure to use the hashtag #CoffeeShopDevos!

Your Beam of Light

Scripture to sip on

In the same way, let your light shine before others, that they may
see your good deeds and glorify your Father in heaven.

Matthew 5:16 NIV

LET'S CHAT ABOUT IT...

Imagine your friends are stumbling around a dark building, unable
to see where they're headed. Meanwhile, you're carrying a flashlight
in your hand—the very light they're desperate for. Your flashlight is
being used to light your way; however, it's bright enough to light the
way for your friends, too.

Similarly, the world you live in is dark. But the good news? If Christ
is inside of you, His light is as well. This verse says, "let your light
shine before others, that they may see your good deeds and glorify
your Father in heaven." You hold the "flashlight" some of your friends
may be searching for.

Your beam of light shines forth any time you share the gospel, pray
for someone who is hurting, or offer encouragement to a discouraged
friend. Even a simple smile to a stranger can radiate Christ's light
and pierce through their darkness.

LET'S THINK ABOUT IT...

How can you offer your flashlight to the dark world around you?

LET'S PRAY ABOUT IT...

Lord, place before me people who are desperate for the beam of light I carry inside. Amen.

TODAY'S DARE

Talk to someone at school who looks as though they could use a friend.

A SHOT OF INSPIRATION

I'm a little pencil in the hand of a writing God, who is sending a love letter to the world.

Mother Teresa

Join the conva! Inspired by today's chat? Share what you learned! Snap a photo of this book (or the drink you're sipping on), and spark a discussion on social media by answering this question:

What are practical ways that Christians can offer light to those who live in darkness?

Be sure to use the hashtag #CoffeeShopDevos!

Raggedy Pajama Pants

"But forget all that—
it is nothing compared to what I am going to do.
For I am about to do something new.
See, I have already begun! Do you not see it?
I will make a pathway through the wilderness.
I will create rivers in the dry wasteland."

Isaiah 43:18–19

LET'S CHAT ABOUT IT...

I own a pair of pajama pants that I refuse to throw away. The material is delicate and lightweight, which has caused the hem to shred. Holes have ripped the fabric into strips. Yet the pants are comfortable. Familiar. The thin material makes them the perfect pajamas to slip on in the summer.

But it's silly to hang on to things that have the life worn out of them.

Are you also clinging to something old rather than embracing the new? Even though the past is familiar, we can't benefit from it. It's been used. God has something far better in store if we'd let go, move on, and trust Him.

Sure, changes can be difficult—but they also brim with possibilities. And even when our lives are in a constant state of motion, the One who never leaves our side is unchanging. So let's step out of yesterday and into the newness of today.

As for the pajama pants—perhaps it's about time I throw those in the trash. ;)

LET'S THINK ABOUT IT...

How can you release the past to God and step into the newness of today?

....

....

....

LET'S PRAY ABOUT IT...

Lord, help me to embrace changes in my life, because I know that releasing the old is the only way I can make room for the new. Amen.

TODAY'S DARE

Are you hanging on to anything from your past, such as old board games or clothes (including pajama pants) that you don't use anymore? Consider donating them to the needy.

A SHOT OF INSPIRATION

Jesus Christ is the same yesterday, today, and forever.

Hebrews 13:8

Join the convo! Inspired by today's chat? Share what you learned! Snap a photo of this book (or the drink you're sipping on), and spark a discussion on social media by answering this question:

Have you experienced difficult changes in your life? What good resulted in leaving the old behind and embracing the new?

Be sure to use the hashtag #CoffeeShopDevos!

Love at First Sip

Taste and see that the Lord is good.
Oh, the joys of those who take refuge in him!

Psalm 34:8

LET'S CHAT ABOUT IT...

"I drank coffee before it was cool." Are you familiar with that saying? It's one I can definitely relate to. I fell in love with coffee at first sip. When I was in preschool.

One morning, I begged my dad to have a sip of his coffee. He only allowed me a taste so I'd realize that I wouldn't like it and never ask again. But after he saw my reaction, he knew I'd become a coffee drinker.

It wasn't until I was a teen that I began to drink coffee almost daily—but even then, I did it because I loved it. The roasted taste and heavenly aroma. I enjoyed how it woke me up in the mornings and helped my creative juices begin to flow.

Even if coffee wasn't cool, I'd still be a fan.

Some try coffee because of the hype, and others, like me, fall in love at the first sip of their parents' coffee. There are others who only drink it for the caffeine.

Similarly, there are multiple reasons why people become Christians. Some might've been influenced by their parents' faith. Some might first experience Christ at youth group with their friends. Yet others have found Him out of desperation to fill their emptiness.

Regardless, once we experience the benefits that come with following Jesus, we're hooked. We become Jesus addicts from the first taste of His goodness and love. Our fire for Him will continue to burn, even if it becomes uncool to follow Jesus.

My devotion to Him is the one addiction I'd never give up!

LET'S THINK ABOUT IT...

Have you experienced the benefits that come from cultivating a relationship with Jesus?

....

....

....

....

LET'S PRAY ABOUT IT...

Lord, help me to grow closer to you. Thank you for the many benefits that come from following you. Amen.

TODAY'S DARE

If you drink coffee (or tea), meet a friend at a coffee shop and discuss the topic of this devotion.

A SHOT OF INSPIRATION

There is a God-shaped vacuum in the heart of every man which cannot be filled by any created thing, but only by God, the Creator, made known through Jesus.

Blaise Pascal

Join the convo! Inspired by today's chat? Share what you learned! Snap a photo of this book (or the drink you're sipping on), and spark a discussion on social media by answering this question:

Share about a time when you tasted firsthand God's goodness and the love He has toward you.

Be sure to use the hashtag #CoffeeShopDevos!

Harvesting a Future

Scripture to sip on

Teach us how short our lives really are
so that we may be wise.

Psalm 90:12 NCV

LET'S CHAT ABOUT IT...

My friends thought I was crazy when I chose to enroll in an online high school. Why would I want to leave them and go virtual? Here's why: I felt called to pursue writing seriously while I was still a teen.

It's commonly assumed teens should spend their youth "living life to the fullest" without worrying too much about their future. But unfortunately, making disastrous decisions isn't going to result in a full life. Our choices will eventually bring forth a crop, whether good or bad.

That's why I wanted to pursue my calling at a young age. I wanted to plant seeds that would reap a good harvest in my future. And I'm glad I did! Otherwise, I wouldn't be where I am in my career today. It's also during my teen years that I built the foundation for my relationship with Christ. I'd be lost without Him.

We aren't guaranteed tomorrow, and we're held accountable for how we choose to spend our time today. Let's grow spiritually, cultivate our gifts, connect with other believers, and reach the lost, determined to bring forth a good harvest for our future.

I speak from experience when I say this: If you spend your youth wisely, your future self will thank you for it!

LET'S THINK ABOUT IT...

What kind of seeds are you planting with the choices you make daily?

LET'S PRAY ABOUT IT...

Lord, help me to be wise with my time and spend my youth planting seeds that will reap a plentiful harvest. Amen.

TODAY'S DARE

Create a time log. As you go about your day, record where you're investing your time. At the end of the day, evaluate this time log and see if you should make any changes to your daily routine.

A SHOT OF INSPIRATION

Time is your most precious gift, because you only have a set amount of it.

Rick Warren

Join the convo! Inspired by today's chat? Share what you learned! Snap a photo of this book (or the drink you're sipping on), and spark a discussion on social media by answering this question:

Why do you think some people believe it's fine for teens to be careless with their time?

Be sure to use the hashtag #CoffeeShopDevos!

Worth the Work

The Lord is good to those who hope in him,
to those who seek him.
It is good to wait quietly
for the Lord to save.
It is good for someone to work hard
while he is young.

Lamentations 3:25–27 NCV

LET'S CHAT ABOUT IT...

When I was a teen, I didn't have a packed social calendar like my sister did while she was in high school. In fact, I decided to enroll in an online school when I was fourteen so I could spend extra time growing in the gifts God gave me.

But I sometimes wondered if my work was ever going to pay off. Was I wasting my time by writing a book that wasn't guaranteed publication? Then I came across this verse. God showed me that I was in the center of His will by seeking Him first. He'd bless me for my diligence, even if I never signed a publishing contract for the book I was writing.

Do you feel called to pursue a passion? Don't wait until graduation to discover your calling. Start now! If you're unsure of where your gifting lies, here's a secret: Put this Scripture into action. Seek Him. Wait for Him. Meanwhile, work hard in all aspects of your life, then watch and see how He blesses your diligence.

In case you're wondering—the book I wrote as a teen? It resulted in my first published novel, *Purple Moon*.

LET'S THINK ABOUT IT...

How can you grow in diligence in your daily work, your gifts, and your relationship with God?

LET'S PRAY ABOUT IT...

Lord, help me to spend my teen years pursuing you, cultivating my gifts, and being diligent in all areas of my work. Amen.

TODAY'S DARE

Spend at least a half hour today working at developing your gifts and/or passions.

A SHOT OF INSPIRATION

Can anything be sadder than work unfinished? Yes: work never begun.

Christina Rossetti

Join the convo! Inspired by today's chat? Share what you learned! Snap a photo of this book (or the drink you're sipping on), and spark a discussion on social media by answering this question:

How can teens make time to discover their gifts and work diligently?

Be sure to use the hashtag #CoffeeShopDevos!

An Unpopular Form of Worship

Scripture to sip on

In all the work you are doing, work the best you can. Work as if you were doing it for the Lord, not for people.

Colossians 3:23 NCV

LET'S CHAT ABOUT IT...

Math was my least favorite subject in school. The homework often took hours to complete, and I rarely made a 100 on tests.

Is there a subject in school you despise? When we aren't passionate about a task, it's tempting not to give it our best effort. However, having a bitter attitude toward work only makes it worse.

You see, if we perform our work as though we were doing it for God, our perspective can change. Working for God is a form of worship, and when we worship Him, we *can't help* but have joy!

So the next time you have a math test—or whatever form of work you dislike—view it as an opportunity to give God glory. No, it might not feel natural. But I can guarantee you this: The suffering we experience is not nearly as dreadful as the suffering Jesus bore on the cross.

Yes, including math.

LET'S THINK ABOUT IT...

What area of work do you find most dreadful? How can you approach this as if you were working for the Lord?

LET'S PRAY ABOUT IT...

Lord, help me to approach my work as though I were doing it in worship of you. Amen.

TODAY'S DARE

The next time you're faced with a form of work that you dread, use it as an opportunity to put this spiritual lesson into practice. As you work for God, take note of whether or not your attitude toward your work has shifted.

A SHOT OF INSPIRATION

> Whatever your life's work is, do it well.
> Martin Luther King Jr.

Join the convo! Inspired by today's chat? Share what you learned! Snap a photo of this book (or the drink you're sipping on), and spark a discussion on social media by answering this question:

Why do you think God wants us to work as though we are working for Him?

Be sure to use the hashtag #CoffeeShopDevos!

Connected to the Source

"Yes, I am the vine; you are the branches. Those who remain in me, and I in them, will produce much fruit. For apart from me you can do nothing."

John 15:5

LET'S CHAT ABOUT IT...

Have you ever been on your phone or laptop, when suddenly it runs out of battery and dies? Frustrating, right? Our electronics are no good when they don't have power, and the only way they gain this life is when they're plugged in to the source.

It's the same with our walk with God. Our works are as good as nothing—*unless* we're connected to the source, which is Christ. It's the only way to produce work that lasts.

In this verse, Jesus tells us He is the vine and we are the branches. The same principle applies: It's impossible for us to produce lasting fruit unless we remain in Him. Otherwise, our fruit will rot.

We remain in Him by fueling ourselves with His Word and letting the Holy Spirit guide us. The only way we can function properly and fulfill our assignment is to rely on God and stay connected to Him.

If you think it's frustrating when your electronics lose their charge, just imagine how upset Jesus is when He sees us attempting to work on a low battery!

LET'S THINK ABOUT IT...

How can you stay "connected to the source" throughout the day?

LET'S PRAY ABOUT IT...

Lord, help me to stay connected to you throughout the day, because I know my works are useless when I do not have your life flowing through me. Amen.

TODAY'S DARE

Read the entire chapter of John 15.

A SHOT OF INSPIRATION

Without the Spirit of God we can do nothing. We are as ships without wind or chariots without steeds. . . . Like coals without fire, we are useless.

Charles H. Spurgeon

Join the convo! Inspired by today's chat? Share what you learned! Snap a photo of this book (or the drink you're sipping on), and spark a discussion on social media by answering this question:

Can you tell the difference between accomplishing works on your own versus staying connected to God and relying on His help?

Be sure to use the hashtag #CoffeeShopDevos!

Why Can't It Be You?

Scripture to sip on

Jesus looked at them intently and said, "Humanly speaking, it is impossible. But with God everything is possible."

Matthew 19:26

LET'S CHAT ABOUT IT...

From a young age, my parents encouraged my siblings and I to thrive in our gifts. It's their belief in me that compelled me to keep writing. Mom always said to me, "Someone has to be an author, so why can't it be you?" She figured that if my passion was driven by the Lord, then it wasn't her place to burst the bubble.

Dreams often go forgotten and buried. They're not given the life they need—which is faith—to become resurrected. If God is the One who placed the dreams on our hearts to begin with, think of how sad that must make Him! It's discouraging to think about the people who could be reached—if only every Christian had the courage to chase after their God-given dream.

Ask God to show you how to pursue your calling. Then do your part and breathe life into your dream by viewing it through the lens of faith rather than doubt.

In the words of my mom, someone has to be the next author. Actress. President of the United States. Doctor. Astronaut. Missionary. Why can't it be you?

LET'S THINK ABOUT IT...

Is there a dream God has placed on your heart?

LET'S PRAY ABOUT IT...

Lord, I believe you can accomplish the impossible in my life. Help me to view my God-given dreams through the lens of faith rather than doubt. Amen.

TODAY'S DARE

If you hope to achieve your dream, take action! Research what it takes to become a [fill in the blank here], then create monthly and weekly goals that will bring you closer to seeing this dream come to pass.

A SHOT OF INSPIRATION

> The difference between a dreamer and a doer is the amount of action that follows their vision.
>
> Fabienne Fredrickson

Join the convo! Inspired by today's chat? Share what you learned! Snap a photo of this book (or the drink you're sipping on), and spark a discussion on social media by answering this question:

Why is it common for people, including Christians, to neglect their dreams?

Be sure to use the hashtag #CoffeeShopDevos!

Supernatural Qualification

Scripture to sip on

Then I said, "But Lord God, I don't know how to speak. I am only a boy." But the Lord said to me, "Don't say, 'I am only a boy.' You must go everywhere I send you, and you must say everything I tell you to say. Don't be afraid of anyone, because I am with you to protect you," says the Lord. Then the Lord reached out his hand and touched my mouth. He said to me, "See, I am putting my words in your mouth."

Jeremiah 1:6–9 NCV

LET'S CHAT ABOUT IT...

Have you ever felt as though you were unqualified to do something? Maybe you wanted to try out for a sport but talked yourself out of it due to lack of experience. This is how I felt before I began to speak to teens. I felt unqualified to speak due to my introverted personality.

In this verse, Jeremiah is a youth, and he feels called to be a prophet. But he tries to argue with God by telling him he's not a good speaker and is too young. God responds by telling Jeremiah He's putting words in his mouth. God later tells him that He would give Jeremiah a supernatural boldness.

Jeremiah didn't have to trust in his own ability; instead, he received a supernatural qualification to speak.

Can I remind you of how big and powerful God is? We can't do anything through our own effort. We need the Holy Spirit, who is inside of us, to help us.

God never calls us without qualifying us. Rely on Him to help you in your weakness. Then watch and see how He equips you to pursue what you once deemed as impossible.

LET'S THINK ABOUT IT...

Do you often feel unqualified to pursue your calling?

LET'S PRAY ABOUT IT...

Lord, as I begin to discover my calling, help me to trust in your ability rather than mine. Amen.

TODAY'S DARE

Write a list of three things you feel called to pursue in the area of ministry.

A SHOT OF INSPIRATION

Instead, God chose things the world considers foolish in order to shame those who think they are wise. And he chose things that are powerless to shame those who are powerful.

1 Corinthians 1:27

Join the convo! Inspired by today's chat? Share what you learned! Snap a photo of this book (or the drink you're sipping on), and spark a discussion on social media by answering this question:

Why do you think God often qualifies the called rather than vice versa?

Be sure to use the hashtag #CoffeeShopDevos!

Flabby Faith

No, dear brothers and sisters, I have not achieved it, but I focus on this one thing: Forgetting the past and looking forward to what lies ahead, I press on to reach the end of the race and receive the heavenly prize for which God, through Christ Jesus, is calling us.

Philippians 3:13–14

LET'S CHAT ABOUT IT...

I've never been a runner. In elementary school, I was involved in my school's running club. It was torture to run laps outside after school. There were some kids, though, who were competitive and determined to run the biggest number of miles.

That's what is admirable about runners: their determination to press on and beat their previous record.

Paul inspires us to use this exact determination to persevere in our walk with Christ. We're to press forward and keep our eyes on the heavenly prize that we'll receive at the end of the race.

Runners know that if they go too long without running, they might become flabby. To keep building muscle and endurance, they need to continue—despite the temptation to slack or bad weather that might tempt them to stay indoors.

Let's strive to grow in our walk with Christ daily. It might be difficult at first—but after persistence, endurance is built. Muscles develop.

Sounds much more appealing than turning into a flabby Christian, if you ask me!

LET'S THINK ABOUT IT...

How do you press forward in building godliness daily?

LET'S PRAY ABOUT IT...

Lord, help me to run the race you've called me to run and keep my eyes set on you. Amen.

TODAY'S DARE

When's the last time you went running? If the weather permits, put on your running shoes and head outside!

A SHOT OF INSPIRATION

All athletes are disciplined in their training. They do it to win a prize that will fade away, but we do it for an eternal prize. So I run with purpose in every step. I am not just shadowboxing. I discipline my body like an athlete, training it to do what it should. Otherwise, I fear that after preaching to others I myself might be disqualified.

1 Corinthians 9:25–27

Join the convo! Inspired by today's chat? Share what you learned! Snap a photo of this book (or the drink you're sipping on), and spark a discussion on social media by answering this question:

What are some obstacles that prevent Christians from growing in their walk with Christ?

Be sure to use the hashtag #CoffeeShopDevos!

Puppet Strings Tug-of-War

The sinful nature wants to do evil, which is just the opposite of what the Spirit wants. And the Spirit gives us desires that are the opposite of what the sinful nature desires. These two forces are constantly fighting each other, so you are not free to carry out your good intentions.

Galatians 5:17

LET'S CHAT ABOUT IT...

Have you seen a puppet controlled by strings? The puppet's movement is dictated by the puppeteer.

We have two natures constantly at battle over our strings: the Holy Spirit and our sinful nature. When we give the Holy Spirit control, we're guided by Him and remain in God's will.

But if we give the reins to our sinful nature and allow it to dictate our actions and speech, then we'll go down a path we weren't intended to walk.

These two natures are at war. Will we allow the Spirit or our sinful nature to dictate our decisions?

Personally, I'd much prefer to walk a path that leads to life rather than death. Wouldn't you?

LET'S THINK ABOUT IT...

Have you felt the tug of these two natures fighting to "pull your strings"?

LET'S PRAY ABOUT IT...

Lord, I realize two natures are constantly at war in my life. Help me to be guided by the Holy Spirit rather than my flesh. Amen.

TODAY'S DARE

Spend some time today feeding your spirit by reading the Bible, praying, and worshiping God. Then, cut out activities you sometimes partake in that could feed your sinful nature. For example, you might want to avoid exposing yourself to books, TV, and music that could plant sinful thoughts in your mind.

A SHOT OF INSPIRATION

> Instead of using "I'm human" as an excuse to walk in the flesh, let us use "I'm saved" as a reason to walk in the Spirit.
>
> Unknown

Join the convo! Inspired by today's chat? Share what you learned! Snap a photo of this book (or the drink you're sipping on), and spark a discussion on social media by answering this question:

Do you have any practical advice on how Christians can strengthen their spirit nature and weaken their sinful nature?

Be sure to use the hashtag #CoffeeShopDevos!

Everlasting Fruit

Scripture to sip on

Oh, the joys of those who do not
   follow the advice of the wicked,
   or stand around with sinners,
   or join in with mockers.
But they delight in the law of the Lord,
   meditating on it day and night.
They are like trees planted along the riverbank,
   bearing fruit each season.
Their leaves never wither,
   and they prosper in all they do.

Psalm 1:1–3

LET'S CHAT ABOUT IT...

My grandma has a sharper long-term memory than anyone I know. She's in her eighties, but she can remember specific details about old memories, and she shares these stories every time I visit her.

One story in particular has stuck with me. When Grandma was in college, she lived in an apartment with several other girls, many of whom weren't Christians. They'd often make fun of Grandma for not attending parties and for reading the Bible.

But the mocking didn't bother her. She was secure in her faith, and her goal was to please God, not people.

I believe she put this Scripture into action. I've noticed the fruit she's borne. Grandma's the perfect example of a woman who "delight[s] in the law of the Lord." She couldn't care less about partaking in sins that the world deems as cool, and all for the sake of pursuing a relationship with Christ.

If I can follow her example, then I, too, will bear fruit and prosper.

And perhaps God will reward me with a memory as sharp as Grandma's. ;)

LET'S THINK ABOUT IT...

Why is pursuing a relationship with God worth the persecution it could possibly result in?

....

....

....

LET'S PRAY ABOUT IT...

Lord, help me to stay devoted to you, even when others might mock me for my faith. I know the time I spend with you is never spent in vain. Amen.

TODAY'S DARE

My grandma started reading the Bible daily when she was in the fourth grade. She committed to three chapters on weekdays and five chapters on Saturdays and Sundays. This Bible plan helped her read through the entire Bible within a year. Do you follow a Bible reading plan? If not, consider finding a plan you can commit to.

A SHOT OF INSPIRATION

When people tell me I'm "missing out" on life because I'm a Christian—because I do the right thing—all I have to say is, "The reason I choose to live the way I do is because God has something so much better in store for me."

Unknown

Join the convo! Inspired by today's chat? Share what you learned! Snap a photo of this book (or the drink you're sipping on), and spark a discussion on social media by answering this question:

Share a time when you were mocked because of your faith.

Be sure to use the hashtag #CoffeeShopDevos!

Eternal Success

Praise the Lord!
How joyful are those who fear the Lord
   and delight in obeying his commands.
Their children will be successful everywhere;
   an entire generation of godly people will be blessed.
They themselves will be wealthy,
   and their good deeds will last forever.

Psalm 112:1–3

LET'S CHAT ABOUT IT...

Are you an overachiever like I am? Perhaps you, too, find it exhilarating to reach milestones and gain accomplishments. I love to work hard in an effort to chase my dreams. But the truth is, no amount of earthly success will be worth anything in eternity. Sure, we can be seen as prosperous in the world's eyes, but the accomplishment won't profit anything unless it contributes to the kingdom of God.

We often look up to celebrities in the spotlight and applaud them for their talent and hard work; however, God may look at the lady who serves food at the homeless shelter and applaud her for her humility and servant's heart.

When we live our lives aiming for worldly achievements, we might find success in the world's eyes—yet we'll miss out on eternal benefits.

Contributing our gifts to the body of Christ, witnessing to nonbelievers, giving to the needy, imitating Jesus to those around us—this is the kind of success that will lead to *true* prosperity, whether or not that prosperity becomes materialized on earth. Either way, it won't matter, because this world will fade in the blink of an eye.

And only the success that's gained for Christ will last.

LET'S THINK ABOUT IT...

How can you spend more time working toward eternal success?

....

....

....

LET'S PRAY ABOUT IT...

Lord, thank you that you don't view success as the world does, but I also know you delight in rewarding those who work for the kingdom. Help me to aim for eternal success rather than earthly success. Amen.

TODAY'S DARE

When someone wants to be successful, they'll often create a vision that will help them achieve their dreams. Today, write down a dream of yours that will benefit the kingdom. Then, establish goals so you can put this into action.

A SHOT OF INSPIRATION

Aim at heaven and you will get earth thrown in. Aim at earth and you get neither.

C. S. Lewis

Join the convo! Inspired by today's chat? Share what you learned! Snap a photo of this book (or the drink you're sipping on), and spark a discussion on social media by answering this question:

What are specific ways Christians can gain eternal success?

Be sure to use the hashtag #CoffeeShopDevos!

Inherited Creativity

So God created human beings in his own image.
In the image of God he created them;
male and female he created them.

Genesis 1:27

LET'S CHAT ABOUT IT...

When I was only a toddler, I had an itch to create. I'd nag my mom—who was an art teacher—and she'd give me a shoebox filled with age-appropriate art and craft supplies. At a young age, I learned how to create dolls from scratch, finger-paint, draw, and write stories.

I believe this itch to create is within all of us and was placed there by the Creator. When we release creativity, we reflect His image. It's a gift He's given us—a gift we can give back to Him when we use it to glorify God and minister to others. He has messages for us to portray through our paintbrushes, words, instruments, and other tools.

Let's go back to the time when we were preschoolers, when we first experienced the joy of creating, and use the tools He's given us to proclaim His love.

If you start to believe you're not creative, remember this: The One who spoke the universe into existence lives inside of you. You've inherited traits from the Creator of the Universe himself because He's your Father.

Therefore, you are creative.

LET'S THINK ABOUT IT...

How can you use your creativity to glorify God and minister to others?

LET'S PRAY ABOUT IT...

Lord, help me to discover the creative gifts you've planted within me, and show me how I can use them to further your kingdom. Amen.

TODAY'S DARE

Experiment with a new creative outlet! If you've never written a story, try it. If you've never drawn a pencil sketch, find a step-by-step lesson online and follow along. As you unleash your creativity, put on worship music and thank God for your creative inheritance!

A SHOT OF INSPIRATION

To create is to reflect the image of God. To create is an act of worship.

Erwin McManus

Join the convo! Inspired by today's chat? Share what you learned! Snap a photo of this book (or the drink you're sipping on), and spark a discussion on social media by answering this question:

Why do you think people grow up and neglect to unleash creativity like they did as children?

Be sure to use the hashtag #CoffeeShopDevos!

The Greatest Gift

Scripture to sip on

Seek the Kingdom of God above all else, and live righteously, and
he will give you everything you need.

Matthew 6:33

LET'S CHAT ABOUT IT...

What if you had a friend who only liked you because of the gifts you
bought her? Wouldn't you feel a little used?

I wonder if God feels this way about us at times. I wonder if He
feels like we sometimes use Him—so we can gain access to His favor.
Receive benefits that come from salvation. Have access to prayer.

Yes, I do believe He enjoys giving gifts to His children, and He
delights in seeing smiles on our faces. But those gifts alone should not
be our motive for serving Him. This Scripture says we should seek
Him "above all else." We should be motivated to grow in the Lord in
response to His love for us.

The awesome thing is, when we do put Him first, He'll give us
everything we need. But by then we'll be satisfied in our relationship
with God, and those gifts will be pale in comparison to the fulfillment
that comes from serving Him.

Because that alone—the freedom that comes from worshiping God
and pursuing a relationship with Him—is the greatest gift of all.

LET'S THINK ABOUT IT...

Do you seek God out of adoration for Him or a desire for His gifts?

LET'S PRAY ABOUT IT...

Lord, help me to seek you first, because I know the gifts that come from seeking you are nothing compared to the gift of knowing you. Amen.

TODAY'S DARE

How can you give a gift to God today as a way to show Him that He has first place in your heart?
Here are some ideas:

- Tithe at your church.
- Volunteer at a local homeless shelter.
- Create a form of art as a means to worship Him.

A SHOT OF INSPIRATION

So if you sinful people know how to give good gifts to your children, how much more will your heavenly Father give good gifts to those who ask him.

Matthew 7:11

Join the convo! Inspired by today's chat? Share what you learned! Snap a photo of this book (or the drink you're sipping on), and spark a discussion on social media by answering this question:

What does it look like for you to seek God wholeheartedly?

Be sure to use the hashtag #CoffeeShopDevos!

Bunny Trails and Parrot Videos

Scripture to sip on

Therefore, since we are surrounded by such a huge crowd of witnesses to the life of faith, let us strip off every weight that slows us down, especially the sin that so easily trips us up. And let us run with endurance the race God has set before us.

Hebrews 12:1

LET'S CHAT ABOUT IT...

After I enrolled in an online high school, I soon discovered the value of self-discipline. It was tempting to sleep in when I knew I wouldn't receive a tardy slip. (Thankfully I had my mom to drag me out of bed!) I often found myself checking Facebook rather than reading my online textbook.

Now, after years of working for myself, I've mastered the art of self-discipline when it comes to time management. No, it still doesn't come naturally. (I don't think I'll ever be a morning person!) But I've discovered the restraint that results from laziness and the freedom that results from self-control.

In today's technology age, distractions surround us. If we aren't careful, we could easily follow one bunny trail and somehow end up watching a YouTube video of a parrot singing the SpongeBob theme song.

Self-control is a *choice*, not a feeling. It's mastered when we choose to overcome our desires rather than allowing them to control us. So instead of following those alluring bunny trails, let's focus on the trail God has set before us.

It's only then, after the day's work is complete, that we can perhaps reward our diligence by watching a parrot video or two. ;)

LET'S THINK ABOUT IT...

Are you more prone to choosing laziness or self-control when it comes to time management?

_____

_____

_____

LET'S PRAY ABOUT IT...

Lord, help me to stay disciplined so I can focus on accomplishing the work you've set before me. Amen.

TODAY'S DARE

The next time you struggle to stay focused, set a timer for twenty minutes and see how much work you can accomplish. Reward yourself after about an hour or so of work.

A SHOT OF INSPIRATION

> Don't get sidetracked;
> keep your feet from following evil.
> Proverbs 4:27

Join the convo! Inspired by today's chat? Share what you learned! Snap a photo of this book (or the drink you're sipping on), and spark a discussion on social media by answering this question:

In what ways does the enemy distract Christians today from cultivating a relationship with God and working to build His kingdom?

Be sure to use the hashtag #CoffeeShopDevos!

How Loud Is Your Ribbit?

Scripture to sip on

For God has not given us a spirit of fear and timidity, but of power, love, and self-discipline.

2 Timothy 1:7

LET'S CHAT ABOUT IT...

When I was little, it was a trend for kids to collect Beanie Babies (small stuffed animals filled with beans). I was only five when Mom and I, along with a crowd of others, waited outside for a shop to open so we could buy from the new Beanie Babies shipment. It was then announced they were giving away a free Beanie Baby frog to the kid who could "ribbit" the loudest.

Mom felt sorry for me because she knew I wanted the frog, but I was the youngest kid in the crowd, not to mention the shyest. Still, before the microphone was handed to me, she whispered in my ear and said, "If you *really, really* want it, you'll have to ribbit the loudest."

And ribbit the loudest is what I did! Despite my age and quiet demeanor, I shocked everyone when I belted out the loudest ribbit of all. I rose to the challenge and was rewarded the frog.

I remind myself of this story every time I confront an intimidating situation. I can't focus on the size of the mountain; instead, I have to focus on the size of my desire to reach the other side.

God will often call us to step out of our comfort zones. Will we cower in fear or cling to the supernatural power God's given us and overcome? If we really want to obey Him, we'll have to step up to the challenge. Take the microphone.

And belt out our biggest *ribbit*.

LET'S THINK ABOUT IT...

Have you ever backed down from a challenge due to fear?

LET'S PRAY ABOUT IT...

Lord, I don't want to cower in fear because I know you've called me to rise to challenges. Thank you for helping me to overcome. Amen.

TODAY'S DARE

Read about how David overcame the giant Goliath in 1 Samuel 17. Where do you think David found the courage to rise to such a daunting challenge?

A SHOT OF INSPIRATION

It's not the size of the dog in the fight, it's the size of the fight in the dog.

Mark Twain

Join the convo! Inspired by today's chat? Share what you learned! Snap a photo of this book (or the drink you're sipping on), and spark a discussion on social media by answering this question:

Share about a time when you rose to a challenge and overcame a fear. What was the reward?

Be sure to use the hashtag #CoffeeShopDevos!

Frappe

Encouragement to Be Yourself

Nothing but Nutella Frappe

Frappes . . . the perfect way to cool off on a hot summer afternoon. I have many memories of making these cold coffee drinks with my friends when I was a teen, but I never thought to add a favorite hazelnut cocoa spread: Nutella.

If you, too, enjoy relaxing by the pool with your friends and fueling up with caffeinated dessert-like drinks, then go ahead. Treat yourself—and your friends—to this Nothing but Nutella Frappe.

INGREDIENTS

- 1 cup strong coffee
- 3 tablespoons Nutella
- 1/2 cup almond milk
- 2 cups ice

INSTRUCTIONS

1. Brew strong coffee.
2. Melt Nutella in microwave.
3. Blend all ingredients in blender.
4. Pour into glass and serve with a straw.
5. Optional garnish: whipped cream and extra melted Nutella drizzle

Pursue Your Youth

Scripture to sip on

You who are young, make the most of your youth.
Relish your youthful vigor.
Follow the impulses of your heart.
If something looks good to you, pursue it.
But know also that not just anything goes;
You have to answer to God for every last bit of it.

Ecclesiastes 11:9 MSG

LET'S CHAT ABOUT IT...

I homeschooled the majority of my high school years so I could pursue creative writing. But it wasn't easy to leave behind my friends and school, and I soon wondered if I'd made the right decision.

One day, I discovered this Scripture, and truth sank into my heart. God showed me I was using my teen years to prepare for my future. I was planting seeds that would eventually result in my career and ministry.

When I was sixteen, I was offered a publishing contract for my young adult novel. It was then published three years later. This wouldn't have been possible if I hadn't pursued my youth by spending my teen years wisely. It's because of this decision that I've had the opportunity to minister to others through my writing at an early age.

How are you pursuing your youth? What interests and hobbies could you go ahead and get your feet wet in? There's no better time than now to begin planting seeds that will reap a good future.

I challenge you to put this Scripture into action. Make the most of your youth. But don't forget the last part of this Scripture, which says, "You have to answer to God for every last bit of it."

LET'S THINK ABOUT IT...

How are you pursuing your youth?

LET'S PRAY ABOUT IT...

God, I surrender my dreams to you and ask for you to use them to accomplish your will. I want my gifts to be a vessel through which your kingdom is spread. Amen.

TODAY'S DARE

Make a list of your hobbies, gifts, and interests. Then, brainstorm possible career and ministry possibilities related to each area.

A SHOT OF INSPIRATION

Each of you has received a gift to use to serve others. Be good servants of God's various gifts of grace.

1 Peter 4:10 NCV

Join the convo! Inspired by today's chat? Share what you learned! Snap a photo of this book (or the drink you're sipping on), and spark a discussion on social media by answering this question:

Do you believe it's wise for teens to get a head start in their ministry and/or future career by beginning early?

Be sure to use the hashtag #CoffeeShopDevos!

Part of the Body

And if the ear says, "I am not part of the body because I am not an eye," would that make it any less a part of the body? If the whole body were an eye, how would you hear? Or if your whole body were an ear, how would you smell anything? But our bodies have many parts, and God has put each part just where he wants it.

1 Corinthians 12:16–18

LET'S CHAT ABOUT IT...

What if your hand tried to perform the task of your foot? Here's an even sillier thought: What if it grew tired of working for you, broke away from the body, and attempted to work for itself instead? The hand is useless unless it's connected to the rest of the body. Even though it's common sense, we often neglect to remember this as it applies to the body of Christ.

Our role in the body—which is the church—is to perform our specific function. It's impossible for us to fulfill an assignment that God didn't assign to us. Our works are dead when we break away from the body and attempt to use our gifts for our own benefit.

Have you viewed your gift in light of the body of Christ? Did you know He's given you a specific purpose that will further His kingdom? Your gifts and talents weren't chosen at random; they were hand selected by the Creator.

If each of us were to fulfill our specific roles, think about how much stronger the body would become. It wouldn't just walk; it would *run*!

So let's stop comparing ourselves. Instead, let's discover our role in the body and use our gifts to benefit the kingdom rather than ourselves.

Besides . . . there's only so far a hand can go on its own.

LET'S THINK ABOUT IT...

How could your gifts further the body?

LET'S PRAY ABOUT IT...

Lord, help me to discover my role in the body of Christ so I can further your kingdom. Amen.

TODAY'S DARE

Read 1 Corinthians 12.

A SHOT OF INSPIRATION

If you don't make your unique contribution to the Body of Christ, it won't be made.

Rick Warren

Join the convo! Inspired by today's chat? Share what you learned! Snap a photo of this book (or the drink you're sipping on), and spark a discussion on social media by answering this question:

How can Christians discover their role in the body of Christ?

Be sure to use the hashtag #CoffeeShopDevos!

Confidence vs. Arrogance

Scripture to sip on

Humble yourselves before the Lord, and he will lift you up.

James 4:10 NIV

LET'S CHAT ABOUT IT...

Growing up, I watched almost every season of the singing reality show *American Idol*. The singers who stood out to me weren't the ones who had the most powerful voices; instead, they were the ones who had talent, yet remained humble. But it annoyed me when the judges told these humble contestants to have more confidence.

The thing is—it's possible to be both humble *and* confident. Yet when we don't stand on a foundation of humility, our confidence can easily give way to arrogance.

There's nothing wrong with being confident. But our gifts are just that: gifts. Nothing is ours to take pride in. We would still be dust if it weren't for God breathing life into us. So if we want to brag, we should brag about Him and what He's done in our lives.

When Christ came to earth in the flesh, He had every reason to be arrogant. Yet He chose to make His appearance as a baby. He was born amongst farm animals and grew up in a humble home. His goal in ministry was to bring glory to His Father.

Shouldn't that be ours, too? Besides, when we attain humility, this Scripture says God will lift us up.

But first, we need to lower ourselves by bowing down to Christ, humbled before the Lord.

It's only then that He can lift us higher than we could imagine.

LET'S THINK ABOUT IT...

How often do you give God the glory for your talents?

_____

_____

_____

LET'S PRAY ABOUT IT...

Lord, help me to lower myself in humility before you so I can accomplish the work you've given me without claiming praise. Amen.

TODAY'S DARE

Take time to humble yourself before God today by thanking Him for the gifts He's given you and giving Him the glory He deserves.

A SHOT OF INSPIRATION

Humility is nothing but the disappearance of self in the vision that God is all.

Andrew Murray

Join the convo! Inspired by today's chat? Share what you learned! Snap a photo of this book (or the drink you're sipping on), and spark a discussion on social media by answering this question:

How can Christians remain both humble and confident in their gifts?

Be sure to use the hashtag #CoffeeShopDevos!

Embrace Your Uniqueness

Scripture to sip on

For we are God's masterpiece. He has created us anew in Christ Jesus, so we can do the good things he planned for us long ago.

Ephesians 2:10

LET'S CHAT ABOUT IT...

When I was in middle school, I thought something was wrong with me. I didn't have the same interests my peers did, and I wasn't as outgoing as most of my friends were. But I soon realized my unique qualities weren't something to be ashamed of; they were to be embraced.

God chose my personality and characteristics because He knew they'd help me carry out my purpose. If I'd allowed the enemy to keep me ashamed, I wouldn't be doing what I'm doing today. I wouldn't be a writer. And if I didn't embrace my role as a writer, I wouldn't have the opportunity to speak into the lives of others.

Are you ashamed of the unique way God crafted you? Have you tried to be someone else? Remember: When you try to be someone else, you're not only neglecting your true self; you're also sacrificing the potential God has planted within you. The potential to rise to your calling, reach others through your gifts, and make a difference.

Yet when you fully accept yourself and step into who God has created you to be, there's no telling the kind of impact you'll make for His kingdom!

LET'S THINK ABOUT IT...

Have you embraced who God has created you to be?

LET'S PRAY ABOUT IT...

Lord, help me to embrace who you've created me to be so I can step into my potential and make an impact for your kingdom. Amen.

TODAY'S DARE

Write a list of the personality traits, characteristics, and gifts that you're grateful for. Any time you begin to compare yourself to someone else, take out this list. Remind yourself of who you are in God's eyes and thank Him for the unique way He made you.

A SHOT OF INSPIRATION

You are a creation of God unequaled anywhere in the universe. God never made anyone else exactly like you, and He never will again.

Norman Vincent Peale

Join the convo! Inspired by today's chat? Share what you learned! Snap a photo of this book (or the drink you're sipping on), and spark a discussion on social media by answering this question:

Why is it tempting for us to compare ourselves to others and pretend to be someone we're not?

Be sure to use the hashtag #CoffeeShopDevos!

Inward Appearance

Scripture to sip on

But the Lord said to Samuel, "Don't judge by his appearance or height, for I have rejected him. The Lord doesn't see things the way you see them. People judge by outward appearance, but the Lord looks at the heart."

1 Samuel 16:7

LET'S CHAT ABOUT IT...

Don't you wish our outer beauty could be a reflection of our inner beauty? If that were the case, our culture would be more focused on beautifying our character and godliness rather than our outer shell. But instead, the media constantly paint a picture of how we should look, then they sell products that can help to alter our physical appearance.

It's upsetting that we're brainwashed into believing our looks aren't good enough. It's sickening that our culture puts more of an emphasis on outer beauty than inner beauty.

But God looks at the heart. If He's the only One we're aiming to please—and if He crafted us perfectly—why do we try to modify His original piece of art? The only beauty we'll give account for in eternity is our godliness.

There's nothing wrong with feeling beautiful and confident. But rather than wasting our energy attempting to measure up to the world's impossible standard of beauty, let's instead pour that devotion into "pampering" our character and godliness.

Because in the end, that's the only kind of beauty that will capture the eyes of Christ.

LET'S THINK ABOUT IT...

How much time do you spend on your outward appearance versus your inward appearance?

LET'S PRAY ABOUT IT...

Lord, help me devote my energy into building my inward beauty rather than attempting to alter my outward appearance. Amen.

TODAY'S DARE

Have you seen a fashion "in and out" trend list? Why not create one that focuses on cultivating your inner appearance?
Here's a start:

Out . . .	In . . .
• Bad language	• Encouraging others
• Gossip	• Compassion
• Judging others	• Empathy and understanding
• Back-talking parents	• Obeying authority

A SHOT OF INSPIRATION

Charm is deceptive, and beauty does not last;
but a woman who fears the Lord will be greatly praised.

Proverbs 31:30

Join the convo! Inspired by today's chat? Share what you learned! Snap a photo of this book (or the drink you're sipping on), and spark a discussion on social media by answering this question:

According to Scripture, what do you believe is God's definition of true beauty?

Be sure to use the hashtag #CoffeeShopDevos!

True Worth

Obviously, I'm not trying to win the approval of people, but of God.
If pleasing people were my goal, I would not be Christ's servant.

Galatians 1:10

LET'S CHAT ABOUT IT...

When I was in middle school, MySpace was the most popular form of social media among my friends. This social media platform gave us the option to order our top friends from greatest to least. Girls would often measure their popularity status based on how many "top friends" they were listed in.

MySpace is no longer trendy—but it's been replaced with other forms of social media. And some girls now base their worth on the number of Instagram followers they have and how many likes their pictures receive.

It's part of our human nature to crave attention and acceptance. Yet we're searching to fulfill this longing for acceptance in the wrong places.

The opinion of humans doesn't define our worth. Our only goal—as this Scripture says—should be to win the approval of God. He doesn't measure our worth based on the number of friends we have. He chose us and stamped His approval on us even before we were created. How freeing is that?

When we step into our identity as a child of God, then even if we *do* become popular, it'll have no value to us.

Because the acceptance we were searching for was attained the day we viewed ourselves through the eyes of Christ.

LET'S THINK ABOUT IT...

Do you try to satisfy your longing for acceptance by seeking the approval of people?

LET'S PRAY ABOUT IT...

Lord, when I have a longing for acceptance, help me to turn to you. Amen.

TODAY'S DARE

Struggling to discover your identity in Christ? Declare the following statements that are found in the Bible.

I am a child of God (Ephesians 1:3–8).

I am loved (John 3:16).

I am forgiven (1 John 1:9).

I am Christ's friend (John 15:15).

I am a masterpiece (Ephesians 2:10).

I am a new creation (2 Corinthians 5:17).

I am fearfully and wonderfully made (Psalm 139:14 NIV).

I am chosen (Ephesians 1:4–5).

A SHOT OF INSPIRATION

If you know who you are in Christ, it won't matter so much to you what other people think.

Joyce Meyer

Join the convo! Inspired by today's chat? Share what you learned! Snap a photo of this book (or the drink you're sipping on), and spark a discussion on social media by answering this question:

Why do you think the enemy aims to attack our identity in Christ?

Be sure to use the hashtag #CoffeeShopDevos!

Fog Ahead

Scripture to sip on

And I am certain that God, who began the good work within you, will continue his work until it is finally finished on the day when Christ Jesus returns.

Philippians 1:6

LET'S CHAT ABOUT IT...

"What are your plans after high school?"

Even when I was going into my senior year, I still didn't know how to answer this question. How was I supposed to make such a pivotal decision?

If your road ahead is also unclear—almost as though fog has dimmed your vision—you're not the only teen who feels that way. There are many teenagers who graduate high school and still have no idea what they're interested in. Sometimes our calling reveals itself little by little rather than all at once. But as we pursue God and let Him guide us through life, He'll open up the way before us.

Meanwhile, do what you can to tap into your potential. Take into consideration the desires that have been placed on your heart, your favorite subjects in school, and your general interests. Get your feet wet in various areas. As you do this, God may just reveal the next step He wants you to take.

So if it seems as though fog has prevented you from seeing the road ahead, grasp God's hand. Work where He's planted you, follow Him, and keep your mind open to possibilities.

As long as you remain by God's side, His light will provide just enough clarity to help you take your next step.

LET'S THINK ABOUT IT...

How can you do your part in discovering your calling and acting in obedience to God's guidance?

_____

_____

_____

LET'S PRAY ABOUT IT...

Lord, thank you that as I remain by your side, you will provide just enough light for my next step. Amen.

TODAY'S DARE

Take the Myers-Briggs® personality test online. What career options are suitable for your personality type?

A SHOT OF INSPIRATION

Faith isn't a feeling. It's a choice to trust God even when the road ahead seems uncertain.

Dave Willis

Join the convo! Inspired by today's chat? Share what you learned! Snap a photo of this book (or the drink you're sipping on), and spark a discussion on social media by answering this question:

Do you have advice for other teens who are struggling to discover their calling?

Be sure to use the hashtag #CoffeeShopDevos!

Wildest Dreams

Scripture to sip on

God can do anything, you know—far more than you could ever imagine or guess or request in your wildest dreams!

Ephesians 3:20 MSG

LET'S CHAT ABOUT IT...

After my older sister graduated high school, she made a bold move from our home in South Carolina to New York City. Her plans to attend Fashion Institute of Technology and pursue modeling seemed crazy at the time; besides, she was only 18 and had never even been in an airplane before!

Even though some people admired Tara for chasing her dreams, there were others who didn't understand. What made her believe this wild dream could actually come true?

I believe it was her faith in God. He placed the dream on her heart, and He paved the way before her. She knew she could trust His provision.

God has rewarded Tara's faith and has blessed her for being a light in the modeling industry. She's now married to a worship leader at Hillsong New York City church and has lived in New York City for nine years. What would've happened if she'd neglected to pursue God's calling for her life?

Your God-given dreams won't always make sense. But when you follow His guidance, you can trust He'll open the way before you.

Then, as you take that leap of faith, watch and see how He rewards your faith and does "far more than you could ever imagine or guess or request in your wildest dreams!"

LET'S THINK ABOUT IT...

Is there a crazy dream God has placed on your heart?

LET'S PRAY ABOUT IT...

Lord, I believe you placed the dreams on my heart for a reason. Help me to have faith in your guidance and provision in this area. Amen.

TODAY'S DARE

Have a crazy dream? If so, consider starting a dream journal. You can write specific prayers about this dream and record your progress and milestones. Someday, you can read through these entries and witness how God rewarded your faith.

A SHOT OF INSPIRATION

> What I do know is that there are two kinds of pain in this life: risk and regret. I'd rather live with the first than the second.
>
> Holley Gerth

Join the convo! Inspired by today's chat? Share what you learned! Snap a photo of this book (or the drink you're sipping on), and spark a discussion on social media by answering this question:

Why do some Christians neglect their God-given dreams?

Be sure to use the hashtag #CoffeeShopDevos!

Running the Wrong Race

Scripture to sip on

Pay careful attention to your own work, for then you will get the satisfaction of a job well done, and you won't need to compare yourself to anyone else.

Galatians 6:4

LET'S CHAT ABOUT IT...

Comparison is an easy trap to fall into. Once we've fallen, it's only a matter of time before we become jealous—and before you know it, we begin to doubt ourselves and become ungrateful for the gifts we've been given.

We're not called to comparison. When we do this, we miss out on appreciating the unique way that God created us. We instead become focused on what we *don't* have and neglect to use our own potential.

Comparison kills—our confidence. Our joy. Our potential. Our self-esteem. What good can come from this? And besides, why are we comparing ourselves when we were called to be set apart?

God has set before each of us a unique race. But if we're constantly comparing ourselves to others, we'll become too preoccupied to notice and appreciate our uniqueness. And if we don't step into the fullness of our potential, then guess what? We could possibly miss out on all that God has in store for us.

You're the only one who is equipped to run your unique race. How sad would it be to miss out on your calling simply because you were too busy attempting to run someone else's race?

LET'S THINK ABOUT IT...

Have you experienced the damaging effects that result from comparison?

LET'S PRAY ABOUT IT...

Lord, help me to focus on running my own race. Thank you for the unique way you created me, and help me to embrace my potential so I can step into all that you have in store for me. Amen.

TODAY'S DARE

The next time you're with a group of friends, ask everyone to write a special characteristic about every person in the group. Each girl should then go home with a pile of encouraging notes. Keep your notes on hand any time you're tempted to compare yourself!

A SHOT OF INSPIRATION

Comparison will consistently cloud the clarity of God's call on your life.

Robert Madu

Join the convo! Inspired by today's chat? Share what you learned! Snap a photo of this book (or the drink you're sipping on), and spark a discussion on social media by answering this question:

How can Christians focus on running their own race rather than comparing themselves to others?

Be sure to use the hashtag #CoffeeShopDevos!

Inside-Out Makeup

Scripture to sip on

Don't be concerned about the outward beauty of fancy hairstyles, expensive jewelry, or beautiful clothes. You should clothe yourselves instead with the beauty that comes from within, the unfading beauty of a gentle and quiet spirit, which is so precious to God.

1 Peter 3:3–4

LET'S CHAT ABOUT IT...

I have my first live TV interview in a few days. Yesterday, my cousin, a makeup artist, taught me how to apply my makeup for the interview. I'm not going to lie—the results amazed me. The way she expertly highlighted and defined my features for the bright lights and cameras was perfect.

I don't believe there's anything wrong with wearing makeup—but what happens when I don't have it as a mask to hide behind? Will I still feel confident and comfortable in my natural, unaltered appearance?

Our culture places a big emphasis on outer beauty. We love to pore over makeup tutorials online and post selfies when we've mastered the cat-eye look just right. It feels good to receive compliments on our appearance—but in the end, I don't want that alone to be my goal. To turn the heads of others. Instead, I want to make a different kind of impact. This kind of impact comes from applying "inside-out makeup":

Instead of just lipstick, I want to wake up every morning and apply joy to my lips.

Instead of just blush, I want my face to glow with gentleness.

Instead of just mascara, I want to apply a thick layer of compassion toward everyone I see.

That way, I can capture the attention of those around me. No, not because I've discovered a new way to apply my outer makeup, but because I've put this Scripture into action and have clothed myself with a "beauty that comes from within." It's only when I master this "look" that I'll feel completely confident in my beauty.

Even if I go an entire day without wearing my outer makeup.

LET'S THINK ABOUT IT...

How can you spend more time applying inside-out makeup in the mornings?

LET'S PRAY ABOUT IT...

Lord, when I come in contact with others, help them to be captivated by my inside-out makeup that radiates from within. Amen.

TODAY'S DARE

Snap a selfie of you without wearing any makeup and post it on social media. Take it a step further by answering this devotion's convo question below!

A SHOT OF INSPIRATION

That's the thing about inner beauty: unlike physical beauty, which grabs the spotlight for itself, inner beauty shines on everyone, catching them, holding them in its embrace, making them more beautiful too.

Unknown

Join the convo! Inspired by today's chat? Share what you learned! Snap a photo of this book (or the drink you're sipping on), and spark a discussion on social media by answering this question:

Why is it sometimes hard for us girls to be comfortable going a day without wearing makeup?

Be sure to use the hashtag #CoffeeShopDevos!

Fingerprints of God

Scripture to sip on

For we are God's masterpiece.

Ephesians 2:10

LET'S CHAT ABOUT IT...

There's a picture that has hung on my parents' refrigerator for years. It's a photo taken on Easter morning when I was fifteen. I wore a spring dress—which is typical on Easter, of course. But what *wasn't* so typical was the white shirt I wore beneath it.

When I look back at the picture now, I cringe. The funny thing is, my older sister had advised me not to wear a shirt beneath my dress. But I thought it was cute! And apparently I didn't care whether or not it was in style.

Fashion has never been a strong suit of mine (pun not intended!). I'd prefer to decide what to wear based on my personal taste and the comfort factor. Even though there have been times when I've wished I could take after my sisters' fashion sense, I've realized there's freedom in being yourself. Our unique personalities, interests, and tastes are reflected in the various ways we express ourselves—and it's this expression of ourselves that allows us to leave our individual fingerprints on the world.

Each of us is God's masterpiece, and He reflects His image in His creation. With that in mind, when we give ourselves permission to be ourselves, we become a reflection of Christ—His original creation. Our fingerprint is actually *His* fingerprint expressed through ours.

So go ahead—wear a T-shirt beneath your dress if you think it's cute. Who knows? You may just start a new fashion trend!

LET'S THINK ABOUT IT...

Do you give yourself permission to be yourself?

LET'S PRAY ABOUT IT...

Lord, thank you that I'm a masterpiece created by your hands. Help me to reflect you when I express myself. Amen.

TODAY'S DARE

Give yourself permission to express yourself today.
Here are some ideas . . .

- Go to the mall and buy a new outfit that expresses your style.
- Redecorate your bedroom; try moving the furniture around for a fresh new look.
- Make jewelry uniquely designed by you.

As you do this, thank God for the unique way He has chosen to reveal himself through you.

A SHOT OF INSPIRATION

You have all you need within you to become the best version of yourself.

Mastin Kipp

Join the convo! Inspired by today's chat? Share what you learned! Snap a photo of this book (or the drink you're sipping on), and spark a discussion on social media by answering this question:

Have you ever neglected to be yourself in order to gain acceptance?

Be sure to use the hashtag #CoffeeShopDevos!

Neglected Tools

Go after a life of love as if your life depended on it—because it does. Give yourselves to the gifts God gives you. Most of all, try to proclaim his truth.

1 Corinthians 14:1 MSG

LET'S CHAT ABOUT IT...

Pretend you're helping to build a youth building for your church. Someone gives you a hammer and tells you to be in charge of reinforcing the foundation. However, you decide not to. Why? Because you would be embarrassed for the loud noise the hammer makes to bring attention to yourself. So instead of doing your job, you ignore the tool you've been given and neglect your assignment.

Now let's apply this to real life. The youth building is the body of Christ, and the tool you've been given is your gift. You aren't called to use this gift to bring attention to yourself; rather, you've been given an assignment. One that will be a witness to the world and help to build the body. If that's the case, why would you want to neglect your gift? Sure, you might bring attention to yourself by using it, but that's not a legitimate reason to ignore this tool.

Cultivating our gifts doesn't have to be about ourselves. It's exciting to watch our dreams come to pass, yes—but our ultimate aim is to build the kingdom.

So let's give ourselves to the gifts God has given us. Let's raise our hammers and reinforce the foundation. If the act of doing this brings attention to ourselves, so what? We'll then have the perfect opportunity to share about our faith!

LET'S THINK ABOUT IT...

Have you believed the lie that it's self-centered to tap into your gifts and pursue your dreams?

LET'S PRAY ABOUT IT...

Lord, I don't want to neglect the tool I've been given to build your kingdom. If I receive attention, help me to use it as an opportunity to share about my faith. Amen.

TODAY'S DARE

If you've neglected your "tool," take it out today and find one way you can spend time using it.

A SHOT OF INSPIRATION

I wouldn't say it's being selfish to pursue a calling that God has placed on your heart. I would say it's being obedient.

Cindi McMenamin

 Inspired by today's chat? Share what you learned! Snap a photo of this book (or the drink you're sipping on), and spark a discussion on social media by answering this question:

Why do you think some Christians believe it's self-centered to pursue their dreams?

Be sure to use the hashtag #CoffeeShopDevos!

Force behind the Pebble

Scripture to sip on

But you belong to God, my dear children. You have already won a victory over those people, because the Spirit who lives in you is greater than the spirit who lives in the world.

1 John 4:4

LET'S CHAT ABOUT IT...

For the past several months, I've traveled to various writing conferences across the country and have taught workshops to writers—most of whom were probably twice my age, at least.

This isn't in my comfort zone. In fact, even though I've been speaking publicly for three years, it's still a feat that I can only conquer through Christ. I often feel like I'm David against Goliath when I go to these conferences.

David, who was a youth, had to face a towering giant. His only weapon? A tiny pebble. Obviously his confidence wasn't placed in his height or in his pebble, so where did his confidence lie? In the One who was greater than he.

And it's because of his faith in the Lord that he won the victory. It's the force behind David's pebble that killed the enemy. I highly doubt that "force" could've come from David!

So when we face our giants—whether the giant is a fear, hardship, or a battle—we don't have to measure it against our own strength. Let's instead place our confidence in the One who lives inside of us.

If we do, then the force behind our pebble will not be the result of our own strength. And it's this force, the result of our faith, that will cause the giant to tumble to the ground.

LET'S THINK ABOUT IT...

What do the giants in your life look like?

LET'S PRAY ABOUT IT...

Lord, when I face giants in my life, help me to find my confidence in you, because I know You are greater than any challenge I confront on this earth. Amen.

TODAY'S DARE

David volunteered to defeat the giant. When you're presented with an opportunity to volunteer—whether it's at church, school, or even at home—don't measure the challenge against your own strength. Instead, if God wants you to step up to the plate, even if it's uncomfortable, place your confidence in Him. Then watch and see how your faith will be rewarded.

A SHOT OF INSPIRATION

The key question in life is not "How strong am I?" but rather "How strong is God?"

Max Lucado

Join the convo! Inspired by today's chat? Share what you learned! Snap a photo of this book (or the drink you're sipping on), and spark a discussion on social media by answering this question:

Have you confronted a difficulty that seemed too large for your strength?

Be sure to use the hashtag #CoffeeShopDevos!

Hammered Confidence

Scripture to sip on

So God created human beings in his own image.
In the image of God he created them;
male and female he created them.

Genesis 1:27

LET'S CHAT ABOUT IT...

My older sister is four years older than I am, so growing up and attending the same schools, I often felt like I had to live in her shadow. Tara was the social butterfly. Cheer captain. Every report card of hers was refrigerator-worthy. It didn't help that she was drop-dead gorgeous, too! As an insecure tween, my self-esteem suffered when I felt like I had to measure up to her.

Of course, it wasn't true that I was being compared to her. This was a lie from the enemy that he used to hammer my self-esteem.

If we aren't confident in our individuality, we'll compare ourselves to others in a negative light. Little by little, our confidence will be hammered. How can we shield ourselves from this hammering and stand tall in who we are?

By viewing ourselves through the eyes of Christ. When we believe the truth of who He says we are, our confidence will be built on the foundation of the Word. It'll become so strong that the enemy's attempts to hammer us down will be useless.

Let's use the Word as a weapon to fight back and reclaim our confidence. Then we'll see the beauty of our own individuality and experience the life that Christ died for us to enjoy.

LET'S THINK ABOUT IT...

How can you fight back against the enemy's attacks and reclaim your confidence?

LET'S PRAY ABOUT IT...

Lord, help me to believe the truth about who you say I am so my confidence doesn't become hammered by the enemy. Amen.

TODAY'S DARE

If you struggle with believing the truth about who you are in God's eyes, write down the following statements and declare them throughout the day:

He says I am . . .
Loved (1 John 4:9–11)
Beautiful (Psalm 139:14)
Valued (Romans 5:8)
Victorious (1 Corinthians 15:57)
Conqueror (Romans 8:37–39)
Redeemed (Colossians 1:14)

A SHOT OF INSPIRATION

The most beautiful women I've ever observed are those that have exchanged a self-focused life for a Christ-focused one. They are confident, but not in themselves. Instead of self-confidence, they radiate with Christ confidence.

Leslie Ludy

Join the convo! Inspired by today's chat? Share what you learned! Snap a photo of this book (or the drink you're sipping on), and spark a discussion on social media by answering this question:

Why do you think the enemy tries to attack our confidence?

Be sure to use the hashtag #CoffeeShopDevos!

Lies vs. Truth

What shall we say about such wonderful things as these? If God is
for us, who can ever be against us?

Romans 8:31

LET'S CHAT ABOUT IT...

I recently found this journal entry I wrote when I was fifteen:

> *Stop letting others affect you! In order to grow the way God
> wants you to, you have to stop letting things affect you so much,
> or they're just winning. They'll be in control of your life, not
> you. Let go. God has a future for you. Just be yourself.*

Trust me: I know words can hurt. Others can use their mouths
to tear you apart and make you feel worthless. That's how I felt at
that age. I wrote this journal entry as a form of therapy—I wanted
to remind myself not to believe the lies of others or let their judgments affect me.

It's impossible to please everyone. Why waste the energy? Our only
aim should be to please God and become who He's created us to be.
We're going to fail if we allow others to keep us from being ourselves
and pursuing our calling.

When we choose to believe lies from others, our belief will feed
those lies; yet when we believe the truth God has spoken over us
instead, our faith will feed that truth. It's whatever we feed that will
have the most power over us.

I'm glad I chose to focus on the truth of who God says I am.
Because now, I can't even recall most of the lies that were spoken
over me. I chose not to feed them, so they shriveled up and became
powerless.

God's love has the ability to erase the lies others have spoken over
you—but it'll only happen when you choose to feed the truth rather
than those lies.

LET'S THINK ABOUT IT...

What are you feeding the most: lies or truth?

LET'S PRAY ABOUT IT...

Lord, thank you that you are for me, so no one can come against me. Help me to believe your truth rather than the lies spoken by others. Amen.

TODAY'S DARE

Take out your journal and write down the truth of who God says you are.

A SHOT OF INSPIRATION

The whole world can ignore me and treat me as if I weren't there at all, but God has picked me out to be His very own.

Neva Coyle

Join the convo! Inspired by today's chat? Share what you learned! Snap a photo of this book (or the drink you're sipping on), and spark a discussion on social media by answering this question:

How can we move past the hurtful words others have spoken over us?

Be sure to use the hashtag #CoffeeShopDevos!

Create a Path

Scripture to sip on

Seek his will in all you do,
and he will show you which path to take.

Proverbs 3:6

LET'S CHAT ABOUT IT...

I didn't get my driver's license until I was a senior in high school. Not because I failed the test multiple times, and not because my parents wouldn't let me, but because I didn't have the desire to drive until then.

I've never been one to "follow the system"; in fact, I've never understood the system. Why try to fit into a mold if it wasn't created for me? Why should I do what everyone else does if it requires being someone I'm not? Some may consider this to be a free-spirited way of thinking. I believe it's how we were called to live—a life in direct obedience to Christ, even if it means doing things differently.

I don't advise that you disobey authority for the sake of "staying true to who you are." God's given us authority to help guide us into the life He's called us to live.

But if you feel pressured—from the world or from friends—to reframe yourself simply to fit into a specific system, you may want to reevaluate where you stand. Are you headed on the path God has created for you? Or abandoning it for the sake of following the crowd?

Seek God's will. Let Him show you which path to take.

Even if it means holding off on getting your driver's license until you're a senior in high school. ;)

LET'S THINK ABOUT IT...

Are you following the path God has set out for you?

LET'S PRAY ABOUT IT...

Lord, as I seek your will, make evident the path I should take. I don't want to sacrifice who I am for the sake of following the crowd. Amen.

TODAY'S DARE

Evaluate where you stand. Are you headed in the direction of the crowd in an effort to fit in? If so, what can you do today that will help you get back on your own path?

A SHOT OF INSPIRATION

Do not go where the path may lead, go instead where there is no path and leave a trail.

Ralph Waldo Emerson

Join the convo! Inspired by today's chat? Share what you learned! Snap a photo of this book (or the drink you're sipping on), and spark a discussion on social media by answering this question:

Why is it tempting to follow the crowd rather than seek God's will for our lives?

Be sure to use the hashtag #CoffeeShopDevos!

Drained by Discouragement

Scripture to sip on

"For I know the plans I have for you," says the Lord. "They are plans for good and not for disaster, to give you a future and a hope."

Jeremiah 29:11

LET'S CHAT ABOUT IT...

Have you experienced the draining effects of discouragement? I have. There are times when the enemy tries to convince me I don't have a purpose. The longer I allow him to convince me of this, the weaker I become in my fight against him. If I let him continue, this discouragement can eventually give way to depression.

Any time I face these times of discouragement—when I become too weak to even open my Bible—I confide in my mom, and she helps me see the big picture. She reminds me of the promises in the Word. And as I grasp these promises, my strength is restored. These promises have the power to loosen the grip of discouragement.

If you, too, experience times of draining discouragement—times when you're not convinced there's a purpose in your life—reclaim your strength in Scripture. It says you were created with a purpose, with an intention, and have a future to look forward to.

As you do this, discouragement will lose its hold and become washed away by the powerful promises from your Father.

LET'S THINK ABOUT IT...

Where do you turn during times of discouragement?

LET'S PRAY ABOUT IT...

Lord, thank you for the promises in your Word that remind me that you created me with a purpose. Remind me to turn to you any time I experience the draining effects of discouragement.

TODAY'S DARE

In need of encouragement? Look up these promises:

Jeremiah 29:11
Psalm 138:8
Romans 8:28
Habakkuk 2:3
Jeremiah 1:5
Philippians 4:13
Psalm 57:2
2 Timothy 1:9
Ephesians 2:10
1 Corinthians 1:27

A SHOT OF INSPIRATION

The remedy for discouragement is the Word of God. When you feed your heart and mind with its truth, you regain your perspective and find renewed strength.

Warren Wiersbe

Join the convo! Inspired by today's chat? Share what you learned! Snap a photo of this book (or the drink you're sipping on), and spark a discussion on social media by answering this question:

Why do you think Christians often face times of discouragement?

Be sure to use the hashtag #CoffeeShopDevos!

YOLO

Scripture to sip on

You will show me the way of life,
granting me the joy of your presence
and the pleasures of living with you forever.

Psalm 16:11

LET'S CHAT ABOUT IT...

You've probably heard the term YOLO, or "You Only Live Once."
Growing up, my mom would remind my sisters and me to keep this
perspective. She wanted us to choose a life we'd enjoy and make decisions that would benefit our future. Because it's true—life's too short.
It's even shorter compared to eternity. Why settle for a life we aren't
passionate about?

That's not to say we won't experience suffering. But God wants
us to make the most of the time we've been given. He wants us to
experience the joy of living in His presence!

So as you move into the future He has planned for you, ask yourself, *What kind of life will I pursue—a life I despise, or one filled
with passion?*

I believe God wants us to live a life of passion—passionate about
Him. Passionate about sharing His love. And passionate about pursuing our calling. Life's too short for anything less, and we aren't even
guaranteed our next breath.

Besides, this day we've been given? It's a gift from the Creator. I
don't know anyone who gives a gift without expecting the recipient
to receive it with joy.

LET'S THINK ABOUT IT...

How will your daily decisions help you experience a life you're passionate about?

....

....

....

LET'S PRAY ABOUT IT...

Lord, thank you for the gift of a new day. Help me to enjoy this gift and make decisions that will lead me into the future plans you have for me. Amen.

TODAY'S DARE

Listen to the song "Thrive" by Casting Crowns.

A SHOT OF INSPIRATION

Even so, I have noticed one thing, at least, that is good. It is good for people to eat, drink, and enjoy their work under the sun during the short life God has given them, and to accept their lot in life. And it is a good thing to receive wealth from God and the good health to enjoy it. To enjoy your work and accept your lot in life—this is indeed a gift from God.

Ecclesiastes 5:18–19

Join the convo! Inspired by today's chat? Share what you learned! Snap a photo of this book (or the drink you're sipping on), and spark a discussion on social media by answering this question:

What does it look like for you to live life to the fullest?

Be sure to use the hashtag #CoffeeShopDevos!

Macchiato

Healing for
Heartache

Maple Marshmallow Macchiato

The macchiato is another coffee drink I prefer to enjoy during cold seasons. In Italy, a café macchiato includes espresso and only a touch of milk. However, in America, we typically enjoy this drink with a little extra milk—and, of course, flavored syrups.

The two flavors I chose for this macchiato, maple and marshmallow, are guaranteed to bring back your favorite autumn memories of bonfires, pumpkin carving, and corn mazes.

INGREDIENTS

- 1 shot espresso (or 1/4 cup strong coffee)
- 1 tablespoon maple syrup
- 2/3 cup milk
- 1 tablespoon marshmallow syrup
- Pinch of ground cinnamon

INSTRUCTIONS

1. Brew espresso (or strong coffee).
2. Stir maple syrup into milk.
3. Steam milk until frothy.
4. Pour milk into a separate mug, using spoon to hold back froth.
5. Pour espresso (or strong coffee) into milk.
6. Cap off macchiato with layer of froth.
7. Drizzle marshmallow syrup on top and add pinch of ground cinnamon.

Piecing a Heart Back Together

Scripture to sip on

The Lord is close to the brokenhearted;
he rescues those whose spirits are crushed.

Psalm 34:18

LET'S CHAT ABOUT IT...

I was nineteen years old when I experienced my first real breakup.

I had dated a guy for two years—although it felt like longer. We'd known each other since we were toddlers, and our families were close friends. Yet even though we had already dreamt about the future together, God started showing me that this guy wasn't the one He planned for me to marry.

The breakup was tough, especially since we went from being together almost constantly to hardly ever seeing or talking to each other.

After devoting so much of my heart to this relationship, the breakup was almost like losing a loved one, but I knew it had to happen. For a few months after the breakup, there was a gap—not only in my life, but in my heart. A gap caused by giving away pieces of my heart and not having them back.

But you know what? No heartbreak is too big that God's love can't repair.

Any time I missed the time with my ex, I turned to God. His arms provided comfort. His love washed over my heart until it was restored and repaired.

A relationship with Jesus is life-giving—and the best part?

He's the only One who is guaranteed never to break our hearts.

LET'S THINK ABOUT IT...

If you've experienced a heartbreak, how can you bring those pieces to God and allow Him to restore your heart to wholeness?

LET'S PRAY ABOUT IT...

Lord, thank you for piecing my heart back together. Help me to experience the life-giving relationship you offer. Amen.

TODAY'S DARE

Craving God's affection? Pour your heart out to Him in worship. Find a worship album to play, then spend time reading the Word, talking to God, and basking in His presence.

A SHOT OF INSPIRATION

Broken things can become blessed things if you let God do the mending.

Beth Moore

Join the convo! Inspired by today's chat? Share what you learned! Snap a photo of this book (or the drink you're sipping on), and spark a discussion on social media by answering this question:

How can Christians cultivate a life-giving relationship with Jesus?

Be sure to use the hashtag #CoffeeShopDevos!

Love for the Unloved

There was no sparkle in Leah's eyes, but Rachel had a beautiful figure and a lovely face. Since Jacob was in love with Rachel, he told her father, "I'll work for you for seven years if you'll give me Rachel, your younger daughter, as my wife."

Genesis 29:17–18

LET'S CHAT ABOUT IT...

Imagine having a crush on someone—then finding out he's in love with your sister because of her beauty.

Leah's been there (Genesis 29). She knows what it feels like to be overlooked. Jacob only had eyes for her sister, Rachel. When their father deceived Jacob and gave him Leah to marry rather than Rachel, he became furious.

Ouch.

Can you relate? Perhaps you, too, were rejected by a guy. Or maybe even a parent.

We often exhaust ourselves in our quest to gain acceptance and affection from others. Thankfully, there's One love that *doesn't* require work. This love sees us as we are and deems us worthy.

Jesus' death on the cross reminds us we're loved, despite our imperfections. His love is greater than our flaws. And rather than our value earning us His love, instead it's His love that gives us our value.

Later, God saw Leah was unloved and hurting, so he allowed her to give birth instead of Rachel.

God has compassion on us, too, when we're forsaken by others. Let's turn to Him with our battered hearts. Because when others kick us out of their lives, Jesus invites us in. His love will make up for our lack of human love.

We never have to worry about God shunning us.

Because no flaw can erase a love that's eternal.

LET'S THINK ABOUT IT...

Have you accepted God's love for you?

LET'S PRAY ABOUT IT...

Lord, thank you that I'm free to be who You've created me to be. Help me to know the fullness of your love so my heart will be made whole. Amen.

TODAY'S DARE

Listen to "Reckless Love" by Steffany Gretzinger.

A SHOT OF INSPIRATION

> Even if my father and mother abandon me,
> the Lord will hold me close.
>
> Psalm 27:10

Join the convo! Inspired by today's chat? Share what you learned! Snap a photo of this book (or the drink you're sipping on), and spark a discussion on social media by answering this question:

Has the imperfect love of humans caused you to have a morphed view of God's love?

Be sure to use the hashtag #CoffeeShopDevos!

Wounded by Words

Scripture to sip on

He heals the brokenhearted
and bandages their wounds.
Psalm 147:3

LET'S CHAT ABOUT IT...

"Sticks and stones may break my bones but words will never hurt me."
Are you familiar with this saying? Although it's a nice idea to not be
affected by words, let's face it: Words hurt. When we're the target of
a weapon, it pierces our skin. Stings. Leaves a mark.

And words often feel a lot like weapons.

It's not fun to live with a wound created by the words of others.
And when the wound doesn't heal, the area remains sensitive. The
sting returns any time someone barely touches it.

A serious wound can't heal itself—and the longer it goes untreated,
the more likely it is to cause an infection.

Painful words often cause damage. If we don't seek healing, the
pain can lead to bitterness. Resentment. Unforgiveness. Anger. Hy-
persensitivity. So how can we go about finding healing?

By turning to our Father. He never turns away when a child comes
to Him with a wound. Only His tender hands have the power to stitch
us back together. His loving presence takes away the sting of the pain,
the cleansing power of His Word washes away the filth and dirt, and
the peace radiating from His love gives us strength to forgive the one
who caused the wound.

So even though words may cause pain, we don't have to live with
the wound. Not when our heavenly Father is the Master Surgeon
himself.

LET'S THINK ABOUT IT...

When someone causes you pain, do you turn to Jesus for healing?

....

....

....

....

LET'S PRAY ABOUT IT...

Lord, thank you that you alone have the power to cleanse the wounds caused by others. Amen.

TODAY'S DARE

Next time someone hurts you with their words—whether intentional or not—think twice before you speak. Instead, try to hold your tongue, then find someplace you can go by yourself and ask God to heal the wound. He can then give you the strength to forgive the person who caused it.

A SHOT OF INSPIRATION

O Lord, if you heal me, I will be truly healed.

Jeremiah 17:14

Join the convo! Inspired by today's chat? Share what you learned! Snap a photo of this book (or the drink you're sipping on), and spark a discussion on social media by answering this question:

What kind of damage can result if we neglect to receive God's healing power for our wounds?

Be sure to use the hashtag #CoffeeShopDevos!

Grief Forever Gone

Scripture to sip on

"He will wipe every tear from their eyes, and there will be no more death or sorrow or crying or pain. All these things are gone forever."

Revelation 21:4

LET'S CHAT ABOUT IT...

My granddaddy passed away when I was thirteen.

It didn't seem fair. Why couldn't he have lived until I graduated high school? Or married? Had kids? His love for God was contagious, and he never ceased to make me laugh. But Granddaddy was here one moment, then gone the next.

When we lose a loved one, an ache is carved inside of us when we realize there's nothing we can do to have that person back in our life. Yet even though it was tough to experience this grief, a hope lit up those dreary days. I knew I'd see Granddaddy again. This life is only a mist in comparison to eternity.

God can relieve the aches in our hearts that have been carved by grief. As much as we may miss our loved ones, it's possible to live without them.

Because the only relationship we absolutely *need* is a relationship with Jesus.

When we reach heaven, not only will we be reunited with those who have gone before us, but we will also have our tears wiped away by the fingers of Christ. According to this Scripture, grief will be gone. There will be no more pain . . . *forever.*

Sounds like a *really* long time, don't you think?

LET'S THINK ABOUT IT...

Is there an ache in your heart leftover by grief? How can you fill this with God's love and seek Him for the strength to move on?

_____

_____

_____

LET'S PRAY ABOUT IT...

Lord, thank you for helping me endure grieving seasons of my life. I know I can find restoration in my immovable relationship with you and in the promise of a pain-free eternity. Amen.

TODAY'S DARE

Make a point to spend time with those you love today. As you do, thank God for the time He's given you with them.

A SHOT OF INSPIRATION

And now, dear brothers and sisters, we want you to know what will happen to the believers who have died so you will not grieve like people who have no hope. For since we believe that Jesus died and was raised to life again, we also believe that when Jesus returns, God will bring back with him the believers who have died.

1 Thessalonians 4:13–14

Join the convo! Inspired by today's chat? Share what you learned! Snap a photo of this book (or the drink you're sipping on), and spark a discussion on social media by answering this question:

If you've experienced grief, where did you find the strength to move on?

Be sure to use the hashtag #CoffeeShopDevos!

Crater of Loneliness

And I am convinced that nothing can ever separate us from God's love. Neither death nor life, neither angels nor demons, neither our fears for today nor our worries about tomorrow—not even the powers of hell can separate us from God's love.

Romans 8:38

LET'S CHAT ABOUT IT...

When I was a teen, I chose to have a few close friends rather than several friends. But at times, I felt like I had no one. I'd be alone at home fighting loneliness while others my age were partying on the weekends.

Loneliness can creep in on us all—whether we're by ourselves or in a room full of people. It's that cold, dark emptiness that whispers lies into your ear. Lies that make you believe you're not important, or that no one cares about you.

We were meant to have a connection with others. But more than that, we were created for intimacy with Jesus. Even if we have *no one*, we can find the connection we crave through a deep relationship with Him. Because we could have all the friends in the world and *still* be lonely without Him.

Only God's presence, Jesus' love, is big enough to fill the emptiness. So the next time you fall into the deep pit of loneliness, cry out to God. Let Christ's love draw you closer to Him as you cultivate a deep friendship with Him.

Trust me, earthly relationships can't come close to the fulfillment found through intimacy with Christ.

LET'S THINK ABOUT IT...

Where do you turn when you experience loneliness?

174

LET'S PRAY ABOUT IT...

Lord, help me to turn to you when I experience loneliness. I want to develop a deep friendship with you, because only your love is big enough to fill this emptiness. Amen.

TODAY'S DARE

As you go through the day, remain in communication with Jesus. You don't have to wait until you go to bed at night before you say your daily prayers. He's closer than the air you breathe and is with you throughout every step of your day.

A SHOT OF INSPIRATION

I am never lonely when I am praying, for this brings me into companionship with the greatest friend of all—Jesus Christ.

Billy Graham

Join the convo! Inspired by today's chat? Share what you learned! Snap a photo of this book (or the drink you're sipping on), and spark a discussion on social media by answering this question:

Why do you think we were created with an emptiness that can only be fulfilled through a relationship with Jesus?

Be sure to use the hashtag #CoffeeShopDevos!

Attachment-Free Living

Scripture to sip on

Your life is like the morning fog—it's here a little while, then it's gone.

James 4:14

LET'S CHAT ABOUT IT...

My mom and I went out to breakfast yesterday morning, and during our conversation, we somehow came around to the subject of death. She shared with me about how God has always helped her deal with grief, especially when it came to losing her dad. Even though it was difficult to live without him, she knew his death wasn't the end; rather, it was only a door into eternity.

I admire Mom for keeping the perspective that life is temporary. She always reminds me that our treasures aren't of this world; therefore, we shouldn't get too attached to anything earthly. This includes our relationships and earthly treasures. Because if we can't live without someone or something, then what happens if we really have to face life without that attachment?

The only One we can't live without should be Christ. He's the only attachment we should have because He's the only One who remains constant.

Death isn't the end. It's a door into eternity. And eternity is far more real than our life on earth.

So let's loosen our grip on things of earth and instead cling to our relationship with Christ. If He's the only One we need to survive, then we're set for eternity.

Literally.

LET'S THINK ABOUT IT...

Is your relationship with Christ the only thing you can't live without?

LET'S PRAY ABOUT IT...

Lord, help me not to become too attached to anything in this world, because you're the only One who will remain. Amen.

TODAY'S DARE

Read Ecclesiastes 1–2. Why do you think Solomon referred to this life as "meaningless"?

A SHOT OF INSPIRATION

My home is in heaven. I'm just traveling through this world.

Billy Graham

Join the convo! Inspired by today's chat? Share what you learned! Snap a photo of this book (or the drink you're sipping on), and spark a discussion on social media by answering this question:

How can you go about living this life without attachments?

Be sure to use the hashtag #CoffeeShopDevos!

An Unchanging Friend

Scripture to sip on

Jesus Christ is the same yesterday, today, and forever.

Hebrews 13:8

LET'S CHAT ABOUT IT...

I've always chosen to have a few best friends rather than several. Because of this, I cherished those friendships. But it also makes it much harder when that person disappears from my life. Thankfully, I've never lost a friend due to an argument, but I have grown apart from friends whom I was once close with.

The end of a friendship can be as difficult as the end of a romantic relationship. But some friends are only meant to be in our lives for a season. Instead of longing for the person to return, we should instead appreciate the memories and look forward to the new relationships God will bring in our future.

Besides, only one friendship in this life is permanent. And that is our relationship with Christ.

So as we walk through the various seasons of life—and as God brings us new friends—let's cherish these moments and keep in mind that they may not be with us forever. And that's okay. Because there is only One whose friendship we need to continue in this life. Only One who sticks with us throughout every season.

And that is the friendship we have with our Savior, Jesus Christ.

LET'S THINK ABOUT IT...

In what ways does Jesus possess all the qualities of a true friend?

LET'S PRAY ABOUT IT...

Lord, thank you for being the only friend who never leaves my side. Amen.

TODAY'S DARE

Create a memory jar with your best friend! The next time you're together, find a big glass jar for each of you. You can then fill this jar with pictures, movie ticket stubs, birthday cards from each other, etc. Over time, you'll have a jar filled with mementos that can help you look back on and cherish the time you've spent with each other.

A SHOT OF INSPIRATION

I no longer call you slaves, because a master doesn't confide in his slaves. Now you are my friends, since I have told you everything the Father told me.

John 15:15

Join the convo! Inspired by today's chat? Share what you learned! Snap a photo of this book (or the drink you're sipping on), and spark a discussion on social media by answering this question:

Why do you think God brings some friendships into our lives only for a season?

Be sure to use the hashtag #CoffeeShopDevos!

When Life Doesn't Make Sense

If we live, it's to honor the Lord. And if we die, it's to honor the Lord. So whether we live or die, we belong to the Lord.

Romans 14:8

LET'S CHAT ABOUT IT...

When I was thirteen, a guy I'd gone to school with was in a car accident. He was killed instantly. Even though I wasn't close to him, the news came as a shock—for me and my entire community. Why would God take the life of a thirteen-year-old? He could've still had a bright future ahead. What good could possibly result from this?

Often, when we don't understand tragedies, we attempt to find answers to these questions. But when this searching leads us to a dead end, we can grow bitter. We can become angry toward God for not providing an answer and for allowing the tragedy to happen. But how's this response going to change the event?

Yes, it can be frustrating when life doesn't make sense. But we can exhaust ourselves if we constantly ask why. It'll only lead to more confusion and resentment, both of which are easy traps to fall into when we're hurt.

Instead of growing weary by asking why—and weakening our faith in the process—let's instead find hope in the answers God *does* provide in His Word: That He is good. Faithful. Trustworthy. He'll never leave us. We can trust in His sovereign ability to work all things together for good for those who love Him (Romans 8:28).

As long as we live in a fallen world, we are prone to tragedies. But there's one thing we can count on, and that is the endless love God has for His children. He carries us through the pain.

And His love cannot be diminished even by the most tragic event on earth.

LET'S THINK ABOUT IT...

Have you ever found yourself asking why to life's tragedies? What resulted from this?

....

....

....

LET'S PRAY ABOUT IT...

Lord, even when life doesn't make sense, I trust in your sovereignty. Your Word provides all the answers I'll need in this life. Amen.

TODAY'S DARE

As I wrote this, the song "It Is Well With My Soul" by Bethel Music started playing on my radio. I don't think it's a coincidence! Take a moment to listen to this song, then research the story behind the hymn.

A SHOT OF INSPIRATION

"My thoughts are nothing like your thoughts," says the Lord.
    "And my ways are far beyond anything you could imagine.
For just as the heavens are higher than the earth,
    so my ways are higher than your ways
    and my thoughts higher than your thoughts."

Isaiah 55:8–9

Join the convo! Inspired by today's chat? Share what you learned! Snap a photo of this book (or the drink you're sipping on), and spark a discussion on social media by answering this question:

How do you trust in God's unending love, even when tragedies occur?

Be sure to use the hashtag #CoffeeShopDevos!

Living after Losing

Scripture to sip on . . .

"For I am about to do something new.
See, I have already begun! Do you not see it?
I will make a pathway through the wilderness.
I will create rivers in the dry wasteland."

Isaiah 43:19

LET'S CHAT ABOUT IT...

When my eighth grade English class studied the biography and poetry of Emily Dickinson, I was fascinated by her life story.

After several of Dickinson's family members passed away, she became depressed and wouldn't leave the house. But why did the death of her loved ones have to result in the figurative "death" of her own life?

Many people believe she was mentally ill. Even so, if I were to find myself in that situation, I'd hope I could find a way to continue living. But this isn't easy. Whether it's the death of a loved one or the death of a relationship, friendship, or a dream, it can be tough to move on. Where can we find the healing power that can speak life back into our heart?

That kind of life-giving power is only attained through the help of the Holy Spirit. Jesus died so we could live life abundantly—yes, even after a loss.

It's natural to grieve. But afterward, let's set our gaze on the sunrise that beams over the horizon. Let's remind ourselves this isn't the end. Because as long as there is breath in our lungs, we have a purpose for our life. A plan that has yet to be completely fulfilled.

Life is too short to live it with a dead heart.

LET'S THINK ABOUT IT...

If you've experienced loss, how can you move on and step into the future God has in store for you?

LET'S PRAY ABOUT IT...

Lord, only your healing love has the power to breathe life back into my heart. Help me move forward from loss and step into my future. Amen.

TODAY'S DARE

Read 2 Samuel 12:15–23. What did David do after he found out about the death of his child?

A SHOT OF INSPIRATION

> To all who mourn in Israel,
>   he will give a crown of beauty for ashes,
> a joyous blessing instead of mourning,
>   festive praise instead of despair.
> In their righteousness, they will be like great oaks
>   that the Lord has planted for his own glory.
>
> Isaiah 61:3

Join the convo! Inspired by today's chat? Share what you learned! Snap a photo of this book (or the drink you're sipping on), and spark a discussion on social media by answering this question:

How does our salvation in Christ give us a purpose to keep living and provide a hope for the future, even after loss?

Be sure to use the hashtag #CoffeeShopDevos!

One Who Understands

The Lord is a shelter for the oppressed,
a refuge in times of trouble.

Psalm 9:9

LET'S CHAT ABOUT IT...

When I was in middle school, I often felt misunderstood. I had a yearning to find someone who could understand me and accept me for who I was.

It's this yearning that drove me into the arms of Christ.

I grew up in a Christian home, but it wasn't until then that I cultivated a relationship with Christ. This relationship was the one I'd been searching for.

Jesus understood me, even when I felt no one else did. Jesus wiped my tears. Jesus listened to my vents. Jesus comforted me when others hurt me. And when I felt invisible after going through an entire day of school without talking to anyone, I could go home and know God saw me. More than that, He'd walked with me throughout the entire day. He wanted to be with me, even though I felt like no one else did because of my reserved disposition.

When we experience heartache—when we feel like no one could ever understand our pain—we can find solace in the fact that Jesus understands. But He not only understands; His heart aches for ours. He hurts when we hurt.

When we use the pain as a means to draw us closer into His embrace, then this relationship will be what gives us the strength to carry on.

LET'S THINK ABOUT IT...

Does the pain you experience compel you to get to know your healer?

_____

_____

_____

LET'S PRAY ABOUT IT...

Lord, thank you for understanding me even when no one else does. I want the pain I experience to compel me to know you more. Amen.

TODAY'S DARE

Create your own private space for your quiet time. This can be in a comfy chair in your bedroom, in an empty closet, or on a hammock in your backyard. Wherever it is, use this space to confide in Christ and draw closer to Him.

A SHOT OF INSPIRATION

> You keep track of all my sorrows.
> You have collected all my tears in your bottle.
> You have recorded each one in your book.
>
> Psalm 56:8

Join the convo! Inspired by today's chat? Share what you learned! Snap a photo of this book (or the drink you're sipping on), and spark a discussion on social media by answering this question:

How can a relationship with Christ provide the strength we need to carry on in the midst of heartache?

Be sure to use the hashtag #CoffeeShopDevos!

Heart Handled with Care

Above everything else guard your heart,
because from it flow the springs of life.

Proverbs 4:23 ISV

LET'S CHAT ABOUT IT...

The heart is our source of life; therefore, if it stops beating, then we stop breathing. Common knowledge, right? It's why we do what we can to lead healthy lives and protect our hearts.

But why do we often neglect to handle our emotional heart with the same care? This Scripture tells us to keep it guarded because "from it flows the springs of life." Yet we often don't think twice before we give another piece of it away in a relationship.

Our hearts have been bought with a price. They're saved through the blood of Christ. It's this salvation that pumps blood through our veins. Our hearts are far too valuable to be treated with neglect. That's why we must do what we can to keep them healthy.

But despite how hard we try, there will be times when our hearts are abused. Some might not handle them with care. Others might pierce them with their words. Unlike our physical hearts, when our emotional ones stop beating, it doesn't mean we have to stop living.

When we experience attacks on our hearts, let's not hesitate to hand them over to God. He'll handle our hearts with care.

Besides, if Jesus went to the grave so our hearts could be saved, don't you know He can be trusted to make them whole once again?

LET'S THINK ABOUT IT...

If you're experiencing heartache, how should you begin your healing process?

LET'S PRAY ABOUT IT...

Lord, I trust you will handle my heart with care. Teach me how I can keep it guarded from the wrong people, because I know you went through great lengths to purchase it. Amen.

TODAY'S DARE

Find a piece of jewelry—whether it's a purity ring, heart bracelet, or cross necklace—that will remind you to keep your heart guarded from the wrong people.

A SHOT OF INSPIRATION

"I will be your God throughout your lifetime—
    until your hair is white with age.
I made you, and I will care for you.
    I will carry you along and save you."

Isaiah 46:4

Join the convo! Inspired by today's chat? Share what you learned! Snap a photo of this book (or the drink you're sipping on), and spark a discussion on social media by answering this question:

What are practical ways we can keep our hearts guarded without becoming too overprotective?

Be sure to use the hashtag #CoffeeShopDevos!

Bullying Games

Scripture to sip on

Jesus said, "Father, forgive them, for they don't know what they are doing." And the soldiers gambled for his clothes by throwing dice.

Luke 23:34

LET'S CHAT ABOUT IT ...

When I was a kid, I attended a sleepover with two of my friends. Even though I was friends with both of them—or so I thought—these girls spent the entire sleepover poking fun at me. As if it were a game. Apparently they didn't realize how badly this "game" hurt me . . . or maybe they didn't care.

I'll never understand why some people find their joy in making others squirm. Or why some people choose to leave others out on purpose, making them feel neglected and rejected.

Are you familiar with the pain that comes from mockery? It might make you feel like something's wrong with you. But even if all your friends walk out on you, there's One who never leaves your side.

Not only does Jesus stick with us, but He understands our pain. He continues, to this day, to be the target of persecution. People mock Him. Despise Him. Reject Him. Ridicule Him.

Yes, Jesus knows the pain. The empathy and compassion He has toward us is what compels Him to hold our hands as we walk through persecution. In Him, we find confidence to keep our heads held high. And as His love pours into us, it'll overflow into the lives of others.

Then, even as we continue to be teased and rejected, we can find strength to respond the same way Jesus did when He was persecuted on the cross: with forgiveness. Not because the bullies deserve it, but because they don't know what they're doing.

And only this love will enable us to win any "game" we may find ourselves thrown into.

LET'S THINK ABOUT IT...

Do you turn to God when you experience persecution?

LET'S PRAY ABOUT IT...

Lord, thank you for giving me the strength to walk through persecution. Fill me with your love so I can face those who mock me. Amen.

TODAY'S DARE

Try to win the next "game" of bullying you find yourself thrown into. How? Instead of attempting to harm the bullies in return, ask for God's strength to see them through eyes of love. It's this love that will make it easier for you to forgive those who have hurt you.

A SHOT OF INSPIRATION

"God blesses you when people mock you and persecute you and lie about you and say all sorts of evil things against you because you are my followers."

Matthew 5:11

Join the convo! Inspired by today's chat? Share what you learned! Snap a photo of this book (or the drink you're sipping on), and spark a discussion on social media by answering this question:

How can we find strength to persevere when we're bullied?

Be sure to use the hashtag #CoffeeShopDevos!

Reason for Breaking

For everyone has sinned; we all fall short of God's glorious standard. Yet God, in his grace, freely makes us right in his sight. He did this through Christ Jesus when he freed us from the penalty for our sins.

Romans 3:23–24

LET'S CHAT ABOUT IT...

Some people draw the conclusion that God causes tragedies and inflicts punishment on our lives when we disobey Him. If so, wouldn't we experience blows of punishment constantly? But Jesus took the punishment upon himself so we could receive atonement.

God sent His Son because He loves us. Jesus bore the weight of the punishment we deserve. Because of this, it would be pointless for God to cause us to suffer on earth as a penalty for our sins.

It would diminish the power of the cross.

Christ bled so we could be healed. Our sins nailed Him to the cross so we could receive grace. He died so we could have abundant life.

Yet even though we don't receive the condemnation we deserve for our sins, this doesn't mean our sins will stand uncorrected. God will sometimes allow us to experience trials and tests to discipline us and correct our behavior. In the end, this discipline is for our *good* rather than *harm*.

So when we experience suffering, let's not turn away from our loving Father in anger. If we come to Him with our broken hearts, He can take the suffering we've experienced—what the enemy meant for harm—and transform it into a new beginning.

Just like He did on the cross.

LET'S THINK ABOUT IT...

Have you believed the lie that God causes us pain to punish us for sins?

LET'S PRAY ABOUT IT...

Lord, I know you are not the cause for my broken heart; in fact, only you have the power to mend my pain. Thank you for sending your Son so I could receive grace. Amen.

TODAY'S DARE

If you've been carrying around a broken heart caused by suffering, take it to God and ask Him to make it new. You may then want to consider speaking with a parent, counselor, mentor, or youth leader and discuss the next steps you should take toward healing.

A SHOT OF INSPIRATION

He canceled the record of the charges against us and took it away by nailing it to the cross.

Colossians 2:14

Join the convo! Inspired by today's chat? Share what you learned! Snap a photo of this book (or the drink you're sipping on), and spark a discussion on social media by answering this question:

If sin is the cause for tragic events—which began at the fall of humankind in the Garden of Eden—why do you think God frequently gets the blame?

Be sure to use the hashtag #CoffeeShopDevos!

Free Bail

The thief's purpose is to steal and kill and destroy. My purpose is to give them a rich and satisfying life.

John 10:10

LET'S CHAT ABOUT IT...

Imagine being trapped in a prison cell, enveloped in your own filth and misery. Metal bars keep you from experiencing the freedom you long for. Then one day, the prison guard unlocks your cell and gives you some great news: Someone has paid your bail! You no longer have to live in bondage. You now have the keys to freedom.

It'd be silly to remain in misery, don't you think? And yet, many of us choose to do just that. Jesus paid the price for our freedom. We don't have to live in the filth of our sins. We don't have to bear the weight of our broken hearts. He took our shame, guilt, despair, and brokenness so we could be made whole. The choice is ours: Will we remain in the prison cell of our bondage or experience a fulfilled life?

Let's grasp our Father's hand as He pulls us out. Let's accept this gift with open hands and a grateful heart.

And step into the light of freedom.

LET'S THINK ABOUT IT...

How can you begin the process of releasing your misery to God so He can help you experience abundant life?

LET'S PRAY ABOUT IT …

Lord, I know I don't have to live in bondage because you paid the price so I could have a "rich and satisfying life." Help me to step into that freedom. Amen.

TODAY'S DARE

Consider buying a cross necklace so you can be reminded daily of your freedom in Christ.

A SHOT OF INSPIRATION

For the wages of sin is death, but the free gift of God is eternal life through Christ Jesus our Lord.

Romans 6:23

Join the convo! Inspired by today's chat? Share what you learned! Snap a photo of this book (or the drink you're sipping on), and spark a discussion on social media by answering this question:

What would it look like for you to remain in bondage rather than step into freedom?

Be sure to use the hashtag #CoffeeShopDevos!

The Best Medicine

Scripture to sip on

A cheerful heart is good medicine,
but a broken spirit saps a person's strength.

Proverbs 17:22

LET'S CHAT ABOUT IT...

As a diabetic, I have to take insulin to manage my blood sugar. If I don't, my blood sugar climbs higher and higher. When that happens, it's nearly impossible to be productive. My energy is sapped. My brain is foggy. My motivation is lacking.

Sounds like a broken spirit, doesn't it? When we have a taste of depression and discouragement, it's as though someone has sapped our strength, just like this Scripture says.

Our energy is low. We can't think clearly. Our motivation lags.

According to this verse, we must have cheerful hearts. The same way insulin keeps my blood sugar in a normal range, cheerful hearts strengthen our spirits.

As Christians, we *always* have a reason to cheer. We can rejoice because of our salvation. We can find purpose for our lives through discovering our roles in God's Kingdom. We can love ourselves when we understand the vast love God has for us. We can appreciate who we are when we step into our identity in Christ. And we can have a deep, unspeakable joy when we take advantage of the benefits of salvation.

This life will always give us a reason to become discouraged. But as long as God's on the throne, and as long as we have breath in our lungs, we have a reason to hope and rejoice. It's by His light we can have cheerful hearts.

And it's this life-restoring medicine that will renew our strength once again.

LET'S THINK ABOUT IT...

Where do you turn when you become discouraged?

LET'S PRAY ABOUT IT...

Lord, help me to keep a cheerful heart so my spirit won't become sapped. Thank you for bringing meaning to my life. Amen.

TODAY'S DARE

If you're struggling with depression, confide in a parent or trusted mentor and consider seeking professional help.

A SHOT OF INSPIRATION

But you, O Lord, are a shield around me;
you are my glory, the one who holds my head high.

Psalm 3:3

Join the convo! Inspired by today's chat? Share what you learned! Snap a photo of this book (or the drink you're sipping on), and spark a discussion on social media by answering this question:

Why do you think Christians sometimes become depressed even though we always have a reason to hope?

Be sure to use the hashtag #CoffeeShopDevos!

The Right Kind of Fuel

Even if my father and mother abandon me,
the Lord will hold me close.

Psalm 27:10

LET'S CHAT ABOUT IT...

Ever tried to fill a gas tank with water? Of course not. A car needs to be filled with a certain type of gas in order for it to function properly. Sure, we can fill it with water, but we'll be in for a disappointment. It needs the *right* kind of fuel.

Similarly, our hearts have a void that only God's love can fill. We can attempt to fuel it with other things, but only His love enables it to function properly. Human love just doesn't work the same way God's does.

In fact, others will hurt us. Abandon us. Forsake us. When this happens, the void in our hearts deepens. We then may try to seek the love of others to fill it—then we're let down, once again, when we realize it's still not enough to fulfill us.

Perhaps God created the void in our hearts for a reason. So we could come to Him and realize only His love can help us persevere.

Let's take a break from seeking love from others and instead let our hearts become immersed in God's love. As His affection pours into our void, we'll gain the power we need to keep going.

And then we'll realize it was His love we were thirsty for all along.

LET'S THINK ABOUT IT...

Have you attempted to seek affection from others in order to fill the void that was created for God's love?

196

LET'S PRAY ABOUT IT...

Lord, help me not to seek to fill this void with anything other than your love, because only your love has the power to fulfill me. Amen.

TODAY'S DARE

Listen to the song "God-Shaped Hole" by Plumb.

A SHOT OF INSPIRATION

Don't love money; be satisfied with what you have. For God has said,
"I will never fail you.
I will never abandon you."

Hebrews 13:5

Join the convo! Inspired by today's chat? Share what you learned! Snap a photo of this book (or the drink you're sipping on), and spark a discussion on social media by answering this question:

Share about a time when you personally experienced God's love.

Be sure to use the hashtag #CoffeeShopDevos!

Blank Chapters Ahead

Scripture to sip on

Whatever is good and perfect is a gift coming down to us from God our Father, who created all the lights in the heavens. He never changes or casts a shifting shadow.

James 1:17

LET'S CHAT ABOUT IT...

The other day, my best friend from middle and high school called me. We spent over an hour talking on the phone and reminiscing over memories I'd forgotten about. It made me nostalgic. When we were sixteen, her family unexpectedly moved to another state. I went from hanging out with her every week to seeing her about once every year or two.

Changes are tough. As a teen, I'm sure you've had your fair share of them.

Friends come and go. Older siblings move out and get married. You may change schools. During the whirlwind, you might long to cling to everything you've left behind. The absence in your life creates a certain kind of sadness. Nostalgia.

But you know what? We weren't meant to stay stuck in our previous chapters. If we do that, we may miss out on the highlights of today.

There are blank chapters ahead that have yet to be written. Memories that have yet to be made. It doesn't mean we can't at times reread our previous chapters—but when we do, let's be careful that it doesn't make us resent the present. And instead of constantly looking back, let's look forward to what God has already written for us in our forthcoming chapters.

As an avid book lover, trust me when I say this: There's nothing quite like the anticipation that comes with turning the page to a new chapter in a good book!

LET'S THINK ABOUT IT...

Do you find yourself rereading your previous chapters too often?

LET'S PRAY ABOUT IT...

Lord, help me to look forward to the forthcoming chapters rather than remain in yesterday. Amen.

TODAY'S DARE

Create a collage on a large poster board throughout the new year or school year. You can use this to display pictures and mementos. That way, you can keep track of the year's highlights and look forward to filling the blank spaces with new memories.

A SHOT OF INSPIRATION

Jesus Christ is the same yesterday, today, and forever.

Hebrews 13:8

Join the convo! Inspired by today's chat? Share what you learned! Snap a photo of this book (or the drink you're sipping on), and spark a discussion on social media by answering this question:

What kind of harm could result from remaining in yesterday rather than stepping into today?

Be sure to use the hashtag #CoffeeShopDevos!

Permanent Bruises

Scripture to sip on

Make allowance for each other's faults, and forgive anyone who offends you. Remember, the Lord forgave you, so you must forgive others.

Colossians 3:13

LET'S CHAT ABOUT IT...

Have you ever found a bruise on your body and had no idea where it came from? I've had that happen to me often. I might not even find the bruise until I accidentally bump the area again and realize how tender it is.

Thankfully, bruises fade over time. But the bruises that have been left on our hearts aren't exactly the same as the ones left on our legs.

When others hurt us, we're often left in fear of getting hurt again. We become ultra sensitive in the area that caused the pain. Not a fun way to live, is it?

Here's a secret: These bruises don't have to be permanent. We don't have to hobble around, feeling the soreness every time someone touches the bruise.

The first step toward healing can only come through forgiving the person who left the bruise. No, it won't be easy. But how freeing will it be to no longer live in fear of getting hurt again?

So when others let us down, let's turn to Jesus and ask Him to help us forgive. He'll be more than happy to lend us some of the same mercy He extends to us every time we hurt Him.

Then, as we forgive and release the hurt we'd harbored, we'll watch in amazement as the bruise disappears. It'll be erased by the healing ointment of God's love.

And we'll finally find the freedom to trust others once again.

LET'S THINK ABOUT IT...

Are there any bruises on your heart that have been left by others?

_____

_____

_____

LET'S PRAY ABOUT IT...

Lord, help me to take necessary steps toward forgiveness so I can be healed and move past the pain. Amen.

TODAY'S DARE

Listen to the song "Forgiveness" by Matthew West.

A SHOT OF INSPIRATION

Make a quality decision to forgive, and God will heal your wounded emotions in due time.

Joyce Meyer

Join the convo! Inspired by today's chat? Share what you learned! Snap a photo of this book (or the drink you're sipping on), and spark a discussion on social media by answering this question:

Have you struggled with forgiving others in the past?

Be sure to use the hashtag #CoffeeShopDevos!

Cappuccino

All about Relationships

Cacao Coco Cappuccino

Cappuccino is the first coffee concoction I fell in love with. (Thanks, Mom, for letting me take a sip of yours when I was little!) This recipe will create the perfect blend of chocolate (in the form of cacao powder) and coconut. Isn't it nice to enjoy a yummy drink that's created with healthy ingredients?

Be warned: You *may* be left with a foam-induced mustache upon taking that first sip. ;)

INGREDIENTS

- 2 shots espresso (or 1/2 cup strong coffee)
- 1 teaspoon coconut oil (optional)
- 1 teaspoon coconut sugar
- 1 tablespoon coconut syrup
- 1 tablespoon cacao powder (or unsweetened cocoa powder)
- 1/4 cup unsweetened coconut milk

INSTRUCTIONS

1. Brew espresso (or strong coffee).
2. Melt coconut oil in microwave.
3. Add coconut oil, coconut sugar, coconut syrup, and cacao powder (or unsweetened cocoa powder) to espresso (or strong coffee).
4. Steam milk until extra frothy.
5. Pour a small amount of milk into espresso (or coffee), using spoon to hold back froth.
6. Cap off cappuccino with thick layer of froth.
7. Optional garnish: sprinkle of cacao powder (or unsweetened cocoa powder)

The Secret to a Long Life

Scripture to sip on

Children, obey your parents because you belong to the Lord, for this is the right thing to do. "Honor your father and mother." This is the first commandment with a promise: If you honor your father and mother, "things will go well for you, and you will have a long life on the earth."

Ephesians 6:1–3

LET'S CHAT ABOUT IT....

I wasn't rebellious as a teenager, but that doesn't mean I wasn't tempted to disobey my parents. I remember thinking, *Why should I obey them if I know they're wrong?*

Of course, disobedience stems from pride. But what if you think your parents really *are* wrong in their discipline? Is it okay to disobey them when their rules don't seem fair?

We're to obey our parents, "for this is the right thing to do." We aren't supposed to obey them only if we think they're right in their discipline or fair in their rules. We're not just honoring them; we're honoring Christ.

Looking back, I now appreciate the wisdom and discipline my parents gave me, even though I resented it at times. Their boundaries saved me from making decisions that could've resulted in disaster.

So the next time your parents ask you to cancel your plans so you can babysit your younger siblings, pretend it's God you're responding to rather than them.

Then watch and see how He blesses you for doing your part in obeying His Word.

LET'S THINK ABOUT IT...

Would your relationship with your parents be better if you obeyed them more often?

_____

_____

_____

_____

LET'S PRAY ABOUT IT...

Lord, help me to obey my parents even when it's hard. I know that by doing so, I will honor your Word and live the life you've called me to live. Amen.

TODAY'S DARE

Surprise your parents! Do something for them today as a way to tell them thank-you.

Here are some ideas . . .

- Clean the house.
- Pay for them to go on a date.
- Buy them a gift.

A SHOT OF INSPIRATION

Children, always obey your parents, for this pleases the Lord.

Colossians 3:20

Join the convo! Inspired by today's chat? Share what you learned! Snap a photo of this book (or the drink you're sipping on), and spark a discussion on social media by answering this question:

Share a time when your parents' wisdom and authority saved you from making a destructive decision.

Be sure to use the hashtag #CoffeeShopDevos!

Clique-Less

"This is my commandment: Love each other in the same way I have loved you. There is no greater love than to lay down one's life for one's friends."

John 15:12–13

LET'S CHAT ABOUT IT....

When I was in middle school, it seemed like the entire school was separated into cliques. People often acted like someone they weren't simply to fit into their preferred group. I never understood why people would sacrifice who they were for the sake of attaining approval.

But I especially didn't understand why cliques often rejected those who *didn't* fit into their group.

If Jesus came to earth in the flesh again and roamed the halls of your school, how would He act? Would He act holier than thou if an outcast sat at His lunch table? Would He only speak to those who go to church?

Of course not! That's not the way He treated people when He *was* on earth, and it's not how He treats people now. And guess what? He calls us to treat others with the same love we've received from Him. This means we, too, shouldn't turn away from others simply because they don't fit in. Instead, we should show love and acceptance to all, regardless of their popularity status and reputation.

Don't be afraid to break away from cliques—even if you're the only one who becomes clique-less. Jesus calls us to be a light to everyone, and we can't do that if we're confined within the boundaries of a circle.

Trust me: If you go clique-less, the wide variety of new friendships you'll gain will be well worth the sacrifices you might make!

LET'S THINK ABOUT IT...

How can you step outside of your group and be a friend to others?

....

....

....

....

LET'S PRAY ABOUT IT...

Lord, help me to make friends with those who are outside of my circles. Amen.

TODAY'S DARE

Next time you're at school, find a stranger to sit with at lunch. Who knows, you might just meet your next best friend!

A SHOT OF INSPIRATION

Dare to reach out your hand into the darkness, to pull another hand into the light.

Norman B. Rice

Join the convo! Inspired by today's chat? Share what you learned! Snap a photo of this book (or the drink you're sipping on), and spark a discussion on social media by answering this question:

What kind of harm could come from sticking with a clique?

Be sure to use the hashtag #CoffeeShopDevos!

Attack of a Loved One

Scripture to sip on

But when you are praying, first forgive anyone you are holding a grudge against, so that your Father in heaven will forgive your sins, too.

Mark 11:25

LET'S CHAT ABOUT IT...

My dog bit me on my face when I was in third grade.

It was an incident I didn't see coming. We had a great relationship. But unfortunately, she was in heat and had been playing with my mom when I went outside and stole her attention. Within a split second of petting her, she jumped up and attacked my face, not stopping until Mom forced her off me. This resulted in a visit to the emergency room and fifteen stitches.

During the aftermath—after my face was patched back together—I wasn't sure what hurt worst, the injuries to my face or my heart.

Can you relate? Maybe you've never been bitten by your dog, but you may have been hurt by someone you love. Maybe you still have scars from the attack, just like I do.

How should we react in these situations?

The only way we can begin the healing process is to first forgive the person who caused the scars.

Think of it this way: When we don't forgive the one who hurt us, it's as if we're allowing the wound to remain exposed. Then our wounds can't be stitched back together by the tender hands of the Great Physician, Jesus.

We can only find the strength to forgive at the cross.

Our sins caused Jesus to bleed, too. He still has the scars in His hands where the nails pierced His skin as a reminder. Yet it's because He chose to forgive us that we can now enjoy a relationship with Him. And it's through this overflow of grace that we can pour grace into the lives of those who have hurt us.

Now my scars are barely noticeable. And even though it hurt emotionally as well, I'm glad I chose to move on and didn't let the pain hinder any future relationships . . . with my pets.

LET'S THINK ABOUT IT...

How can you begin the process of forgiving loved ones who have hurt you?

....

....

....

LET'S PRAY ABOUT IT...

Lord, thank you for helping me move past the pain caused by loved ones so I can cultivate healthy relationships. Amen.

TODAY'S DARE

Listen to the song "Losing" by Tenth Avenue North.

A SHOT OF INSPIRATION

To be a Christian means to forgive the inexcusable because God has forgiven the inexcusable in you.

C. S. Lewis

Join the convo! Inspired by today's chat? Share what you learned! Snap a photo of this book (or the drink you're sipping on), and spark a discussion on social media by answering this question:

How can unforgiveness keep us from pursuing healthy relationships?

Be sure to use the hashtag #CoffeeShopDevos!

Deep Wells of Love

Scripture to sip on

Come close to God, and God will come close to you.

James 4:8

LET'S CHAT ABOUT IT....

When I was a teen, even though I wanted to have a boyfriend, I didn't want to date for the sake of dating. Instead, I wanted to find "the one" I was supposed to marry. But I soon began to wonder—how could I be sure that someone was "the one" before I entered the relationship?

So, when the guy I liked asked me out, I decided to date him, even though I wasn't sure if he was my future husband. I gave in to the longing. This resulted in a two-year relationship that ended in heartbreak on both ends.

Just because I had "the longing" to be in a relationship didn't mean it was time for me to meet my future husband. God created me with this longing in my heart—not just so I would be compelled to find the right guy, but so I would pursue a relationship with Him first. His love satisfies in a way that human love can't.

So when we're desperate for affection, rather than seeking to satisfy the thirst in earthly relationships, let's pursue God first and drink from the deep wells of His love. Then, when we're full in our relationship with Jesus, He may decide to bring "the one" into our lives. Not because we're thirsty for affection.

But because we now long to share this overflowing love with someone else.

LET'S THINK ABOUT IT...

Have you entered a relationship in an attempt to satisfy a thirst for affection?

LET'S PRAY ABOUT IT...

Lord, the next time I'm tempted to enter a relationship in order to satisfy this longing for love, remind me to seek you first. Amen.

TODAY'S DARE

Did you know the Bible is God's love letter written to you? If you're thirsty for His love, drink from the following Scriptures:

Romans 8:35–39
1 John 4:16
Ephesians 3:17–19
1 John 4:10
Lamentations 3:22–23

A SHOT OF INSPIRATION

To be loved by God is the highest relationship, the highest achievement, and the highest position in life.

Henry Blackaby

Join the convo! Inspired by today's chat? Share what you learned! Snap a photo of this book (or the drink you're sipping on), and spark a discussion on social media by answering this question:

Do you believe teens should date, even if they aren't sure their boyfriend or girlfriend is "the one"? Why or why not?

Be sure to use the hashtag #CoffeeShopDevos!

Grace for Faults

Always be humble and gentle. Be patient with each other, making allowance for each other's faults because of your love.

Ephesians 4:2

LET'S CHAT ABOUT IT...

When I develop characters for my books, I have to intentionally give them flaws. Otherwise, readers will complain that my characters are too perfect. Not real.

It's funny, because in *real* life, we often expect perfection from our loved ones. I know I'm guilty of this. But it's our human nature to be imperfect. Each of us has flaws—even if we're blind to our own. It's these imperfections that cause us to be disappointed and frustrated with others. When that happens, let's put this Scripture into action in our relationships and make allowance for each other's faults. How?

It'll only be possible through love.

Love gives us the ability to remain humble and gentle with others. Love empowers us to be patient with one another's faults, because Jesus never fails to be patient with ours.

If we do that—if we can give others allowance for their faults—we can expect the relationship to thrive. No, not because the other person is perfect.

But because our *love* is perfect. And it enables us to cover mistakes with grace.

The same way our sins have also been forgotten because of the perfect love of Christ.

LET'S THINK ABOUT IT...

How can you put this Scripture into action in your relationships?

LET'S PRAY ABOUT IT...

Lord, when others let me down, help me to cover their mistakes with grace, because I know you never fail to do that for me. Amen.

TODAY'S DARE

The next time someone disappoints you, take time to ask yourself how Christ would respond to the situation. Show them the same grace you would want Christ to show to you. Then watch and see how a potential argument can be avoided.

A SHOT OF INSPIRATION

For the whole law can be summed up in this one command: "Love your neighbor as yourself." But if you are always biting and devouring one another, watch out! Beware of destroying one another.

Galatians 5:14–15

Join the convo! Inspired by today's chat? Share what you learned! Snap a photo of this book (or the drink you're sipping on), and spark a discussion on social media by answering this question:

How can demanding perfection from another person destroy a relationship?

Be sure to use the hashtag #CoffeeShopDevos!

Selfie-Focused

Don't look out only for your own interests, but take an interest in others, too.

Philippians 2:4

LET'S CHAT ABOUT IT...

Our culture today is a selfie-focused world.

And I'm not just talking about the pictures.

Most of us, including me, can say we go through the day with our minds primarily focused on ourselves. Our needs. Our problems. Our dreams. Even our prayers often become self-focused!

We're born selfish. It goes against our flesh to put others first.

Of course, there's nothing wrong with self-care. But it can become a problem when we're so focused on taking care of our own needs, problems, and dreams that we neglect to notice those who are in need around us.

As Christians, our aim should be to treat others the way Jesus did. When He was on earth, He didn't strive to fulfill His selfish desires; instead, He cared for the sick, needy, and poor.

When we look out only for our own interests, we'll only take care of ourselves. But when we look out for the interests of others as well, as this Scripture instructs, not only will we express God's love, but we'll also receive a heavenly (and possibly an earthly) reward (see Proverbs 19:17). When we take care of others, God will be sure to take care of us.

So let's go against the culture's norm. Let's learn how to become an others-focused society.

Don't worry—we can still take selfies from time to time. ;)

LET'S THINK ABOUT IT...

How often do you take an interest in the needs and desires of others?

LET'S PRAY ABOUT IT...

Lord, help me to be like Jesus to those around me and become others-focused, even when it goes against my fleshly desires. Amen.

TODAY'S DARE

As you go through the day, learn to become aware of the needs of others: your parents, siblings, teachers, classmates, friends, strangers—and yes, even those you might not necessarily like.

Here are some ideas:

- Pay for a friend's lunch.
- Help a sibling with their homework.
- Run an errand for your mom.

A SHOT OF INSPIRATION

If you help the poor, you are lending to the Lord—
and he will repay you!

Proverbs 19:17

Join the convo! Inspired by today's chat? Share what you learned! Snap a photo of this book (or the drink you're sipping on), and spark a discussion on social media by answering this question:

What are some of the dangers that could result from a self-focused society?

Be sure to use the hashtag #CoffeeShopDevos!

Searching for a True Friend

There are "friends" who destroy each other,
but a real friend sticks closer than a brother.

Proverbs 18:24

LET'S CHAT ABOUT IT...

Growing up, I discovered that it wasn't easy to find true friendships. So instead of continuing to beg God for a friend, I decided to become a friend to others instead—and somehow, this attracted the friends I needed in my life. I made friends with people who had nothing in common with me.

That's when I realized the definition of a true friend: A true friend isn't someone who shares the same interests. It isn't someone who can promote your reputation in some way. And it certainly isn't someone who is fake.

Rather, a true friend is someone we *become* when we express God's love to others. It's someone we become when we get to know a stranger, despite their reputation. It's who we become when we pray for someone. When we can be the shoulder they cry on.

Because when we learn to become a true friend, that's when we'll attract true friends in return.

And even if it's only one true friendship, trust me, that will be far more valuable than having all the fake friendships in the world.

LET'S THINK ABOUT IT...

How can you become more focused on being a true friend rather than finding one?

216

LET'S PRAY ABOUT IT...

Lord, help me to become a true friend, because I know, in doing so, I'll attract the right people in my life. Amen.

TODAY'S DARE

Plan a girls' night! This weekend, make time to show your true friends how much they mean to you. Spend time with them at a coffee shop, movie theater, or mall.

A SHOT OF INSPIRATION

> A friend is always loyal,
> and a brother is born to help in time of need.
> Proverbs 17:17

Join the convo! Inspired by today's chat? Share what you learned! Snap a photo of this book (or the drink you're sipping on), and spark a discussion on social media by answering this question:

What's your definition of a true friend?

Be sure to use the hashtag #CoffeeShopDevos!

Just Like Jesus

Don't be selfish; don't try to impress others. Be humble, thinking of others as better than yourselves.

Philippians 2:3

LET'S CHAT ABOUT IT...

If Jesus came back to earth in the flesh today, don't you think He'd be popular? Crowds of people would swarm around Him, demanding selfies. Reporters would hold microphones to His mouth, demanding answers. But when Jesus was on earth, He didn't have this popularity status—at least not before His ministry began. In fact, He grew up in an average home with an average family. Even His appearance wasn't attention grabbing.

The funny thing is, Jesus knew how important He was. Yet He didn't come across as arrogant, even though His bloodline was royalty. He experienced the worst of human conditions, even though He deserved a crown.

In other words, Jesus didn't try to impress others.

Don't you think He was trying to set a standard of humility for us?

Our goal in life shouldn't be to bring attention to our talent, intelligence, or looks. (Although there's absolutely nothing wrong with being confident!) Instead, our goal should be this: To keep a servant's heart. To bring glory and honor to His name. And to continue the work Jesus started by expressing His love to others.

We're only human. Created from dust. Everything we have, everything we are, was given to us by the Creator.

Besides, even if we *were* popular and received all the attention in the world, we would never be satisfied. Because true satisfaction isn't reached through focusing on ourselves. It only comes from carrying out God's commands to love God and love others.

Just like Jesus did.

LET'S THINK ABOUT IT...

When it comes to relationships, is your attitude "me first" or "them first"?

LET'S PRAY ABOUT IT...

Lord, help me to remain humble, put others first, and be an example of Christ in all of my relationships. Amen.

TODAY'S DARE

Put your reputation at risk like Jesus did. At school, find someone who is typically ignored or bullied and talk with them. Let them see Christ in you as you express His love in your words and actions.

A SHOT OF INSPIRATION

Since God chose you to be the holy people he loves, you must clothe yourselves with tenderhearted mercy, kindness, humility, gentleness, and patience.

Colossians 3:12

Join the convo! Inspired by today's chat? Share what you learned! Snap a photo of this book (or the drink you're sipping on), and spark a discussion on social media by answering this question:

Why do you think God wants us to remain selfless and humble in our relationships?

Be sure to use the hashtag #CoffeeShopDevos!

Putting Out the Flames

Scripture to sip on

Never pay back evil with more evil. Do things in such a way that everyone can see you are honorable. Do all that you can to live in peace with everyone. Dear friends, never take revenge. Leave that to the righteous anger of God. For the Scriptures say,
"I will take revenge;
I will pay them back,"
says the Lord.

Romans 12:17–19

LET'S CHAT ABOUT IT...

Isn't it crazy how when Jesus was persecuted, He could've easily called for the angels to come to His aid? He could've destroyed the soldiers who were persecuting Him. Sent lightning to strike them to prove He was the Messiah.

Instead, He chose to forgive those who were persecuting Him—even as He hung on the cross. Jesus knew justice would be served eventually and the truth would be known. He knew the enemy would be defeated, once and for all.

How many times have you been tempted to seek revenge? Maybe someone at school shared a rumor about you that wasn't true, or perhaps you were picked on by a classmate. When others hurt us, our initial reaction is often to hurt them back. But this Scripture tells us we should refrain from paying back evil with more evil. Doing so is like adding fire to fire; it'll only feed the flames and cause more damage. Instead, we are to "live in peace with everyone."

God is a God of justice; however, His way of "getting revenge" is different from ours. We can trust His way is best.

So the next time someone wrongs us, instead of trying to put out the fire with more fire, let's take out our water hose of peace and douse the fire out. Let's choose to love them in return—just like Jesus did on the cross.

If we do this, the flames will diminish.

Then our Father will take care of the damage it caused.

LET'S THINK ABOUT IT...

If someone has wronged you, how can you respond in peace and love rather than revenge?

....

....

....

....

LET'S PRAY ABOUT IT...

Lord, the next time I'm tempted to seek revenge on someone, remind me to leave the situation in your hands and stay at peace with them. Amen.

TODAY'S DARE

The next time you're tempted to seek revenge on someone, instead give them the revenge of love! Shock them by responding to their hurtful words with a peaceful gesture or words of kindness.

A SHOT OF INSPIRATION

See that no one repays anyone evil for evil, but always seek to do good to one another and to everyone.

1 Thessalonians 5:15 ESV

Join the convo! Inspired by today's chat? Share what you learned! Snap a photo of this book (or the drink you're sipping on), and spark a discussion on social media by answering this question:

When we're wronged, why do you think God wants us to remain at peace and leave revenge to Him instead?

Be sure to use the hashtag #CoffeeShopDevos!

Flaming Tongue

Fire goes out without wood,
and quarrels disappear when gossip stops.

Proverbs 26:20

LET'S CHAT ABOUT IT...

Adding a single spark of flame to a tree can result in a wildfire. The wood feeds the flames, then the fire enlarges and destroys everything in its path.

A single flame becomes an intimidating and powerful force when it's fed with wood.

Likewise, the tongue becomes an intimidating and powerful force when it produces gossip. Even the smallest amount of gossip can produce wildfires of drama. So how can we put out this wildfire? By applying this Scripture and not adding wood to the fire.

It can be tough to cut gossip out of our behavior, especially since we often don't recognize our own gossip! It'll disguise itself as innocent small talk among friends. Sometimes it sneaks up on our tongues, and by the time we've realized the damage our words have caused, it's too late to take them back.

Gossip is as small and harmless as a single flame when ignited to wood; in other words, there's nothing *harmless* about it. And despite the size of the flame, it will eventually produce a wildfire as it spreads.

So let's keep the flame of our tongues contained when we're tempted to join in on gossip. Then, we'll watch and see how—just as this verse says—the drama will be extinguished.

Because a fire will always diminish when it's no longer fed.

LET'S THINK ABOUT IT...

How can you keep the flame of your tongue contained when you're tempted to gossip?

LET'S PRAY ABOUT IT...

Lord, give me the strength to contain my tongue when I'm tempted to gossip. Amen.

TODAY'S DARE

The next time your friends engage in gossip around you, instead of listening and being faced with the temptation to chime in, leave the room. If that's not possible, hold your tongue and ask God to help you not add more wood to the wildfire.

A SHOT OF INSPIRATION

> A troublemaker plants seeds of strife;
> gossip separates the best of friends.
> Proverbs 16:28

 *Join the convo!* Inspired by today's chat? Share what you learned! Snap a photo of this book (or the drink you're sipping on), and spark a discussion on social media by answering this question:

What kind of damage have you witnessed or experienced as a result of gossip?

Be sure to use the hashtag #CoffeeShopDevos!

Identical Friends

Scripture to sip on

Do not be fooled: "Bad friends will ruin good habits."

1 Corinthians 15:33 NCV

LET'S CHAT ABOUT IT...

When my oldest sister was in high school, she and her best friend spoke almost identically. Same accent, similar speech patterns. It was often difficult to tell them apart based on their voice alone.

Have you witnessed this unintentional copycat behavior in your own friendships, or perhaps in the friendships of others? The more we hang out with someone, the easier it'll become for them to rub off on us—and vice versa. You may notice that you've started to act the same, dress the same, and talk the same as your best friend.

This is the reason God wants us to be careful with our friendships. He knows we're prone to copycat those we're surrounded by—even if it's unintentional.

No, this doesn't mean we're supposed to ignore non-Christians out of fear of becoming like them. Instead, we're to apply this verse by not allowing ourselves to be close friends with those who could serve as a bad influence. People who could tempt us to fall away from our faith or take on bad habits.

Instead, let's find friends who can challenge us in our faith, character, and lifestyle. Friendships that can serve as a good influence on us, and vice versa.

That way, when we play the unintentional copycat game, we'll be proud to look, sound, and act like our best friend. ;)

LET'S THINK ABOUT IT...

Do your friendships inspire godly behavior and habits?

....

....

....

LET'S PRAY ABOUT IT...

Lord, give me wisdom to choose the right friendships. Help me to know how to end a friendship—without hurting feelings—if it's not a good influence on me. Amen.

TODAY'S DARE

Start a Bible study with your friends! Choose a day of the week that you and your friends can meet and read through a book of the Bible together. That way, you will challenge one another in your walk with Christ.

A SHOT OF INSPIRATION

> Walk with the wise and become wise;
> associate with fools and get in trouble.
> Proverbs 13:20

Join the convo! Inspired by today's chat? Share what you learned! Snap a photo of this book (or the drink you're sipping on), and spark a discussion on social media by answering this question:

How can we be a good influence on a nonbeliever without allowing them to influence us in a negative way?

Be sure to use the hashtag #CoffeeShopDevos!

God-Ordained Interruptions

Scripture to sip on

Therefore, whenever we have the opportunity, we should do good
to everyone—especially to those in the family of faith.

Galatians 6:10

LET'S CHAT ABOUT IT...

Since I work from home, I have to be strict with my time management.
Interruptions can result in missed deadlines and late-night work sessions. I've learned to be protective of my time.

But when I received a phone call today from a fellow writer, I
couldn't avoid it. After about five minutes, I knew it was going to
be a long conversation. I watched my time slip by.

Not only was the phone call throwing a kink in my daily routine,
but it didn't benefit me in any way.

Finally, as the fellow writer brought the conversation to a close,
she thanked me for my time. She then told me our phone call had
encouraged her to write again.

At this, I felt convicted for being self-focused. So what if the conversation delayed my work and didn't benefit me? It gave me the opportunity
to help someone in need.

How many times have I brushed off God-ordained interruptions
in an attempt to protect my schedule?

Later, I came across this Scripture and was reminded that my life
isn't about me. My priorities should not be me-focused, but I should
view interruptions as opportunities to express God's love.

No, it's not smart to ignore responsibilities. But if God wants us
to help someone, then let's view it as kingdom work rather than an
interruption.

Besides, if we continue to work for our heavenly boss, just think
of how large our kingdom bank accounts will be when we reach
eternity!

LET'S THINK ABOUT IT...

Do you take advantage of the opportunities God gives you to help others?

LET'S PRAY ABOUT IT...

Lord, thank you for sending God-ordained interruptions in my life to remind me not to focus on myself. I want to use every opportunity to be a light for you. Amen.

TODAY'S DARE

Read Matthew 5:41–42. Next time you have a God-ordained interruption, try to go the extra mile for the other person.

A SHOT OF INSPIRATION

The one who blesses others is abundantly blessed;
those who help others are helped.

Proverbs 11:25 MSG

Join the convo! Inspired by today's chat? Share what you learned! Snap a photo of this book (or the drink you're sipping on), and spark a discussion on social media by answering this question:

How can we know the difference between a God-ordained opportunity to help someone and an unnecessary interruption?

Be sure to use the hashtag #CoffeeShopDevos!

Undeserved Love

Scripture to sip on

Love your enemies! Do good to them. Lend to them without expecting to be repaid. Then your reward from heaven will be very great, and you will truly be acting as children of the Most High, for he is kind to those who are unthankful and wicked.

Luke 6:35

LET'S CHAT ABOUT IT...

I love to watch a good movie, but there's one pattern I've noticed spotted in some Hollywood movies. Have you ever noticed how the main character of the story is commonly praised when he or she seeks revenge on the bad guy? This is a reoccurring element in chick flicks especially. These films promote the assumption that it's okay to hurt those who hurt us.

But the Bible tells us otherwise. God wants us to view our enemies through eyes of love. To realize that they're only human, influenced by the enemy. The *enemy* is to blame for the evil acts of this world.

I'm not saying that those who hurt us shouldn't receive blame and take the responsibility; however, it should be the enemy we're *upset* with. Sure, the love you show them might be undeserved. But how many times have you, too, received undeserved love from Christ?

Besides—what if the person who abused you with their words is dealing with abuse at home? What if they've never felt loved? If you choose to reciprocate their evil words with even more evil words, it could make them worse off than they were to begin with. But if you choose to love instead, then who knows? You might be the very reason that person finds Christ!

Plus, when we repay evil with love, this verse says our "reward from heaven will be very great." I'd much prefer a heavenly reward rather than temporary revenge!

LET'S THINK ABOUT IT...

How can you show love and kindness to those who hurt you?

LET'S PRAY ABOUT IT...

Lord, I can't love my enemies without your strength. Thank you for helping me to see them through eyes of love. Amen.

TODAY'S DARE

Read about how Jesus was betrayed by His disciple Judas Iscariot in Matthew 26. What was Jesus' reaction?

A SHOT OF INSPIRATION

If your enemies are hungry, give them food to eat.
If they are thirsty, give them water to drink.
You will heap burning coals of shame on their heads,
and the Lord will reward you.

Proverbs 25:21–22

Join the convo! Inspired by today's chat? Share what you learned! Snap a photo of this book (or the drink you're sipping on), and spark a discussion on social media by answering this question:

When we're wronged, why do you think God wants us to remain in peace and leave revenge to Him instead?

Be sure to use the hashtag #CoffeeShopDevos!

Love Like It's the Last

Scripture to sip on

"This is my commandment: Love each other in the same way I have loved you."

John 15:12

LET'S CHAT ABOUT IT...

My grandpa passed away two days ago. Although he was diagnosed with cancer last month, we didn't expect him to go home to be with the Lord so soon. Since then, my family has been reminiscing over memories and discussing the impact he's made on our lives. But his sudden absence makes me wish I could've clung to those special moments with him longer.

Isn't that always the case? We often don't realize how much someone means to us until they're gone. And no matter how long you spend with a loved one before they pass away, it never seems long enough.

Even though I'm always going to miss my grandpa, his passing has reminded me how fast life is.

If you knew today was your last day to spend with a loved one, would you treat them differently? Would the arguments and grudges be worth the time they steal? I don't want it to take a funeral to make me realize how much someone means to me.

Let's cherish every relationship we've been gifted with today. Not out of fear of death, but because it's what God has called us to do. To love each other the same way He has loved us.

The day will soon come when we'll have a heavenly reunion with other believers—but until then, let's appreciate every second we've been given with our loved ones on earth.

And let's never stop loving each other like it's the last day.

LET'S THINK ABOUT IT...

How often do you show appreciation to your loved ones?

....

....

....

....

LET'S PRAY ABOUT IT...

Lord, thank you for the small amount of time I've been given with my loved ones. Help me to make the most of every moment I have with them. Amen.

TODAY'S DARE

How loud is your love? Read 1 Corinthians 13. Then, take an inventory of how you manifest this definition of love in your relationships.

A SHOT OF INSPIRATION

Dear children, let's not merely say that we love each other; let us show the truth by our actions.

1 John 3:18

Join the convo! Inspired by today's chat? Share what you learned! Snap a photo of this book (or the drink you're sipping on), and spark a discussion on social media by answering this question:

If you've experienced the death of a loved one, how did this loss teach you how to cherish the loved ones still on earth?

Be sure to use the hashtag #CoffeeShopDevos!

The Wrong Family

Scripture to sip on

But those who won't care for their relatives, especially those in their own household, have denied the true faith. Such people are worse than unbelievers.

1 Timothy 5:8

LET'S CHAT ABOUT IT...

Growing up, my older sisters sometimes would tease me by telling me I was adopted. They were joking, of course, and I knew better. But there have been times when I *have* felt like I was adopted. Besides, my sisters and my mom have straight blond hair and blue eyes. I have curly brown hair and brown eyes. I've always been more on the quiet side, whereas the three of them could talk up a storm.

Have you, too, ever felt like you were adopted, even if you weren't? Or if you *were* adopted, do you sometimes feel like you were placed with the wrong family?

The truth is, God placed you with your family for a reason— adopted or not. It wasn't a mistake. Actually, it was intentional.

We're each called to honor God in the role we play in our families. Unfortunately, not everyone abides by this. But even if our family members neglect to show us love, we're still called to fulfill *our* roles as daughters (and sisters) by obeying our parents and caring for our relatives.

The time we've been given with them is short. Let's not spend a second of it wishing we had been placed in another family; instead, let's love our relatives, even if they make it difficult. Not only will we please God, but we'll serve as an example of Christ to them.

Then, we may just discover why God chose our family after all— and realize it wasn't simply a result of a random occurrence.

In fact, it was His plan all along.

LET'S THINK ABOUT IT...

How can you honor God by showing love to your family?

....

....

....

....

LET'S PRAY ABOUT IT...

Lord, thank you for the family you chose for me. Help me to carry out my role to love my relatives, even when it's hard. Amen.

TODAY'S DARE

Read about the responsibilities of each member of the family in Colossians 3:18–25 and Ephesians 5:21–33.

A SHOT OF INSPIRATION

A man ought to live so that everybody knows he is a Christian . . . and most of all, his family ought to know.

D. L. Moody

Join the convo! Inspired by today's chat? Share what you learned! Snap a photo of this book (or the drink you're sipping on), and spark a discussion on social media by answering this question:

Why do you think God designed the family?

Be sure to use the hashtag #CoffeeShopDevos!

The Key to Your Heart

Scripture to sip on

And don't be wishing you were someplace else or with someone else.
Where you are right now is God's place for you. Live and obey and
love and believe right there. God, not your marital status, defines
your life.

1 Corinthians 7:17 MSG

LET'S CHAT ABOUT IT...

When I was in eighth grade, I told my two best friends that I wanted
my next boyfriend to be my future husband. I'll never forget the
strange looks they gave me.

"How are you going to do that?" they asked.

I wasn't sure, but I believed God could help me find the right guy
when it was His timing. I only wanted to date someone I could see
myself marrying one day.

Unfortunately, my plan didn't go exactly the way I'd hoped. I dated
a guy for two years before discovering he wasn't my future husband. I
am, however, grateful that I didn't spend my teen years giving pieces
of my heart away to a string of guys.

The purpose of dating is to prepare for marriage. It's to find the
person we're meant to spend the rest of our lives with. When we
date one guy after another in attempt to keep ourselves from being
single, then we aren't treating our hearts with respect. Playing this
kind of game won't prepare us for marriage, but it *might* prepare
us for divorce.

Your heart was purchased by the blood of Jesus. It's far too valuable to give pieces of it away to guys who won't treat it with care. So
stay prayerful when you find a guy you like, and try to save your heart
for the one whose hands it was designed to fit in.

Our hearts have been saved by grace. Let's keep the lock on them
until just the right time. Your future spouse is the one who has the
key. The key is a cross.

The key is Christ.

LET'S THINK ABOUT IT...

How can you seek God for direction and guidance the next time you're tempted to enter a relationship?

LET'S PRAY ABOUT IT...

Lord, thank you for purchasing my heart and saving it through grace. Help me to keep the lock on it and only give the key to the one I'm supposed to marry. Amen.

TODAY'S DARE

Read the book *When God Writes Your Love Story* by Eric and Leslie Ludy.

A SHOT OF INSPIRATION

Your heart is precious to God: So guard it, and wait for the man who will treasure it.

Unknown

Join the convo! Inspired by today's chat? Share what you learned! Snap a photo of this book (or the drink you're sipping on), and spark a discussion on social media by answering this question:

How can girls keep their hearts locked for their future spouse?

Be sure to use the hashtag #CoffeeShopDevos!

Secret to Peace

Scripture to sip on

Hot tempers start fights;
a calm, cool spirit keeps the peace.

Proverbs 15:18 MSG

LET'S CHAT ABOUT IT...

When I was a kid, my best friend and I argued. Constantly. I don't even know what we fought about, but if others overheard us, they probably wouldn't believe we were best friends! There were even times when we'd call our parents and have them pick us up from the other's house earlier than planned.

I wonder how many more memories we could've made together if it wasn't for our senseless arguments.

Did you know it's possible to keep peace with everyone we come in contact with? We can do this by keeping a "calm, cool spirit," as this verse says. This peaceful spirit is not one that acts on fleshly impulses—such as wanting our own way, reacting with a temper, defending ourselves, or being bossy.

If we "kill the flesh" and stay peaceful, allowing the Holy Spirit to guide our speech, arguments will be prevented. And when the arguments are prevented, we'll gain more quality time with our friends and family.

So the next time someone pushes our buttons, let's refrain from *reacting* and quietly ask the Holy Spirit to help us *respond* in a peaceful manner.

I would've saved myself from much strife if I'd practiced this sooner in life!

LET'S THINK ABOUT IT...

How much time do you spend arguing with your friends and family?

LET'S PRAY ABOUT IT...

Lord, give me the strength to resist fleshly impulses to argue and instead have an ability to stay cool and calm. I don't want pointless arguments to ruin my relationships. Amen.

TODAY'S DARE

The Bible has a lot to say on the subject of keeping peace. Look up these Scriptures:

Proverbs 15:1
Ephesians 4:32
Proverbs 17:14
Proverbs 20:3
James 4:1–2
Ephesians 4:26

A SHOT OF INSPIRATION

Again I say, don't get involved in foolish, ignorant arguments that only start fights. A servant of the Lord must not quarrel but must be kind to everyone, be able to teach, and be patient with difficult people.

2 Timothy 2:23–24

Join the convo! Inspired by today's chat? Share what you learned! Snap a photo of this book (or the drink you're sipping on), and spark a discussion on social media by answering this question:

Have you ever seen an argument destroy a relationship? How could it have been handled differently?

Be sure to use the hashtag #CoffeeShopDevos!

The Relationship Recipe

Love is patient and kind. Love is not jealous or boastful or proud or rude. It does not demand its own way. It is not irritable, and it keeps no record of being wronged. It does not rejoice about injustice but rejoices whenever the truth wins out. Love never gives up, never loses faith, is always hopeful, and endures through every circumstance.

1 Corinthians 13:4–7

LET'S CHAT ABOUT IT...

Do you know of a couple who has a *perfect* relationship? Maybe their Instagram pictures make their relationship appear flawless. I doubt it is. Since we're flawed humans, we should never expect perfection from our loved ones. But even though we might not have *perfect* relationships, we can still cultivate healthy ones. How?

By following the recipe laid out for us in 1 Corinthians 13.

We are to be patient. Kind. Not jealous, boastful, proud, or rude. We shouldn't control, become aggravated, or recall the wrongdoings of others. We should persevere through the highs and lows of any relationship and believe the best about one another.

It might sound impossible. But when we come to know God's unconditional love, we'll have the ingredients required to put this Scripture into action. When we taste of the enduring love He has for us, we'll know what it takes to express that in our relationships.

Then the Holy Spirit can help us sacrifice our fleshly desires and follow God's recipe in 1 Corinthians 13 instead.

No, this might not result in a perfect relationship, but it *will* result in a relationship covered in Christ's perfect love.

LET'S THINK ABOUT IT...

How can you take action and follow this recipe in your relationships?

LET'S PRAY ABOUT IT...

Lord, help me to receive the perfect love you have for me so I can portray this love to others. Amen.

TODAY'S DARE

Do you know of a couple, such as your parents, who have cultivated a healthy relationship? If so, ask them how they've sacrificed their selfish desires by putting 1 Corinthians 13 into action in their relationship.

A SHOT OF INSPIRATION

The secret of loving is living loved.

Max Lucado

Join the convo! Inspired by today's chat? Share what you learned! Snap a photo of this book (or the drink you're sipping on), and spark a discussion on social media by answering this question:

How does the world define healthy relationships, and in what ways does this differ from the recipe for relationships laid out in 1 Corinthians 13?

Be sure to use the hashtag #CoffeeShopDevos!

Espresso

Joy for
Each Moment

Sassy Espresso Sundae

I personally can't handle drinking straight-up espresso. I love the taste of strong coffee, but espresso is a little too concentrated for my liking. So why not change it up a bit—okay, a lot—by transforming it into a sundae instead? The great thing about this recipe is that *you're* the boss. Hence the "sass"!

(And yes, you will need a spoon to "drink" this one.) ;)

INGREDIENTS

- 2 shots espresso (or 1/2 cup strong coffee)
- 1 large scoop of preferred flavored ice cream
- 1 tablespoon of preferred syrup flavor

INSTRUCTIONS

1. Brew espresso (or strong coffee).
2. Scoop ice cream into mug.
3. Pour espresso (or strong coffee) over ice cream.
4. Drizzle syrup over ice cream.
5. Optional garnish: whipped cream, sprinkles, a cherry, chocolate shavings, coffee beans, etc. You're the boss!

Abundant Life

Scripture to sip on

"The thief's purpose is to steal and kill and destroy. My purpose is to give them a rich and satisfying life."

John 10:10

LET'S CHAT ABOUT IT...

Have you ever been advised to live life to the fullest? Our culture encourages us to do it all—travel to new places, gain new experiences, and take risks. Life's short; why not make the most of it?

Jesus also wants us to live a "rich and satisfying life." But what if His definition of "life" is different than ours?

True life is equivalent to *eternal* life, whereas death is equivalent to living in sin. So if we experience the world's version of life yet we don't know Christ, we can still be living in death.

Why seek for the world to grant us "life" when we already have eternal life abiding inside of us? God wants us to enjoy our lives whether we're checking off our bucket list or not. We can do this by living in His perfect will, having an intimate relationship with His Son, storing up heavenly treasures, and loving others. *That* is abundant life. The kind that will lead to true fulfillment and joy.

Eternal life is far more real than this earthly one. If we only live for earth, what will we have to show for it in eternity?

So if you can't take an Alaskan cruise, swim with dolphins, or go skydiving, don't feel like you're missing out on life. If we live for Jesus, we *will* be making the most of this life, as well as the one to come.

And this is the only kind of life that death cannot snatch away from us!

LET'S THINK ABOUT IT...

Have you experienced the abundant life Jesus paid for us to enjoy?

_____

_____

_____

LET'S PRAY ABOUT IT...

Lord, thank you for the price you paid so I could experience abundant life. There's no earthly pleasure that compares to the pleasure of living for you. Amen.

TODAY'S DARE

Write a bucket list that will profit your life in eternity. Here are some ideas:

- Go on a missions trip.
- Start a homeless ministry.
- Lead someone to Christ.

A SHOT OF INSPIRATION

> You will show me the way of life,
> granting me the joy of your presence
> and the pleasures of living with you forever.
> Psalm 16:11

Join the convo! Inspired by today's chat? Share what you learned! Snap a photo of this book (or the drink you're sipping on), and spark a discussion on social media by answering this question:

What does it look like to live life to the fullest as a Christian?

Be sure to use the hashtag #CoffeeShopDevos!

Healthy Minds

Scripture to sip on

And now, dear brothers and sisters, one final thing. Fix your thoughts on what is true, and honorable, and right, and pure, and lovely, and admirable. Think about things that are excellent and worthy of praise.

Philippians 4:8

LET'S CHAT ABOUT IT...

Have you heard the phrase "You are what you eat"? Did you know you are what you dwell on as well? If you feed your mind with thoughts that are filled with junk, such as, *I'm never going to make good grades in school*, then guess what? You'll likely produce just that!

This Scripture tells us to think about things that are "excellent and worthy of praise." Our minds direct our actions, words, moods, and behavior. If we want to produce good works, we first need to feed our minds with healthy nutrients.

If we can't find anything good to think about, let's find reasons to stay grateful. If we *still* can't change our thoughts, let's follow this wise advice from my grandma: "If you can't find anything to be thankful for, then at least be thankful for what you *don't* have." Are you in perfect health? Then thank God that you aren't sick!

Even if we're trudging through dreadful circumstances, we can always thank God for the gifts of our salvation that never diminish— such as peace. Hope. Joy. Love. The promise of heaven.

As we feed our minds with positive nutrients, guess what? The negative will be squeezed out. Soon, we'll notice positive results in our moods, actions, and words, even if we're still experiencing hardships. How?

Healthy food always results in a healthy life.

LET'S THINK ABOUT IT...

Are you feeding your mind the nutrients it needs to thrive?

LET'S PRAY ABOUT IT...

Lord, thank you for giving me the mind of Christ (1 Corinthians 2:16). Help me to feed my mind with healthy nutrients and stay grateful in every season. Amen.

TODAY'S DARE

The next time you have a hard day, make a list of fifteen good things that have happened to you. If you can't think of fifteen, then instead fill your list with reasons to be grateful.

A SHOT OF INSPIRATION

> You will keep in perfect peace
> all who trust in you,
> all whose thoughts are fixed on you!
> Isaiah 26:3

Join the convo! Inspired by today's chat? Share what you learned! Snap a photo of this book (or the drink you're sipping on), and spark a discussion on social media by answering this question:

Have you noticed positive changes result from thinking positive thoughts? Or have you noticed negative changes result from thinking negative thoughts?

Be sure to use the hashtag #CoffeeShopDevos!

Joy in Winter

Not that I was ever in need, for I have learned how to be content with whatever I have. I know how to live on almost nothing or with everything. I have learned the secret of living in every situation, whether it is with a full stomach or empty, with plenty or little.

Philippians 4:11–12

LET'S CHAT ABOUT IT...

There's a certain peace that arises in winter. It's the kind that reminds us to enjoy life's simple moments—such as relaxing inside and sipping hot chocolate while snow falls from the sky.

However, some people don't like how the green leaves that once gave life to trees have fallen to reveal only skeleton-like branches. They don't enjoy how the sunshine that once splashed light into their days becomes replaced with gray skies covered by heavy snow clouds.

What if I told you joy could be found in *every* season of our lives?

Since this world isn't our home, our happiness doesn't depend on circumstances. Instead, our happiness—or rather, our *joy*—stems from our life with Christ. We don't have to wait for the sunshine of spring to splash color into our days when our relationship with Jesus illuminates *every* day. The closer we draw to Him, the more we'll learn to appreciate life's simple moments.

When this happens, don't be surprised if you find yourself viewing winter through a new lens. What was once arctic snow may transform into a grown-up playground; what was once a frozen pond turns into an ice skating rink. Our life with Christ adds fresh joy to every day.

Yes, even the never-ending, bitter days of winter.

LET'S THINK ABOUT IT...

How can your life with Christ add meaning and beauty to your current season?

....

....

....

....

LET'S PRAY ABOUT IT...

Lord, your light adds beauty to every season. Help me to learn how to find joy even in the small moments. Amen.

TODAY'S DARE

Are you facing a dreadful season in your personal life? If so, in your prayer journal, write down a list of ways you can view the situation through a positive lens.

A SHOT OF INSPIRATION

Joy is not the absence of suffering. It is the presence of God.

Robert Schuller

Join the convo! Inspired by today's chat? Share what you learned! Snap a photo of this book (or the drink you're sipping on), and spark a discussion on social media by answering this question:

How does your relationship with Christ bring joy and beauty to your life?

Be sure to use the hashtag #CoffeeShopDevos!

Heavenly Ecstasy

A single day in your courts
is better than a thousand anywhere else!
I would rather be a gatekeeper in the house of my God
than live the good life in the homes of the wicked.

Psalm 84:10

LET'S CHAT ABOUT IT...

Have you ever been on a vacation that made you believe you were in paradise? Perhaps you've visited Hawaii and spent a week lying in a hammock on the coast, reading books and sipping water from a coconut. I bet once you returned home, you longed to escape reality and return to your dreamland.

What if I told you that our real home, our *eternal* home, will be far better than any temporary paradise we've experienced on earth? What if I told you we could have a taste of the peace, hope, and love we will bask in forever, even while we're still on earth?

God's presence will fill the atmosphere in heaven. And guess what? His presence is with us on earth as well. When we draw close to Him, we can bask in His perfect love. We can be filled with joy and saturated in peace. Nothing on earth compares to the heavenly ecstasy we experience in God's presence!

Even when we face suffering, His presence can make any moment sacred. And as we walk through pain, we can find hope in this one fact: This life is temporary. Someday we'll spend eternity in the presence of Jesus—far removed from the troubles of this life.

Then, when we look back at the earthly paradise we once enjoyed, it'll probably look like suffering in comparison to our eternal paradise!

LET'S THINK ABOUT IT...

Have you experienced this "heavenly ecstasy" in God's presence?

248

LET'S PRAY ABOUT IT...

Lord, thank you for preparing a place for those who love you. Thank you for filling me with your love, joy, and peace as I draw closer to you. Amen.

TODAY'S DARE

Listen to the song "I Can Only Imagine" by MercyMe.

A SHOT OF INSPIRATION

> You will show me the way of life,
> granting me the joy of your presence
> and the pleasures of living with you forever.
>
> Psalm 16:11

Join the convo! Inspired by today's chat? Share what you learned! Snap a photo of this book (or the drink you're sipping on), and spark a discussion on social media by answering this question:

How does your relationship with Jesus and the promise of heaven help you persevere?

Be sure to use the hashtag #CoffeeShopDevos!

Life-Giving Medicine

Scripture to sip on

A cheerful heart is good medicine,
but a broken spirit saps a person's strength.

Proverbs 17:22

LET'S CHAT ABOUT IT...

When was the last time you took a dose of life-giving laughter? I'm not talking about the fake kind of laugh, or even a giggle. But the kind of can't-catch-your-breath laugh that gives you an ab workout and leaves you breathless. Did you know these belly laughs can actually lengthen our lives? Not only is this theory supported scientifically, but it's a biblical truth that this joy is healing to the body.

Life often zaps our energy and leaves us with a broken spirit, as this verse says; that's why we need to restore our energy by finding something to laugh at daily.

I believe humor is a gift God's given to help us lighten our load. Laughter reminds us not to take life so seriously. It reminds us that, despite the suffering we've experienced, life goes on—and we can always find something that will make us smile, in spite of the pain.

So the next time we find ourselves stressed, burdened, or discouraged— symptoms of a broken spirit—let's take an extra dose of laughter. As this medicine dissolves into our bloodstream, our strength will be restored. Our frown will be turned around. The endorphins laughter releases will help us breathe easier and think more clearly. Rather than complaining about a stress-induced migraine, we'll instead complain about a laughter-induced bellyache.

Doesn't sound too bad for a free prescription of life-giving medicine, if you ask me!

LET'S THINK ABOUT IT...

How can you find more reasons to laugh throughout the day?

_____

_____

_____

_____

LET'S PRAY ABOUT IT...

Lord, thank you for creating the gift of humor and laughter. When I feel weighed down, remind me to take advantage of this free medicine and find a reason to laugh. Amen.

TODAY'S DARE

Write a prescription for a cheerful heart—things you can do when you're in need of a good laugh.

A SHOT OF INSPIRATION

I have not seen anyone dying of laughter, but I know millions who are dying because they are not laughing.

Dr. Madan Kataria

Join the convo! Inspired by today's chat? Share what you learned! Snap a photo of this book (or the drink you're sipping on), and spark a discussion on social media by answering this question:

Have you witnessed the health benefits of humor in your life or in the life of another?

Be sure to use the hashtag #CoffeeShopDevos!

Independent Joy

But the Holy Spirit produces this kind of fruit in our lives: love, joy, peace, patience, kindness, goodness, faithfulness, gentleness, and self-control.

Galatians 5:22–23

LET'S CHAT ABOUT IT ...

My friends and family know that if they want to make me happy, all they have to do is buy me a new book. Or take me to a coffee shop. New clothes will never make my face light up the way new books will.

But even if I were to lose all of my books—and if I were to stop drinking coffee—I could still have joy. That's because it isn't dependent on anything of this world. Clothes, coffee, books, money, achievements, perfect circumstances . . . none of this can come close to bringing me the joy that comes from the Holy Spirit.

If I live dictated by my fleshly desires, then I'll always look to the world to make me happy; however, when I'm led by the Holy Spirit, my joy will be dependent on my relationship with Christ. When we expect others to keep us happy, relationships will fail. When we expect circumstances to keep us happy, we'll remain disappointed.

Instead, I want the joy that stems from the Holy Spirit. *Independent* joy. The kind that isn't attained by getting more stuff or having perfect circumstances. Because no amount of new things could give me this independent joy.

No, not even a new book or a latte. ;)

LET'S THINK ABOUT IT ...

Is your happiness dependent on the world or your relationship with Christ?

LET'S PRAY ABOUT IT...

Lord, thank you that my joy isn't dependent on anything of this world. Amen.

TODAY'S DARE

Next time you have a bad day, ask yourself, *Am I letting my joy be dependent on my circumstances?* If so, set your gaze on Christ, and thank the Holy Spirit for the joy that comes from knowing Him.

A SHOT OF INSPIRATION

How sweet all at once it was for me to be rid of those fruitless joys which I had once feared to lose! . . . You drove them from me and took their place, You who are sweeter than all pleasure.

Augustine

Join the convo! Inspired by today's chat? Share what you learned! Snap a photo of this book (or the drink you're sipping on), and spark a discussion on social media by answering this question:

How does the world's definition of happiness differ from God's definition of joy?

Be sure to use the hashtag #CoffeeShopDevos!

A Pleasant Aroma

Scripture to sip on

Those who have been ransomed by the Lord will return.
They will enter Jerusalem singing,
crowned with everlasting joy.
Sorrow and mourning will disappear,
and they will be filled with joy and gladness.

Isaiah 35:10

LET'S CHAT ABOUT IT...

Have you ever been around someone who always carries a stench? I'm not referring to a bad smell. I mean the kind of stench that radiates from a bad attitude and negative outlook. And no matter what you do—even if you offer this person deodorant—nothing is strong enough to erase the smell.

We have to be intentional with the aroma we carry. If nothing puts a smile on our face, we should find a reason to smile. For Christians, this shouldn't be a difficult task! Our joy is rooted in our relationship with Christ. He can replace our sorrow and mourning—the "bad stench" we might carry—with joy and gladness. But this won't happen unless we first recognize our own foul stench and ask Him to replace it with a pleasing aroma.

So don't be the person who constantly gives off funk. Instead of grumbling, find reasons to be grateful. Instead of wearing a frown, allow the joy that comes from your relationship with Christ to overflow onto your face.

Then you can be proud if your aroma rubs off on others. And don't be surprised when others ask you for the source of your fragrance so they can smell pleasant, too!

LET'S THINK ABOUT IT...

What kind of aroma do you carry?

_____

_____

_____

_____

LET'S PRAY ABOUT IT...

Lord, my joy stems from my relationship with you. I want this joy to overflow so others can recognize my pleasing fragrance and be compelled to seek you as well. Amen.

TODAY'S DARE

How can you express your joy to someone today?
Here are some ideas:

- Encourage a friend.
- Smile at a stranger.
- Find a reason to laugh with a sibling.

A SHOT OF INSPIRATION

Let your smile change the world, but don't let the world change your smile.

Unknown

Join the convo! Inspired by today's chat? Share what you learned! Snap a photo of this book (or the drink you're sipping on), and spark a discussion on social media by answering this question:

Tell about someone you know whose joy overflows into the lives of those around them.

Be sure to use the hashtag #CoffeeShopDevos!

Rainbow after Rain

Scripture to sip on

For his anger lasts only a moment,
but his favor lasts a lifetime!
Weeping may last through the night,
but joy comes with the morning.

Psalm 30:5

LET'S CHAT ABOUT IT...

My sister's dog used to freak out during thunderstorms. She wouldn't rest until the rain ceased and thunder gave way to silence. Why did she continue to panic during storms even though she'd survived the previous one? It seems like she should've known the storm would eventually die down.

How many times have I reacted the same way to the storms in my life? I should know by now that they don't last forever. Plus, after the rain dies down, there's a certain kind of stillness, a hush, in the atmosphere. It gives me a chance to catch my breath. Then, when it's dry enough to go outside, I often spot a rainbow painted across the sky. One that never ceases to remind me of God's faithfulness.

You see, the storms of our lives are never wasted. The best thing to do when the thunder crashes is to stay still and remind ourselves of God's faithfulness. Because the God who paints a rainbow across the sky after a rainstorm is the same One who can produce joy from our hardships.

Eventually, the sunshine will peek through the clouds, and we'll once again bask in the sunlight of God's goodness and be filled with His joy.

And this joy will far surpass the showers of pain we had to walk through to get there.

LET'S THINK ABOUT IT...

What kind of rainbows has God produced from your previous storms in life?

....

....

....

....

LET'S PRAY ABOUT IT...

Lord, thank you that the storms in my life are never wasted. I believe you can turn the pain in my life into joy. Help me to trust in your faithfulness. Amen.

TODAY'S DARE

Read about the story of Joseph in Genesis 37–45. In what ways did God transform his pain into joy and reward Joseph for his faithfulness?

A SHOT OF INSPIRATION

"He will once again fill your mouth with laughter
and your lips with shouts of joy."

Job 8:21

Join the convo! Inspired by today's chat? Share what you learned! Snap a photo of this book (or the drink you're sipping on), and spark a discussion on social media by answering this question:

Why do you think God sometimes doesn't send the rainbow until after a rainstorm?

Be sure to use the hashtag #CoffeeShopDevos!

A Different Kind of Party

For the Lord is the Spirit, and wherever the Spirit of the Lord is, there is freedom.

2 Corinthians 3:17

LET'S CHAT ABOUT IT...

I wasn't a partier as a teen, but I didn't judge those who partook in that lifestyle. Life can get overwhelming. It can be tempting to let loose and have fun with friends.

But what if there were something more freeing than that? A type of partying that *doesn't* involve drinking until you're sick?

God dwells in the praises of His children (Psalm 22:3). And according to 2 Corinthians 3:17, "wherever the Spirit of the Lord is, there is freedom."

Nothing is more freeing than releasing our burdens to the Lord. We can let loose, knowing we're fully loved and accepted. As we praise Him, joy fills our hearts—a kind that can *never* be attained by alcohol. Plus, we don't have to wait until the weekend. We can worship Him throughout the week.

So instead of searching the world to fill a void and give us the freedom we crave, let's experience how much fun it is to praise God. I believe it's only a sneak peak of the party we'll have in eternity!

Best part? This form of partying *doesn't* result in a hangover.

LET'S THINK ABOUT IT...

Have you experienced the freedom that comes from praise?

LET'S PRAY ABOUT IT ...

Lord, thank you that I can enjoy freedom in your presence. Help me to remember to praise you when I crave release rather than turning to the world. Amen.

TODAY'S DARE

Plan a different kind of party with a group of your friends! Invite them over and spend the evening playing games and socializing. Consider playing music from Hillsong Young & Free to set an atmosphere of praise.

A SHOT OF INSPIRATION

Come, everyone! Clap your hands!
Shout to God with joyful praise!
Psalm 47:1

Join the convo! Inspired by today's chat? Share what you learned! Snap a photo of this book (or the drink you're sipping on), and spark a discussion on social media by answering this question:

Have you experienced the emptiness that comes from partying?

Be sure to use the hashtag #CoffeeShopDevos!

Gifts of Love

Taste and see that the Lord is good.
Oh, the joys of those who take refuge in him!

Psalm 34:8

LET'S CHAT ABOUT IT...

When you love someone, don't you long to express your love to them? Perhaps you enjoy buying them a gift to encourage them when they're discouraged. We find joy in blessing our loved ones and watching their reaction as they open our gifts.

Did you know God delights in blessing His children as well? He's pleased with seeing our faces light up. The joy we receive when we're blessed brings *Him* joy, too.

But what if we don't feel blessed? Perhaps we don't recognize His evidence of love because we're searching for these gifts in the wrong places. Maybe we've become preoccupied with focusing on what we *lack*—such as money or friendships—rather than focusing on what we *do* have, such as a family. Even the small gifts in our everyday lives—the sunrise on your way to school, the beauty of wildflowers—are evidence of His love.

So let's do as this Scripture says and take refuge in Him. That doesn't mean we'll suddenly become prosperous and gain every worldly gift; however, our joy in the blessings God *does* give us will increase. Even the smallest gifts will become larger than the lack in our lives. Why?

Because it's impossible to be discouraged with the blessings God hasn't given us when we're busy appreciating the ones He *has* given us!

LET'S THINK ABOUT IT...

What blessings in your life have you yet to thank God for?

LET'S PRAY ABOUT IT...

Lord, thank you for the many ways you've proven your love for me. Help me to recognize these gifts and stay grateful for them rather than focusing on what I might lack. Amen.

TODAY'S DARE

Share with others the many ways God has blessed you—not to brag about yourself, but to brag about His goodness.

A SHOT OF INSPIRATION

Even when life may be difficult, we should thank God for all He does for us—which we do not deserve.

Billy Graham

Join the conva! Inspired by today's chat? Share what you learned! Snap a photo of this book (or the drink you're sipping on), and spark a discussion on social media by answering this question:

Have you noticed your joy increase when you remain grateful?

Be sure to use the hashtag #CoffeeShopDevos!

Infected with Laughter

Be happy with those who are happy.

Romans 12:15

LET'S CHAT ABOUT IT...

Have you ever caught the bug of laughter? Perhaps your friend started laughing at something random, and you couldn't help but join the roll of laughter. Before long, the laughter deepened. And the funniest part was that neither of you remembered what started the contagious laughter in the first place!

It's a scientific fact that laughter is contagious; in other words, when we hear someone laugh, it triggers a region of the brain that prompts us to join in, even if we don't know the source of it.

I believe this is because God created us for connection. He knew we couldn't do life alone (see Genesis 2:18), which is why we should share life with our friends and family. When we're happy with those who are happy, as this verse says, our joy can increase. Even when we're walking through a difficult season, if we catch a bug of laughter from a loved one, the load we carry becomes lighter. Laughter is a priceless and healthy way to drown out the sorrows and pain in our lives.

So let's surround ourselves with those who can help us find a reason to laugh even on our darkest of days. Let's expose ourselves to those who can infect us with the bug of laughter—the only kind of infection that can actually *lengthen* our lives rather than shorten them!

LET'S THINK ABOUT IT...

How can you intentionally surround yourself with people who can help you stay joyful and enjoy life?

LET'S PRAY ABOUT IT...

Lord, thank you for the gift of laughter. Help me to find people who can bring joy into even the darkest days. Amen.

TODAY'S DARE

Watch a clean comedy film with your friends and/or family.

A SHOT OF INSPIRATION

There is nothing in the world so irresistibly contagious as laughter and good humour.

Charles Dickens

Join the convo! Inspired by today's chat? Share what you learned! Snap a photo of this book (or the drink you're sipping on), and spark a discussion on social media by answering this question:

Is there someone you can always count on to infect you with laughter?

Be sure to use the hashtag #CoffeeShopDevos!

Nourishing Joy

Scripture to sip on

You love him even though you have never seen him. Though you do not see him now, you trust him; and you rejoice with a glorious, inexpressible joy.

1 Peter 1:8

LET'S CHAT ABOUT IT...

I'll never forget the time I hyperventilated when I was fifteen years old. I had been running along the beach in the Florida sun when I collapsed. When the medics arrived and put an oxygen mask on me, I could feel the color return to my face and lips almost immediately. I took my first full breath in what seemed like forever.

I'd never appreciated the gift of oxygen as much as I did in that moment. When the sudden lack of it in my life made me desperate.

Have you experienced that kind of relief? Maybe not the kind that comes from being hooked to an oxygen mask, but the kind that comes from exploding with a good laugh—the first one in far too long. Pain and trials often steal our oxygen, and the lack of joy leaves us suffocating.

Thankfully, as Christians, our faith in Christ provides the nourishing joy we need to breathe clearly. When I was wearing the oxygen mask, I couldn't see the oxygen that restored my body back to health. But I trusted it because I could feel the effects.

Likewise, when we trust God—as this verse says—and when our love for Him grows, we'll begin to feel the effects of His life-giving joy within us.

So the next time the anxieties of life leave us "hyperventilating," let's find our breath again in our relationship with Christ. Let's allow the joy of our salvation, a joy nothing can diminish, to restore us back to health.

Because it's only after we take a fresh breath that we'll regain strength to keep pressing forward.

LET'S THINK ABOUT IT...

Have you experienced the life-giving joy that comes from cultivating a relationship with Christ?

LET'S PRAY ABOUT IT...

Lord, help me to grow in my love for you so I can always have a reason to experience your joy. Amen.

TODAY'S DARE

Hook yourself up to life-giving joy by diving into these Scriptures on God's goodness:

Psalm 34:8	James 1:17
Romans 8:28	Psalm 107:1
Psalm 31:19	Psalm 27:13
Psalm 23:6	Nahum 1:7
Psalm 84:11	

A SHOT OF INSPIRATION

"I have told you these things so that you will be filled with my joy. Yes, your joy will overflow!"

John 15:11

Join the convo! Inspired by today's chat? Share what you learned! Snap a photo of this book (or the drink you're sipping on), and spark a discussion on social media by answering this question:

What's the difference between happiness and joy?

Be sure to use the hashtag #CoffeeShopDevos!

Don't Cry over Spilled Coffee

Scripture to sip on

Do not lose your temper—
it only leads to harm.

Psalm 37:8

LET'S CHAT ABOUT IT...

This morning—as I prepared to leave my house for a writers' conference—something terrible happened.

I spilled my coffee.

Not just any kind of coffee, but my favorite drink from Starbucks: a Guatemala roast pour over with mocha sauce. Over half of the drink leaped out of my cup and onto my carpet.

Although I might sound slightly coffee-obsessed, the new spill on the carpet is the least of my concerns!

It's disappointing, yes—especially because I love to take *good* coffee with me to a writing conference. It gives me the caffeinated-induced energy I need and puts me in the right mood for the day. But instead of crying after this happened (although it was tempting!), I tried to think of worse things that could've happened.

I could've spilled the coffee on my laptop. (It wouldn't have been the first time!) I could've burned myself with the coffee. (Ditto . . .) Or I could've come down with a cold that would've forced me to stay home from the conference.

Doing this helped me view this small inconvenience in the right perspective. It is, after all, just coffee. I don't need it to survive. My joy isn't attached to this drink; it's attached to my relationship with Christ. And unless someone removes me from Him—which will *never* happen—then I'll have everything I need to face the day.

And, I'll admit, it does help to know that I can brew myself another cup before I leave. ;)

LET'S THINK ABOUT IT...

How often do you lose your joy over small inconveniences?

....

....

....

....

LET'S PRAY ABOUT IT...

Lord, thank you that nothing in this world can take away this joy I've found in you. Help me not to lose this joy over small inconveniences in life. Amen.

TODAY'S DARE

When you're tempted to lose your joy over an inconvenience, try thinking of worse things that could've happened.

A SHOT OF INSPIRATION

Don't magnify your problem. Magnify your God. The bigger you make God, the smaller your problems will become.

Joel Osteen

Join the convo! Inspired by today's chat? Share what you learned! Snap a photo of this book (or the drink you're sipping on), and spark a discussion on social media by answering this question:

Share about a time when you lost your joy over a small inconvenience.

Be sure to use the hashtag #CoffeeShopDevos!

More Than Santa

"Until now you have not asked for anything in my name. Ask and you will receive, so that your joy will be the fullest possible joy."

John 16:24 NCV

LET'S CHAT ABOUT IT...

I was the kid who started counting down the days to Christmas beginning in October. I'd write letters to Santa Claus, have Christmas movie marathons, and bake Christmas cookies. And, of course, I loved to scour through the Toys "R" Us catalogs and circle the toys I wanted to add to my Christmas list.

My parents didn't mind it when my sisters and I did this. They didn't spoil us by buying all of the presents on our wish list, but they *did* like to know what we wanted. They found joy in watching us open our presents on Christmas morning.

Did you know God enjoys the same thing?

He invites His children to bring our desires to Him. He doesn't listen to our prayers only when we pray for serious matters. God delights in giving us our hearts' desires, especially when we seek Him first in our lives.

This doesn't necessarily mean we'll receive everything we ask for. He isn't a genie, after all. But when we leave our requests in God's hands, we can trust He knows what's best.

So let's not be shy when it comes to approaching God with our specific requests. Besides, He's the Giver of every good and perfect gift (James 1:17) and finds joy in watching His children open the gifts they asked for.

Yes, even more than Santa Claus.

LET'S THINK ABOUT IT...

Do you reserve your prayer requests for serious matters only? Or do you bring God the desires of your heart?

_____

_____

_____

LET'S PRAY ABOUT IT...

Lord, thank you for caring about the desires of my heart. I place them in your hands and ask that your will be done. Amen.

TODAY'S DARE

Write a list of five desires. Then, as you seek God first, bring these requests to Him. Watch and see how He answers these prayers according to His perfect will and timing.

A SHOT OF INSPIRATION

> Take delight in the Lord,
> and he will give you your heart's desires.
>
> Psalm 37:4

Join the convo! Inspired by today's chat? Share what you learned! Snap a photo of this book (or the drink you're sipping on), and spark a discussion on social media by answering this question:

Share about a time when God granted you a desire of your heart.

Be sure to use the hashtag #CoffeeShopDevos!

The Wrong Latte

Scripture to sip on

Do everything without complaining and arguing.

Philippians 2:14

LET'S CHAT ABOUT IT...

The other day, Starbucks gave me the wrong latte. I didn't notice this until I'd left and it was too late to tell them. I took a sip, expecting to taste the hazelnut latte I'd ordered; instead, I cringed when I sipped a caramel latte instead. Worst part? I've never been a fan of caramel.

When this happened, I was tempted to complain to everyone around me. But you know what I realized? It was a waste of time and energy to drink the latte and complain the entire time. I could learn to love it. Rather than finding fault in the drink, why didn't I thank God for His provision to buy it?

No, life isn't perfect. There will be some baristas who won't get your drink order right, no matter how many times you repeat it in the drive-thru. So why should we make it worse by magnifying the fault? Complaining prevents us from noticing the things we should be grateful for instead.

So let's put this Scripture into action and retrain our brains to bring more attention to the positive rather than the negative. Let's find reasons to thank God rather than whine—because for every complaint, we have a million other reasons to be grateful.

And for every wrong latte we receive, there will be dozens of others that will be just right.

LET'S THINK ABOUT IT...

Do you spend so much time complaining that you miss out on some of the good things in life?

LET'S PRAY ABOUT IT...

Lord, forgive me for complaining. Help me to give more attention to my blessings instead. Amen.

TODAY'S DARE

Can you recall your last complaint? If so, think of five to ten positive things about this situation (or person). Do this every time you find yourself tempted to complain.

A SHOT OF INSPIRATION

Embrace your life, count your blessings, and don't complain about what you don't have.

Joyce Meyer

Join the convo! Inspired by today's chat? Share what you learned! Snap a photo of this book (or the drink you're sipping on), and spark a discussion on social media by answering this question:

How can our perspective change when we focus on blessings rather than complaints?

Be sure to use the hashtag #CoffeeShopDevos!

Labor Pains

Scripture to sip on

"It will be like a woman suffering the pains of labor. When her child is born, her anguish gives way to joy because she has brought a new baby into the world. So you have sorrow now, but I will see you again; then you will rejoice, and no one can rob you of that joy."

John 16:21–22

LET'S CHAT ABOUT IT...

When my mom shares her pregnancy stories with me, she focuses on the labor *highlights* rather than the pregnancy *pain*. She tells me what it was like to feel the baby kicking in her belly, and how exciting it was when her contractions drew closer and closer. She could endure the labor because she set her eyes on the new birth that would soon come.

Then, the pain was overshadowed by joy when she saw the face of her newborn baby.

When Jesus went to the cross, He probably experienced anticipation similar to that of women when they enter into labor. Jesus knew the anguish He'd endure would give way to new birth.

God transformed the darkest day humankind had ever known into a new sunrise, and He can transform our darkest days into new birth as well. We can experience a joy we wouldn't have tasted otherwise had we not gone through the suffering.

So let's cling to the hand that was pierced for our sake. The One who suffered so we could walk through earth with a light that permeates our darkness. Let's find a supernatural joy that comes from setting our eyes on the sunrise that will soon arise.

Someday, joy will overshadow the pain we once knew when we see our Savior's face. According to this verse, *no one* will rob us of our joy.

Not even the memory of our pregnancy pains.

LET'S THINK ABOUT IT...

When you face hardships, how can you build your faith so you can focus on the new joy soon to come?

LET'S PRAY ABOUT IT...

Lord, thank you that our earthly suffering will someday pass. Only you can use it to bring about new birth in my life. I also know the joy I'll experience when I see you will overshadow every memory of earthly pain. Amen.

TODAY'S DARE

Read John 16 and put yourself in the disciples' shoes. If you watched Jesus suffer on the cross, do you think it would've been possible for you to hang on to the hope that you'd see Him again someday?

A SHOT OF INSPIRATION

For we know that all creation has been groaning as in the pains of childbirth right up to the present time. And we believers also groan . . . for we long for our bodies to be released from sin and suffering.

Romans 8:22–23

Join the convo! Inspired by today's chat? Share what you learned! Snap a photo of this book (or the drink you're sipping on), and spark a discussion on social media by answering this question:

Share about a time when you experienced suffering that gave way to new birth.

Be sure to use the hashtag #CoffeeShopDevos!

Crazy in Love

You love him even though you have never seen him. Though you
do not see him now, you trust him; and you rejoice with a glorious,
inexpressible joy.

1 Peter 1:8

LET'S CHAT ABOUT IT...

Have you witnessed someone who is falling in love? It's hard to miss
them as they go about their day wearing a smile on their face. Their
newfound love gives them a deep happiness and brings lightness to
their steps. Even the worst days can become glorious to those falling
in love.

Similarly, when we experience the fullness of love that Christ has
for us, our hearts will swell with love for Him in return. Then, when
we're crazy in love, it's only natural that our joy will double. The
light of His love will brighten our days; this crazy love will demolish
the strongholds of fear and dread in our lives. How? This joy gives
us the supernatural ability to overcome any challenges.

When a couple falls in love, they'll often go through great lengths to
show their love. They express their affection through serving the other
(such as preparing a meal). Similarly, when we fall in love with Christ,
we'll be happy to serve Him. This joy will motivate us to do our best
in every area—at school, in sports, at home, etc. We can overcome
dreadful challenges because of the newfound joy we have in Christ.

However, unlike an earthly relationship, this relationship doesn't
just grant us a temporary happiness. We have access to "glorious,
inexpressible joy." A joy that breathes purpose into our days.

A joy that can only be found through falling head-over-heels, crazy
in love with Jesus Christ.

LET'S THINK ABOUT IT...

How can you fall deeper in love with Jesus so you can attain this eternal joy?

LET'S PRAY ABOUT IT...

Lord, help me to fall deeper in love with you, because I know from this relationship I can attain eternal joy. Amen.

TODAY'S DARE

When you're tempted to have dread or fear, read Nehemiah 8:10 and 1 John 4:18. Remind yourself that the joy you've found in Christ can equip you to face anything, and His perfect love casts out all fear.

A SHOT OF INSPIRATION

"Don't be dejected and sad, for the joy of the Lord is your strength!"

Nehemiah 8:10

Join the conva! Inspired by today's chat? Share what you learned! Snap a photo of this book (or the drink you're sipping on), and spark a discussion on social media by answering this question:

How do you define joy?

Be sure to use the hashtag #CoffeeShopDevos!

Gift of Today

Scripture to sip on

This is the day that the Lord has made.
Let us rejoice and be glad today!

Psalm 118:24 NCV

LET'S CHAT ABOUT IT...

Every morning on the way to school when I was younger, my mom would have my sister and me repeat this Scripture with her. Sometimes, we'd be half awake and yawning or stressing over an upcoming test. But the simple act of reciting this verse reminded us to keep our hearts full of praise as we went about our day.

It's because of this habit that I continue to recite this Scripture almost daily. My mood brightens when I rejoice in the gift of another day.

As Christians, we don't have to wait until our circumstances change before we can be happy. Our joy stems from our relationship with God, and it's expressed as we give thanks to Him. I don't want my circumstances to dictate my mood; rather, I want my praise and thanks to God to dictate my mood. When I thank Him, joy swells within me, and it helps me notice the gifts He has for me throughout the day.

So the next time your alarm wakes you up at six o'clock, rather than groaning and throwing a pillow over your head (am I the only one?), try to praise God instead. And as you go through the day, thank Him for even the smallest gifts He provides along the way.

Even if it's only the simple gift of another day.

LET'S THINK ABOUT IT...

Do you take the time to thank God for His blessings, including the gift of another day?

LET'S PRAY ABOUT IT...

Lord, thank you for the simple gift of another day. Remind me to go throughout my day praising you and focusing on the gifts you've given me. Amen.

TODAY'S DARE

Recite Psalm 118:24 on your way to school every day.

A SHOT OF INSPIRATION

Each moment that we're given is a precious gift from God. We can choose to have a thankful attitude and live each moment full of joy . . . simply because God is good.

Joyce Meyer

Join the convo! Inspired by today's chat? Share what you learned! Snap a photo of this book (or the drink you're sipping on), and spark a discussion on social media by answering this question:

Have you noticed a difference in your mood when you praise and thank God?

Be sure to use the hashtag #CoffeeShopDevos!

Americano

Everyday Issues

Mexican Americano

Do you like to add an extra kick of spice to your coffee drinks? I do. This Americano offers just that—as well as a bit of a change from the typical milk-heavy coffee drinks. That's because Americanos have equal amounts of water and espresso. In other words, they're a lighter alternative to lattes and other espresso drinks; however, the spice in this recipe will give it that extra froufrou coffee flair.

Warning: This drink is not for the faint of tongue! (Is that a thing?)

INGREDIENTS

- 2 shots espresso
- 1/4 cup boiling water
- 1 tablespoon sugar
- 1/2 teaspoon ground cinnamon
- Pinch of nutmeg
- Pinch of cayenne pepper
- 1–2 tablespoons half-and-half

INSTRUCTIONS

1. Brew espresso.
2. Pour water into a mug.
3. Pour espresso over water.
4. Mix in sugar, cinnamon, nutmeg, and cayenne pepper.
5. Pour half-and-half into mug and combine.

Indulging in Brownies

Temptation comes from our own desires, which entice us and drag us away. These desires give birth to sinful actions. And when sin is allowed to grow, it gives birth to death.

James 1:14–15

LET'S CHAT ABOUT IT...

Growing up, my friends and I made brownies at almost every sleepover. I indulged in every bite of the moist, rich chocolate. But there was one problem: Every time I'd promise myself that I'd only have one brownie, the next thing I knew, I'd cram another chocolate square into my mouth.

Then another.

I sometimes couldn't stop until I became sick to my stomach.

Sound familiar? Maybe you, too, told yourself you'd have *just one* taste of _____. (Fill in the blank. And no, it doesn't have to be a type of food or sweets.) But that one "brownie" led to the entire batch—and the consequences of your actions didn't hit you until you felt that first wave of nausea.

In these moments, we often neglect to realize the impact of our decisions. It's as if we're in a trance, and our minds can only think about the pleasure that would arise from giving in.

So instead of remaining in the area of temptation—the kitchen— let's remove ourselves from the aroma of chocolate and find another activity to distract ourselves. However, we can't resist the pull of temptation with our own strength. We need to ask God for the strength to be led by the Sprit rather than our fleshly desires (see Galatians 5:16).

Then we won't have to worry about indulging in an entire batch of brownies. And if we can resist eating that first one, then we won't have a strong craving for more.

This, of course, is only an analogy. There's nothing sinful about enjoying a brownie or two—just make sure to step away from the kitchen before you get a stomachache!

LET'S THINK ABOUT IT...

Do you remove yourself from settings that could lead to temptation?

LET'S PRAY ABOUT IT...

Lord, give me the strength to remove myself from places of temptation. Amen.

TODAY'S DARE

Read about how David gave in to temptation and the consequences that followed in 2 Samuel 11–12. What kind of destruction resulted from his sinful choices?

A SHOT OF INSPIRATION

In all temptations let us consider not what he [Satan] offers, but what we shall lose.

Richard Sibbes

Join the conva! Inspired by today's chat? Share what you learned! Snap a photo of this book (or the drink you're sipping on), and spark a discussion on social media by answering this question:

Have you witnessed or experienced the destruction that can result from giving in to temptation?

Be sure to use the hashtag #CoffeeShopDevos!

The Best GPS

Scripture to sip on

If you go the wrong way—to the right or to the left—you will hear a voice behind you saying, "This is the right way. You should go this way."

Isaiah 30:21 NCV

LET'S CHAT ABOUT IT...

You're probably faced with several different paths you could take after graduation. But if you're anything like I was, then I doubt you already have your entire future mapped out. It doesn't help when you receive conflicting advice from multiple people—some voices telling you to go one way, and others advising you to go another.

With so many paths and voices, it's no wonder teens often feel directionless. When this happens, bring your life-altering decisions to God. Allow Him to become your GPS. He's the only One who can see the bird's-eye view of your life, and He'll guide you step-by-step.

So as you approach a crossroads, don't allow yourself to become confused by the conflicting GPS voices in your life; instead, seek His guidance. God's direction might be a whisper compared to the shouting voices of others. He may speak to you in multiple ways: through His Word, the wisdom of respected authority figures, as well as the inward leading of the Holy Spirit.

His voice is the only one you can trust wholeheartedly. Sometimes, the decisions God calls us to make won't make sense. But if we know we're following His guidance, then we can step out in faith and trust the path will lead us to the right destination.

Besides, even the best GPS on the market can't compare to God's navigational skills. ;)

LET'S THINK ABOUT IT...

How do you seek God's guidance?

LET'S PRAY ABOUT IT...

Lord, when I approach a crossroad, help me to hear your voice telling me which path to take. Amen.

TODAY'S DARE

Are you at a decision-making point in your life? If so, write a list of pros and cons for each path. But keep in mind that God's direction might not always make sense.

A SHOT OF INSPIRATION

The Lord says, "I will guide you along the best pathway for
your life.
I will advise you and watch over you."

Psalm 32:8

Join the convo! Inspired by today's chat? Share what you learned! Snap a photo of this book (or the drink you're sipping on), and spark a discussion on social media by answering this question:

Share about a time when you followed God's guidance, even if it didn't make sense in the natural. What were the results?

Be sure to use the hashtag #CoffeeShopDevos!

Stamp of Approval

Scripture to sip on

He came into the very world he created, but the world didn't recognize him. He came to his own people, and even they rejected him.

John 1:10–11

LET'S CHAT ABOUT IT...

As a writer and an actress, I've had my fair share of rejection. Even though I've learned to take this as rejection of my *work* rather than who I am, it can still sting. Especially since I've had a tendency to be a people pleaser.

We long to be accepted—whether it's within a group of friends, a cheerleading squad, or in the area of pursuing our dreams. But we can't go through life and *not* be rejected. It's impossible to please everyone.

After realizing this, I finally learned a secret to handling rejection. Rather than wasting my energy attempting to please, I should instead remain true to who I am and the work God's called me to do. He is, after all, the only One I'll ultimately have to give account to when this life is over.

This has taken a load off my shoulders. I no longer have to go through life striving to jump through man-made hoops, then being devastated if I fall flat on my face. Instead, when I get rejected, I can remind myself of who I am in God's eyes. My life is no longer dictated by the opinions of others.

Because the only One I care to please has already stamped His approval on me—far before anyone else ever had the chance to disapprove.

LET'S THINK ABOUT IT...

Do you live your life striving to please others or God?

LET'S PRAY ABOUT IT...

Lord, help me to stay true to who I am and aim to please you only. Amen.

TODAY'S DARE

The next time you're hurt from a rejection, look up the following Scriptures:

Genesis 1:31
2 Corinthians 10:18
Romans 14:18
1 Corinthians 4:5
Psalm 118:6–9
2 Timothy 2:15

A SHOT OF INSPIRATION

Fear of man is the enemy of the fear of the Lord. The fear of man pushes us to perform for man's approval rather than according to God's directives.

Paul Chappell

Join the convo! Inspired by today's chat? Share what you learned! Snap a photo of this book (or the drink you're sipping on), and spark a discussion on social media by answering this question:

Have you ever tried to jump through hoops to gain acceptance? What was the result?

Be sure to use the hashtag #CoffeeShopDevos!

Too Connected to Connect

Scripture to sip on

For the world offers only a craving for physical pleasure, a craving for everything we see, and pride in our achievements and possessions. These are not from the Father, but are from this world.

1 John 2:16

LET'S CHAT ABOUT IT...

Something awful happened.

My iPhone stopped working. I've had to go a few days without it. I thought I'd be miserable, but it's freeing! I've read more books and have connected more with those around me. It's also eye-opening to realize how often I reach for it—as a way to pass time—then realize I don't have it.

There's nothing wrong with having my smartphone. I need it to communicate. I need my laptop for work. But too much of anything can become a bad thing. It's possible to be so connected with online life that I miss out on living my *real* life.

I'm "too connected" if . . .

Technology creates a division between me and my friends and family.

Technology keeps me from communicating with God.

I die every time my phone does.

I turn to technology to fulfill every desire rather than God's Word. (Sad? Watch a funny cat video. Lonely? Text your best friend. Bored? Kill time on social media.)

Technology tempts me to sin.

Technology keeps me from noticing the small moments in life.

Technology becomes an idol.

I don't want to reach the end of my life and realize I didn't look up from my screen long enough to appreciate and cherish every moment that passed. Even though being without my iPhone is annoying, it's not the end of my life.

But it *will* be if I'm too connected virtually and don't connect with life outside of my screens.

LET'S THINK ABOUT IT...

Do you feel incomplete when you're without technology?

LET'S PRAY ABOUT IT...

Lord, thank you that I don't need technology to survive. Help me to recognize when I'm too disconnected from my real life. Amen.

TODAY'S DARE

Take a break from technology. Use the extra time to build relationships with those around you.

A SHOT OF INSPIRATION

Technology is a useful servant but a dangerous master.
Christian Lous Lange

Join the convo! Inspired by today's chat? Share what you learned! Snap a photo of this book (or the drink you're sipping on), and spark a discussion on social media by answering this question:

How can we disconnect from our virtual lives and connect more with our real lives?

Be sure to use the hashtag #CoffeeShopDevos!

Idol of the Heart

Some people make idols, but they are worth nothing.
People treasure them, but they are useless.

Isaiah 44:9 NCV

LET'S CHAT ABOUT IT...

Have you ever been obsessed with a certain celebrity or band? I think we've all been there. I know I have. I've also witnessed what can happen when the obsession spins out of control.

I once had a friend who admired a certain band so much that she began to dress and apply her makeup like the lead singer. Soon, the way she spoke became darker—similar to the singer's. I watched as my friend transformed from a sweet girl to someone of dark thoughts and appearance—all because of this band's influence.

There's nothing wrong with being a fan of something or someone, but we need to be careful that this passion doesn't take the place of Jesus in our hearts.

You see, we've been created with an urge to worship someone or something. And oftentimes, we seek to fill this craving with other passions and people. But the longing inside was meant to be fulfilled through worshiping our Father.

So let's choose to make *Him* the object of our worship. He's the only one who is worthy of our attention, adoration, and devotion. As we become obsessed with Jesus, we'll begin to reflect His image to those around us. Our speech will transform. Our character will look more like His. Why? Because our lives will always mirror the idols of our hearts.

Personally, there's no one I'd rather reflect than my Savior!

LET'S THINK ABOUT IT...

Is there anything or anyone in your life that could potentially become an idol?

LET'S PRAY ABOUT IT...

Lord, remove from my heart any passion or person that could take the place of you. You're the only one deserving of my adoration, affection, and devotion. Amen.

TODAY'S DARE

Listen to the song "Clear the Stage" by Jimmy Needham.

A SHOT OF INSPIRATION

Idolatry is seeking security and meaning in someone or something other than God.

A. R. Bernard

Join the convo! Inspired by today's chat? Share what you learned! Snap a photo of this book (or the drink you're sipping on), and spark a discussion on social media by answering this question:

What are some of the most common forms of idols today?

Be sure to use the hashtag #CoffeeShopDevos!

Distorted Reflection

You made my whole being;
you formed me in my mother's body.
I praise you because you made me in an amazing
and wonderful way.
What you have done is wonderful.
I know this very well.

Psalm 139:13–14 NCV

LET'S CHAT ABOUT IT...

When I was a tween, I didn't understand those who said they hated their bodies. What did they mean? And what caused them to dislike their bodies so much?

But as I grew into my teen years, I became exposed to messages that told me there was only one version of a perfect body. These messages distorted my reflection in the mirror.

The enemy deceives us into wearing a false pair of lenses—the kind that demolishes our self-confidence by altering our reflection. He tries to make us believe that our value, beauty, and worth are attached to what we see in the mirror.

Let's put on a new lens and believe the truth about who *God* says we are: No, we are not our shirt size or the number on the scale; yes, we have been crafted in an "amazing and wonderful way."

That is the lens we should view ourselves through. God's Word has the final say. His truth smashes the lies of the world.

The next time you find yourself ashamed of your reflection, put on your new lens. Not the lens of the world, but the lens of the Word.

The only lens that will reveal your *true* reflection.

LET'S THINK ABOUT IT...

What lens do you view yourself through—the lens of the world or the Word?

LET'S PRAY ABOUT IT...

Lord, help me to view myself through the lens of the Word rather than the world. Amen.

TODAY'S DARE

Write a list of three to five lies about your appearance you've believed through the world's lens. Then, strike a line through each lie. In its place, write the following truths based on the corresponding Scripture:

My body has been purchased with a high price. (1 Corinthians 6:20)

I've been made in an amazing and wonderful way. (Psalm 139:13–14)

I am valuable, and God gave careful attention to every detail of my body. (Luke 12:7)

My beauty is not attached to my physical appearance. (1 Peter 3:4 and 1 Timothy 2:10)

I am God's masterpiece. (Ephesians 2:10)

A SHOT OF INSPIRATION

Don't copy the behavior and customs of this world, but let God transform you into a new person by changing the way you think.

Romans 12:2

Join the convo! Inspired by today's chat? Share what you learned! Snap a photo of this book (or the drink you're sipping on), and spark a discussion on social media by answering this question:

Why do you think the enemy strives to destroy our self-confidence?

Be sure to use the hashtag #CoffeeShopDevos!

Sustaining Diet

Scripture to sip on

And this world is fading away, along with everything that people crave. But anyone who does what pleases God will live forever.

1 John 2:17

LET'S CHAT ABOUT IT...

When I was eight, my parents bought our family a package of ice cream sandwiches.

They vanished within a couple of days.

My parents asked my sisters and me how many we'd each eaten. My sisters only had one each. Me?

I'd scarfed down about four sandwiches a day.

Thankfully, my parents prevented that from happening again; otherwise, who knows how much weight I could've gained!

When we feed our bodies with junk, we reap the consequences of poor health. Likewise, when we constantly feed our minds with junk—such as trashy TV, movies, magazines, books, and music—it's going to influence us in a negative way.

So let's replace the junk food on our shelves with cleaner TV, movies, magazines, books, and music. That way we can be satisfied and empowered rather than sluggish and overweight.

Thankfully, I eat much healthier than I did as a kid, and I don't feel deprived at all. In fact, I'm now disgusted when I think about the diet I used to have. I crave food that will give my body *life* rather than *death*.

So if you've been dealing with "health issues" recently, perhaps it's time to take inventory of the junk food stashed away in the cabinets of your mind and hidden in your internet browser history.

And especially be careful with those addicting ice cream sandwiches!

LET'S THINK ABOUT IT...

How can you cut "junk food" out of your mind's diet and replace it with healthier "foods" instead?

LET'S PRAY ABOUT IT...

Lord, help me to honor you in the media and entertainment I expose myself to. Help me to cut out "foods" that may be harmful to my spiritual health. Amen.

TODAY'S DARE

Have a movie night with your friends! But instead of watching a cheap chick flick or vulgar comedy, why not pop in an inspirational film? Here are some of my favorites:

Soul Surfer	*October Baby*
The Song	*I'm Not Ashamed*
Wildflower	*God's Not Dead*
Priceless	

A SHOT OF INSPIRATION

> I will refuse to look at
> anything vile and vulgar.
> Psalm 101:3

Join the convo! Inspired by today's chat? Share what you learned! Snap a photo of this book (or the drink you're sipping on), and spark a discussion on social media by answering this question:

What kind of impact does our diet (TV, music, books, etc.) make on our lifestyle, worldview, and behavior?

Be sure to use the hashtag #CoffeeShopDevos!

Dressed to Impress

And I want women to be modest in their appearance. They should wear decent and appropriate clothing and not draw attention to themselves.

1 Timothy 2:9

LET'S CHAT ABOUT IT...

When we're head-over-heels in love with someone, we strive to do everything we can to show our devotion. It brings us joy to express our adoration to this person. Others will often witness our devotion to this person because of the way we serve them.

Just as a couple serves each other when they're in love, I, too, want my adoration for Jesus to penetrate everything I do. I want to worship Him in the way that I speak. Behave. Love others. In my character. And in my obedience to the Word.

Which includes the way I dress.

Being modest is a reflection of our hearts. It's a reflection of our love for our Savior. We should want to please and honor Him more than we want to dress inappropriately. Does this mean we can't wear clothes that are fashionable and make us feel confident? Of course not! But ultimately, our aim shouldn't be to gain the attention of others as much as to bring attention to our Father in everything we do, including the way we dress.

No, dressing modestly isn't about being legalistic. It's not about hiding our bodies, and it's not a religious duty; rather, it's an *opportunity* to show adoration to our Father and respect to ourselves.

So when we choose our outfits for the day, let's ask ourselves, *Who are we dressing to impress?*

LET'S THINK ABOUT IT...

When you choose your outfits, who do you seek to impress?

LET'S PRAY ABOUT IT...

Lord, I want to dress in a way that impresses you rather than the world. Thank you for the opportunity I have to show my adoration to You. Amen.

TODAY'S DARE

Search your closet and dressers. Is there a piece of clothing that might be considered inappropriate? If so, consider throwing it away. Then, reward yourself by going on a shopping spree! (My favorite place to buy modest and fashionable clothes is Altar'd State.)

A SHOT OF INSPIRATION

We cannot give our hearts to God and keep our bodies for ourselves.

Elisabeth Elliot

Join the convo! Inspired by today's chat? Share what you learned! Snap a photo of this book (or the drink you're sipping on), and spark a discussion on social media by answering this question:

Why do you think it's important to dress in a way that honors God rather than the world?

Be sure to use the hashtag #CoffeeShopDevos!

Permanent Memories

Scripture to sip on

So I recommend having fun, because there is nothing better for people in this world than to eat, drink, and enjoy life. That way they will experience some happiness along with all the hard work God gives them under the sun.

Ecclesiastes 8:15

LET'S CHAT ABOUT IT...

When I was a teen, I loved hanging out with my older cousin, Josh—probably because his unrestrained, immature humor made me feel like a little kid again. We could have fun doing the silliest things, such as taking a trip to the Dollar Store to buy Play-Doh and junk food. (Who doesn't love Play-Doh?) Or riding our scooters late at night in his neighborhood . . . while wearing our pajamas. (Okay, so maybe we were both slightly immature for our age!)

The point is, when I hung out with my friends as a teen, we always found unique ways to have fun together. And thankfully, none of the memories were erased from alcohol.

The assumption that being a Christian must be boring, since you can't partake in a partying lifestyle, is entirely wrong. Being a Christian isn't restricting; it's freeing! You can still party, but you won't have to worry about doing or saying something you'll regret later. Or waking up with a hangover. Or spending the night with your head in a toilet.

Why limit your fun by engaging in activities that could result in damaging consequences and erased memories? There are far more activities we can do with our friends that *don't* involve taking alcohol-induced risks.

I'm grateful I can look back and laugh over the memories I made with my friends as a teen . . . even though it *is* a little embarrassing to recall the prank calls my friends and I used to make. ;)

LET'S THINK ABOUT IT...

What do you and your friends do for fun?

....

....

....

LET'S PRAY ABOUT IT...

Lord, show me how I can hang out with my friends and have fun in a way that pleases you. Amen.

TODAY'S DARE

If you and your friends tend to engage in the same activities when you hang out, maybe it's time to brainstorm new ideas.
Here are some suggestions:

- Have a picnic at a park.
- Do a DIY project.
- Make a dessert together.

A SHOT OF INSPIRATION

If you hope for happiness in the world, hope for it from God, and not from the world.

David Brainerd

Join the convo! Inspired by today's chat? Share what you learned! Snap a photo of this book (or the drink you're sipping on), and spark a discussion on social media by answering this question:

Why do you think it's commonly believed that Christians can't have fun?

Be sure to use the hashtag #CoffeeShopDevos!

Healthy for God's Glory

Scripture to sip on

So whether you eat or drink, or whatever you do, do it all for the glory of God.

1 Corinthians 10:31

LET'S CHAT ABOUT IT...

Growing up in the south, it was a necessity to have the following items in every home-cooked meal: biscuits, a fried meat or veggie, and sweet tea. I assumed meals that weren't starchy—you know, *health* food (gasp!)—tasted like cardboard.

If my older sister hadn't become a health coach and poured her newfound wisdom about nutrition into my family, my diet probably wouldn't look much different today. It's because of this, as well as my diagnosis of Type 1 Diabetes, that my eyes were opened and I had a reason to adjust my diet.

Our bodies are the temples of the Holy Spirit (see 1 Corinthians 6:19–20). It's our responsibility to care for them. How can we fulfill our assignments in life and live out our days if we're battling health issues caused by poor diets? The way we treat our bodies is yet another way we show respect to our Father.

Now that I fuel my body with food that brings life, I don't have a desire to return to the diet I once knew. No amount of fried food in the world can give me the satisfaction of eating a nutritious meal. Actually, I now crave healthy food and am disgusted by the junk I used to eat!

We don't deprive ourselves when we make good choices with our diets. It's the opposite: We deprive ourselves of the fuel our body needs to thrive when we choose a poor diet. So let's glorify God with our bodies. If you do this, don't be surprised if you find that you never want to return to the foods you once knew.

Yes, even if you grew up on starchy southern cooking.

LET'S THINK ABOUT IT...

What's your attitude toward health food and exercise?

LET'S PRAY ABOUT IT...

Lord, help me to glorify you in all that I do, including the way I care for my body. Amen.

TODAY'S DARE

Make a healthy dish with a friend! Find a new recipe online. Here are a few of my favorites:

Baked spaghetti squash
Fish tacos
Cauliflower pizza

A SHOT OF INSPIRATION

God created it. Jesus died for it. The Spirit lives in it. I'd better take care of it.

Rick Warren

Join the convo! Inspired by today's chat? Share what you learned! Snap a photo of this book (or the drink you're sipping on), and spark a discussion on social media by answering this question:

How can Christians honor God by caring for our bodies?

Be sure to use the hashtag #CoffeeShopDevos!

Counterfeit Buzz

Scripture to sip on

Don't be drunk with wine, because that will ruin your life. Instead, be filled with the Holy Spirit, singing psalms and hymns and spiritual songs among yourselves, and making music to the Lord in your hearts.

Ephesians 5:18–19

LET'S CHAT ABOUT IT...

Have you ever seen a counterfeit dollar bill? It might look like the real deal. But good luck trying to buy a pack of gum with it!

A counterfeit can never replace the real thing. It's a wannabe, and it doesn't carry the same value as the *real thing*. Similarly, the enemy has attempted to counterfeit some of the perks of being a Christian. One of these counterfeits comes in the form of getting high.

People often become hooked on alcohol or drugs in attempt to escape from reality. Depressed? Alcohol will help you momentarily forget your troubles and have fun. Anxious? Smoking weed can help you loosen up and relax.

But we don't need to drink to achieve that high. When we become "hooked" on the Holy Spirit, we experience a better buzz. The fruits of the Spirit are peace, love, and joy, among others (see Galatians 5:22–23). And being filled with the Spirit can be fun as well! Ephesians 5 tells us to make music and sing among ourselves. We can enjoy ourselves when we're rejoicing in the Lord, especially when we're rejoicing with other brothers and sisters in Christ. And rather than running away from our troubles, we actually become stronger as we gain supernatural strength to conquer them through the Holy Spirit.

So instead of getting a superficial high, let's become addicted to spending time with Jesus. Then we'll experience for ourselves the "buzz" that comes from being filled with the Holy Spirit, and we'll realize that cheap imitations just won't do.

Because counterfeits will never be the same as the real thing.

LET'S THINK ABOUT IT...

Have you experienced the peace, love, and joy that come from being filled with the Holy Spirit?

LET'S PRAY ABOUT IT...

Lord, any time I have a desire to escape my troubles through a counterfeit high, help me to turn to you and become filled with the Holy Spirit instead. Amen.

TODAY'S DARE

Plan a party with your friends—but instead of serving alcohol, create a coffee bar, and experiment with the recipes in this book!

A SHOT OF INSPIRATION

Christ is a substitute for everything, but nothing is a substitute for Christ.

Harry Ironside

Join the convo! Inspired by today's chat? Share what you learned! Snap a photo of this book (or the drink you're sipping on), and spark a discussion on social media by answering this question:

Have you experienced the benefits that come from being filled with the Holy Spirit?

Be sure to use the hashtag #CoffeeShopDevos!

Just a Bite

Don't use foul or abusive language.

Ephesians 4:29

LET'S CHAT ABOUT IT...

If you grew up in the church, you've probably heard the story about the Garden of Eden a hundred times: Eve took a bite of the forbidden fruit. It seemed harmless, despite the fact that God had commanded her to avoid it. Adam saw Eve take a bite of this fruit, so he figured, why shouldn't he?

Humans aren't very different than Adam and Eve were back then. We're often convinced that "just a bite" isn't harmful, especially since *everyone else is doing it*. Besides, what could possibly go wrong?

Well, let's see. The entire human race has suffered ever since. I don't know about you, but I'd rather not know the disaster that could result from disobeying God's Word!

Often, it's the "small" sins that can lead to the biggest consequences. The Bible's clear we're to avoid "foul or abusive language."

Yes, words are just words—but it's the power behind these strong words that God detests. Even if no one is hurt from a curse word I might choose to say, I'm still disobeying God's Word. And when I disobey God's Word, then I don't treat it with respect. Disobedience will always reap harm rather than reward.

If you struggle in this area, it's never too late to seek God's forgiveness and begin with a clean slate. If you continue to find yourself spewing out abusive language, you might want to take inventory of what you're feeding yourself (music, TV, books, friend influences, etc.).

Next time you're tempted to just say one cuss word, take a moment to look around. See the evil in the world? It was sparked by one person's decision to disobey. One person's decision to have *just a bite*.

Let's never underestimate the damage that could result from the tongue!

LET'S THINK ABOUT IT...

Do your words reflect your respect and adoration toward God?

....

....

....

LET'S PRAY ABOUT IT...

Lord, put a guard over my tongue. I want to only speak words that please you. Amen.

TODAY'S DARE

The Bible has a lot to say about the power of the tongue. Look up the following verses:

Ephesians 4:29   James 3:10
Proverbs 13:3   James 1:26
Colossians 3:8   1 Peter 3:10

A SHOT OF INSPIRATION

> Those who control their tongue will have a long life;
> opening your mouth can ruin everything.
>
> Proverbs 13:3

Join the convo! Inspired by today's chat? Share what you learned! Snap a photo of this book (or the drink you're sipping on), and spark a discussion on social media by answering this question:

In what ways can curse words cause harm?

Be sure to use the hashtag #CoffeeShopDevos!

Voice of a Giant

David replied to the Philistine, "You come to me with sword, spear, and javelin, but I come to you in the name of the Lord of Heaven's Armies—the God of the armies of Israel, whom you have defied."

1 Samuel 17:45

LET'S CHAT ABOUT IT...

How do you think Goliath responded when he saw David, a boy, coming toward him? According to Scripture, Goliath, the giant, sneered at him, teased him, and cursed him.

Read the story in 1 Samuel 17. How differently do you think this story would've played out if David had allowed Goliath's taunts to intimidate him? What if the giant's voice became louder than God's?

When the bullies who tease us attempt to knock us down in order to keep us from rising higher, let's allow the voice of God to speak louder. Because when we choose to rely on His power, we can rise higher. We become the giant when God's on our side.

I'm glad David didn't let the giant's taunts hold him back. Instead of defeat, he chose victory. Instead of running away in fear, he ran toward the giant with confidence.

Likewise, the bullies in our lives become drained of power when we find our confidence in Christ. Their words are drowned out by a greater voice that has far more authority than any earthly giant's: The voice of the Most High.

LET'S THINK ABOUT IT...

Which voice has the most authority in your life?

LET'S PRAY ABOUT IT...

Lord, help me to listen to your voice rather than the voice of bullies. Amen.

TODAY'S DARE

Facing bullies? Proclaim the following statements based on Scripture:

"I have power and love and self-control." (2 Timothy 1:7)

"I am more than a conqueror through Christ." (Romans 8:37)

"I am strong and courageous." (Joshua 1:9)

"I will not fear or dread them." (Deuteronomy 31:6)

"I can do all things through Him who strengthens me." (Philippians 4:13)

"I put on the full armor of God to resist the fiery darts of the enemy." (Ephesians 6:10–18)

"I will not be afraid or discouraged, because God will strengthen and help me." (Isaiah 41:10)

"The Lord is always with me and I will not be shaken." (Psalm 16:8)

"God is my strength and has given me victory." (Isaiah 12:2)

"God is for me and no one can be against me." (Romans 8:31–39)

A SHOT OF INSPIRATION

So be strong and courageous!
Deuteronomy 31:6

Join the convo! Inspired by today's chat? Share what you learned! Snap a photo of this book (or the drink you're sipping on), and spark a discussion on social media by answering this question:

If you've been bullied, how did you respond?

Be sure to use the hashtag #CoffeeShopDevos!

Hope for the Outcasts

Scripture to sip on

"But many who are the greatest now will be least important then,
and those who seem least important now will be the greatest then."

Mark 10:31

LET'S CHAT ABOUT IT...

Think of the most popular girl in your school. Has she been blessed
with good looks and a vibrant personality? Does she have thousands
of followers on Instagram?

Unfortunately, what the world views as important is actually considered meaningless in God's eyes. The number of friends we have
and achievements we gain don't account for anything when they're
only used to bring glory to ourselves.

So why do so many of us still strive to be labeled as popular? Why
do I often find myself wishing I could have more followers on social
media when I know it'll account for nothing in the end?

When we reach the end of our short lives on earth, Jesus isn't going
to ask us how many followers we had on social media; He's going to
ask us how many of those lives we touched.

He's not going to applaud us for becoming famous during our lifetime; He's going to ask us how we used our spotlight to bring Him glory.

He's not going to ask us how many trophies and awards we received; He's going to ask us how we used our gifts to build the body
of Christ.

So even if we're outcasts on earth, if we spend our lives focused
on pleasing God rather than people, we'll be deemed as important in
eternity. And the life we'll have after death is far more real than the
short amount of time we have on earth.

LET'S THINK ABOUT IT...

Are you more focused on achieving earthly popularity or pleasing
Christ?

LET'S PRAY ABOUT IT...

Lord, help me not to view popularity as something of value, because I know earthly importance is fleeting and will account for nothing in eternity. Instead, I want to spend my life focused on pleasing you. Amen.

TODAY'S DARE

Write down ways you can use social media to touch lives, and how you can use your gifts to build the body of Christ.

A SHOT OF INSPIRATION

There are no rewards at the end of life for wealth, fame, accomplishment, or beauty. There is reward for faithfulness.

Lecrae

Join the convo! Inspired by today's chat? Share what you learned! Snap a photo of this book (or the drink you're sipping on), and spark a discussion on social media by answering this question:

How can Christians become more focused on attaining eternal riches than earthly popularity?

Be sure to use the hashtag #CoffeeShopDevos!

E for Effort

Work hard so you can present yourself to God and receive his approval. Be a good worker, one who does not need to be ashamed and who correctly explains the word of truth.

2 Timothy 2:15

LET'S CHAT ABOUT IT...

When I was in high school, I wasn't fond of math. So, before taking a test, I already expected that I wouldn't answer every question correctly. This assumption gave me the results I'd anticipated. But what would've happened if I had raised my standards and worked harder?

You see, the lack of a natural ability to solve math equations—as well as my lack of passion for the subject—resulted in Cs and Bs rather than As. However, I'm sure I could've raised these grades if I'd tried harder by working with a tutor and spending more time studying.

What good would this have done?

Well, it would've raised my GPA. I could've had the satisfaction that comes from a job well done. But more than that: I would've gained God's approval, as this verse says, by working harder and putting forth my best effort.

You might not understand why it's necessary to study some subjects in school. But even if there are certain subjects that don't come naturally for you, this will allow room to work harder. The purpose shouldn't be just to please parents and teachers, but to honor God and worship Him.

First of all, you need to believe it *is* possible to rise higher and conquer these challenges through Christ (see Romans 8:31–39). Then, even if you still don't receive a good grade, God will approve of your hard work.

Besides, it's much more rewarding to receive a hard-earned B than an easy A.

LET'S THINK ABOUT IT...

Is there a subject(s) in school that you could work harder in?

....

....

....

....

LET'S PRAY ABOUT IT...

Lord, thank you for the opportunity to learn. Help me to work hard in every subject and excel in my efforts. Amen.

TODAY'S DARE

Devote at least an extra half hour every day this week to working harder on your homework and studying early for tests.

A SHOT OF INSPIRATION

Continuous effort—not strength nor intelligence—is the key to unlocking our potential.

Winston Churchill

Join the convo! Inspired by today's chat? Share what you learned! Snap a photo of this book (or the drink you're sipping on), and spark a discussion on social media by answering this question:

How have you reaped rewards from working hard in school?

Be sure to use the hashtag #CoffeeShopDevos!

Knots of Confusion

Scripture to sip on

We destroy every proud obstacle that keeps people from knowing God. We capture their rebellious thoughts and teach them to obey Christ.

2 Corinthians 10:5

LET'S CHAT ABOUT IT...

Did you ask countless "philosophical" questions when you were a kid? I did, too. One day, I asked my older sister what caused thunderstorms. Her response? "Thunderstorms happen when Jesus and Satan play kickball in heaven." It didn't occur to me that Satan probably wouldn't be in heaven—or friends with Jesus, for that matter.

You still might have questions of your own, such as "Why did God give us free will?" "How did Noah feed all of those animals?" It can get frustrating when the Bible doesn't clearly spell out answers. But you know what it *does* spell out?

The fact that it provides everything we need to live on this earth, know God, and make it to heaven.

Sure, it's fine to ask questions. Our Creator created our curious minds for a reason. But if we keep asking too many—especially the kind that cannot be answered through a Bible study—then we can create a tangled mess of confusion. Doubts thrive in these knots of confusion, and over time, they'll crowd out our faith.

Our limited knowledge keeps us humble. It reminds us we're only human and serve a God who is far greater than we can comprehend.

So, let's destroy every knot of confusion—every thought that might lead us away from our faith—and concentrate on obeying Christ.

Then our faith will have room to grow. The transformation we experience through our walk with Christ—and the love, peace, and joy we come to know in His presence—will put our wandering minds at ease. My faith is all I need to make it to heaven. Maybe then I'll ask God these questions.

Perhaps I'll begin with the one about thunderstorms.

LET'S THINK ABOUT IT...

How often do you allow your wandering mind to create knots of confusion and doubts?

LET'S PRAY ABOUT IT...

Lord, I don't want to create knots of confusion that could give way to doubts. Thank you for the ways you've confirmed your love for me. Amen.

TODAY'S DARE

If you'd like to have research to validate your faith, consider reading *The Case for Christ: Student Edition* by Lee Strobel.

A SHOT OF INSPIRATION

Jesus didn't come to tell us the answers to the questions of life; he came to be the answer.

Timothy Keller

Join the convo! Inspired by today's chat? Share what you learned! Snap a photo of this book (or the drink you're sipping on), and spark a discussion on social media by answering this question:

How has God confirmed His love for you?

Be sure to use the hashtag #CoffeeShopDevos!

Chains of Shame

"So if the Son sets you free, you are truly free."

John 8:36

LET'S CHAT ABOUT IT...

I went through a season in my teen years when I was ashamed of myself. I didn't appreciate my appearance or personality. My sisters had smooth blond hair. Mine was brown and frizzy. I tried to lighten and straighten my hair rather than embrace my curls and appreciate my natural color.

I longed to be different, yet it was impossible to change who I was. Have you experienced the anger that comes from self-shame? Maybe you, too, are ashamed of yourself. Or perhaps you're ashamed of sins you've committed.

If we aren't careful, this shame can give way to anger, and anger can lead to self-abuse, which may then manifest itself in various forms: Eating disorders. Addictions. Self-harm. We'll lose respect for ourselves. The enemy will blind us from our own value. Every time we listen to his lies, it's as if he wraps another chain around our wrists—and the more we agree with his lies, the more in bondage we become to self-shame.

These chains are far too heavy to break free from with our own strength.

In fact, it took the death of Christ to take back our freedom.

His blood poured out on the cross was to bring about your healing. Every bruise inflicted upon his body was tolerated because of His overwhelming love for you. He knew every sin you'd commit, yet He still chose to bear your punishment.

As we find our worth and forgiveness at the feet of Jesus, these chains will loosen. We'll be free to run into His loving arms—restored and whole. Not because we're perfect or sinless.

But because Jesus saw our flaws and sins and still, He said, "*You are worth dying for.*"

LET'S THINK ABOUT IT...

Do you struggle with self-shame?

LET'S PRAY ABOUT IT...

Lord, it's because of your death that I can break free from the chains of shame. Thank you for taking my place on the cross. Amen.

TODAY'S DARE

If you struggle with self-abuse, talk with a parent or trusted adult. Consider applying for Mercy Multiplied, a nonprofit Christian organization that helps young women reclaim their freedom in Christ.

A SHOT OF INSPIRATION

> But he was pierced for our rebellion,
> crushed for our sins.
> He was beaten so we could be whole.
> He was whipped so we could be healed.
>
> Isaiah 53:5

Join the convo! Inspired by today's chat? Share what you learned! Snap a photo of this book (or the drink you're sipping on), and spark a discussion on social media by answering this question:

Why do you think the enemy tries to blind young women from seeing their worth in Christ?

Be sure to use the hashtag #CoffeeShopDevos!

Connected to the Head

Scripture to sip on

Christ is also the head of the church,
which is his body.

Colossians 1:18

LET'S CHAT ABOUT IT...

As a kid, I wasn't crazy about children's church. Apparently I thought I was too old for it—so when my older sisters grew out of children's church, I decided that I, too, would transition into "big church."

Even though I was only seven years old.

I soon realized this *big church* wasn't as fun as kids' church. They didn't play games, sing fun songs, or watch *Veggie Tales*. The pastor seemed to drone on forever, and his sermons flew over my head. I'd count down the minutes until we could eat at Sonny's BBQ.

During this time, I dreaded church. It wasn't until I reached my middle school years that I developed a relationship with God and actually had a *desire* to attend.

When we view church as a religious obligation, we'll most likely find it dreadful. But it's far more than a building Christians go to every Sunday as a means to polish their Christian label.

God designed church to be a place where His body could join together and connect with Him. *We* are the body; *He* is the head. The body becomes stronger when we're connected as a whole and take a stand against the enemy. However, we're fruitless if we decide to break away from the rest of the body.

So rather than hitting our snooze alarms on Sunday mornings, let's pull ourselves out of bed and be grateful for the opportunity to join with other believers and grow in our walk with Christ.

Besides, a body can't gain optimum health until each part takes its role seriously.

LET'S THINK ABOUT IT...

What is your attitude toward church?

....

....

....

....

LET'S PRAY ABOUT IT...

Lord, help me to take my role in church seriously and be grateful for the opportunity to grow in my walk with you. Amen.

TODAY'S DARE

If you're not involved in your church, visit your church's website to search for ways to get connected with other believers. You could join their youth group, a small group, or a Bible study.

A SHOT OF INSPIRATION

The human body has many parts, but the many parts make up one whole body. So it is with the body of Christ.

1 Corinthians 12:12

Join the convo! Inspired by today's chat? Share what you learned! Snap a photo of this book (or the drink you're sipping on), and spark a discussion on social media by answering this question:

How has attending church furthered your walk with Christ?

Be sure to use the hashtag #CoffeeShopDevos!

Decaf

Finding
Rest

Dark Decaf

Desperate times call for desperate measures. And when I'm desperate for coffee—in the evening, or in those times when I've had too much caffeine already—I bring out my decaf. Even though it tastes similar to the real stuff, the lack of caffeine somehow weakens the taste. In my opinion, at least. That's why I like it rich and dark.

So if you want to avoid caffeine, or if you need some rich bean juice to accompany you as you read at night, then this drink might just fit the bill.

INGREDIENTS

- Dark roast decaf coffee
- 1 tablespoon honey
- 2 tablespoons half-and-half

INSTRUCTIONS

1. Brew coffee.
2. Mix in honey.
3. Pour in half-and-half and stir.

Cranky without Caffeine

"Blessed are those who hunger and thirst for righteousness, for they shall be satisfied."

Matthew 5:6 ESV

LET'S CHAT ABOUT IT...

I can get cranky without my daily caffeine fix. My brain becomes foggy. It's almost impossible to think clearly. My head feels like a semitruck hit me. It's not a good thing to be addicted to caffeine—but those side effects *do* make it harder to stop having caffeine every day, wouldn't you agree?

Now, let's look at the side effects I often experience when I don't have my daily quiet time with God: My mood isn't the brightest. I'm unable to view the day's events from His perspective. My mental and spiritual energy are weakened.

People often joke about how they're unable to make conversation until they've had their morning cup of coffee. What if we treated our daily quiet time with the same importance? What if we decided not to speak to anyone until we spent time with our Creator and allowed Him to fill us with His Spirit?

Not only does this "spiritual caffeine" keep us from experiencing negative side effects, but the benefits of spending daily time alone with God are endless! We can have constant peace, joy, help, comfort, love, and more. The simple act of drinking in God's presence is enough to satisfy our every longing.

Yes, I love coffee. But I'd choose my time with Jesus over my intake of java any day.

Let's strive to become as protective over our time with God as we are our daily cup of brew. Let's become addicted to our "spiritual caffeine fix."

Then, if we ever skip our quiet time and our friends see that we're acting cranky, they won't assume it's due to a lack of caffeine; rather, they'll simply whisper among each other, saying, "Don't mind her. She hasn't had her time with Jesus yet."

LET'S THINK ABOUT IT...

Do you have quiet time because you feel like it's your duty, or because you love Jesus so much that you can't wait to spend time with Him?

LET'S PRAY ABOUT IT...

Lord, give me a hunger and a thirst for righteousness and a heart that yearns to seek you daily above all else. Amen.

TODAY'S DARE

Set a timer for thirty minutes. Don't check your phone, email, or social media. Put your focus entirely on God and see how He satisfies your thirst during this time.

A SHOT OF INSPIRATION

All I need today is a little bit of coffee and a whole lot of Jesus.

Unknown

Join the convo! Inspired by today's chat? Share what you learned! Snap a photo of this book (or the drink you're sipping on), and spark a discussion on social media by answering this question:

How has your daily quiet time strengthened your relationship with Christ?

Be sure to use the hashtag #CoffeeShopDevos!

Messages from Creation

Scripture to sip on

The heavens proclaim the glory of God.
The skies display his craftsmanship.
Day after day they continue to speak;
  night after night they make him known.
They speak without a sound or word;
  their voice is never heard.
Yet their message has gone throughout the earth,
  and their words to all the world.

Psalm 19:1–4

LET'S CHAT ABOUT IT...

God's majestic creation is a reflection of His goodness. He paints these sights daily—not because He has to, but because He loves us that much. Throughout His Creation, He whispers His love to our hearts. According to this Scripture, His messages are woven throughout nature.

Think about it:

Outer space reminds us that God's vastness is far beyond our comprehension.

Painted sunrises and sunsets remind us of His loving-kindness.

Freshly fallen snow reminds us of His gentle peace.

Flowers remind us that He forms beauty in all shapes, colors, and sizes.

Oceans remind us of the immeasurable expanse of His love for us.

And all of earth reminds us that God gives careful attention to every detail of His creation.

Spending time in His creation gives us insight into the very character of our Creator. And as we spend more time in nature, we may even hear God's message speaking to our hearts. Perhaps that's the reason He chose to surround us with this majestic creation to begin with:

So it could point us to the Creator.

LET'S THINK ABOUT IT...

How often do you spend time in God's creation?

....

....

....

....

LET'S PRAY ABOUT IT...

Lord, thank you for the gift of your creation and the opportunities it gives me to know you better. Amen.

TODAY'S DARE

Spend time outside today! Here are some ideas: Take your dog on a walk in the park, swim in a lake, or go on a hike.

As you do this, keep your ears open to the messages God might be speaking to you through His creation.

A SHOT OF INSPIRATION

For ever since the world was created, people have seen the earth and sky. Through everything God made, they can clearly see his invisible qualities—his eternal power and divine nature. So they have no excuse for not knowing God.

Romans 1:20

Join the convo! Inspired by today's chat? Share what you learned! Snap a photo of this book (or the drink you're sipping on), and spark a discussion on social media by answering this question:

What's your favorite sight in nature? Does it remind you of a specific quality of the Creator?

Be sure to use the hashtag #CoffeeShopDevos!

Love Made Personal

And I pray that you and all God's holy people will have the power to understand the greatness of Christ's love—how wide and how long and how high and how deep that love is. Christ's love is greater than anyone can ever know, but I pray that you will be able to know that love. Then you can be filled with the fullness of God.

Ephesians 3:18–21 NCV

LET'S CHAT ABOUT IT...

I grew up hearing about the story of the gospel—how God loved me so much that He sent His Son to die for me (see 1 John 4:9). But there's a difference between understanding this love with your mind and knowing it with your heart.

It wasn't until I was fifteen that I had my first personal taste of the greatness of His Love. I was at a summer youth camp, and the worship band played the song "How He Loves" by John Mark McMillan. The lyrics spoke straight to my heart and ushered me into God's presence.

Remember when you were a kid, how safe and comforted you felt when you were held by your parents? That's how it felt—as if I were held in God's embrace. I never wanted to leave the security of His presence.

God's Word is His love letter to His children. He's given His Word to us so we can learn about Him and get to know Him. It's the foundation of our walk with Christ.

But let's be careful that we don't become so caught up in *learning* about God's love that we neglect to *experience* it for ourselves. Because it's those experiences—when we get to know our Savior personally and feel His loving arms wrap around us—that the truth of the Bible becomes tangible.

The next time you have your quiet time, I pray that, just as this verse says, you'll come to know the greatness of His love.

A love deeper than any of us could comprehend.

LET'S THINK ABOUT IT...

Have you personally experienced God's love?

....

....

....

....

LET'S PRAY ABOUT IT...

Lord, thank you that your love for me is more than I can fathom. Help me to experience the fullness of this love on a daily basis. Amen.

TODAY'S DARE

Listen to "How He Loves" by John Mark McMillan.

A SHOT OF INSPIRATION

Refuse to be content with just the knowledge of God, but insist on experiencing His presence.

Kerri Weems

Join the convo! Inspired by today's chat? Share what you learned! Snap a photo of this book (or the drink you're sipping on), and spark a discussion on social media by answering this question:

Share about a time when God's love became personal.

Be sure to use the hashtag #CoffeeShopDevos!

Why Worship?

Shout with joy to the Lord, all the earth!
Worship the Lord with gladness.
Come before him, singing with joy. . . .
For the Lord is good.
His unfailing love continues forever,
and his faithfulness continues to each generation.

Psalm 100:1–2, 5

LET'S CHAT ABOUT IT...

Do you love your parents only because of what they give and provide for you? I hope not!

Likewise, our worship to God shouldn't be conditional, based on tangible evidence of His goodness in our lives. Nothing can add or take away from who He is. And if His love for us is unconditional, shouldn't our love for Him be unconditional as well?

"We love Him because He first loved us" (1 John 4:19 NKJV). His love is freely given; therefore, our worship should be freely poured out to Him in response. Not because He *needs* our praise, but because our hearts can't help but worship Him.

When we raise our hands in worship, it's an act of surrender and praise. It's a symbolic way to say, "I am nothing without you." Worship is an invitation for Him to take control of our lives and have His way within us. We're reminded that we serve a God who is far greater than *any* problem we might face on this earth. His perfection negates the imperfection in our lives.

So what's the purpose of worship? It's simple: to act upon our natural instinct as humans.

Besides—we're going to spend all of eternity praising and worshiping our Father. Why not go ahead and start now?

LET'S THINK ABOUT IT...

Where does your focus lie during worship at church?

LET'S PRAY ABOUT IT...

Lord, help me to remain in a state of worship to you. I am nothing without you; yet in you, I am complete. Amen.

TODAY'S DARE

Spend some time worshiping God today—whether you're in the car, doing chores, or in your bedroom.

These are some of my favorite worship artists/bands: Lauren Daigle, Bethel Music, Hillsong United, Kari Jobe, and Jesus Culture.

A SHOT OF INSPIRATION

Know that when you praise and worship God and fully appreciate all that He is, you open up a channel through which more of His love pours into your heart.

Stormie Omartian

Join the convo! Inspired by today's chat? Share what you learned! Snap a photo of this book (or the drink you're sipping on), and spark a discussion on social media by answering this question:

What does worship mean to you?

Be sure to use the hashtag #CoffeeShopDevos!

Prescription for Peace

Scripture to sip on

Don't worry about anything; instead, pray about everything. Tell God what you need, and thank him for all he has done. Then you will experience God's peace, which exceeds anything we can understand. His peace will guard your hearts and minds as you live in Christ Jesus.

Philippians 4:6–7

LET'S CHAT ABOUT IT...

When I was fifteen, I hyperventilated and collapsed while running along the beach on my family's first day of vacation. My face turned white, my lips became purple, and I couldn't grasp a full breath. At the hospital, I was told I was dehydrated, my blood sugar was low, and I was diagnosed with vagal response syndrome (which means your body is triggered to faint easily).

After this happened, it was as if fear wrapped its claws around my neck. I became terrified of it happening again. I limited my exercise because the rapid breathing made me feel like I might hyperventilate. This fear tormented me while I watched an intense movie at the theater, drove my car, or rode a bike.

Have you felt choked by anxiety? The stronghold of its grip can keep us from enjoying our lives to the fullest. The only way to break free is by taking our prescription for peace.

I'm not just talking about medication (although that can help, too). But even more powerful is the Word of God. This Scripture lays out how we can access peace when anxiety threatens to choke us: 1) Pray about everything. 2) Tell God what you need. 3) Thank Him for all He's done.

As I began to take this "prescription," fear's grip loosened. Christ's peace guarded my heart and mind. It was only His peace that helped me breathe and enjoy life again.

Thankfully, this medicine doesn't involve any risk of harmful side effects. ;)

LET'S THINK ABOUT IT...

Do you ever feel crippled from fear or anxiety?

....

....

....

....

LET'S PRAY ABOUT IT...

Lord, help me to remember to take your prescription for peace any time I face fear, worry, or anxiety. Only your peace has the power to break their strongholds on my life. Amen.

TODAY'S DARE

Write down three things you're worried about or afraid of. Leave them in God's hands. Thank Him for His sovereign control, and allow His peace to replace the stronghold of fear.

A SHOT OF INSPIRATION

"I have told you all this so that you may have peace in me."

John 16:33

Join the convo! Inspired by today's chat? Share what you learned! Snap a photo of this book (or the drink you're sipping on), and spark a discussion on social media by answering this question:

When has fear kept you from enjoying your life?

Be sure to use the hashtag #CoffeeShopDevos!

Full Charge

This is what the Sovereign Lord,
the Holy One of Israel, says:
"Only in returning to me
and resting in me will you be saved.
In quietness and confidence is your strength."

Isaiah 30:15

LET'S CHAT ABOUT IT...

You have to plug in your phone every now and then so it can function, right? It can't go too long without running out of power. We, too, can only go so long before we need to recharge our batteries—not just through sleep and rest, but through spiritual nourishment from our Father.

When we rest in God and feed on His Word, we're refreshed and revived. We don't have to handle the weight of this world on our own. In fact, God gladly takes the weight off of us and puts it on himself instead. He'll then equip us to face our problems through His perspective and strength.

We weren't meant to do this life on our own. We need to recharge by spending time with our Father.

Even Jesus, when He was on earth, needed to break away from His work to spend time with His Father. How much more do you think we need this?

So rather than waking up and jumping head on into our days, let's take time to be still. Let's refresh ourselves in the Word of God and "plug in" to His presence. Then we'll see how much we better we function when we run on a full charge rather than low.

Now, excuse me while I plug in my laptop. After all, I can only work for so long before it loses its charge and dies on me. ;)

LET'S THINK ABOUT IT...

Do you recharge your batteries daily?

LET'S PRAY ABOUT IT...

Lord, I can't face this life on my own. Thank you for giving me the spiritual nourishment I need as I rest in you. Amen.

TODAY'S DARE

Schedule your daily quiet time. Whether it's thirty minutes before you go to bed at night or an hour in the morning, try to make this time with God a priority—just like you might make it a point to plug in your phone every night.

A SHOT OF INSPIRATION

Ten minutes spent in the presence of Christ every day, aye, two minutes, will make the whole day different.

Henry Drummond

Join the convo! Inspired by today's chat? Share what you learned! Snap a photo of this book (or the drink you're sipping on), and spark a discussion on social media by answering this question:

Have you experienced the exhaustion that comes from running low on your spiritual batteries?

Be sure to use the hashtag #CoffeeShopDevos!

Room for Rest

On the seventh day God had finished his work of creation, so he rested from all his work. And God blessed the seventh day and declared it holy, because it was the day when he rested from all his work of creation.

Genesis 2:2–3

LET'S CHAT ABOUT IT...

I love staying productive. However, if I keep working without taking a break, then I compromise the quality of my work. The passion fades, and my brain turns to mush.

God knows the importance of rest; He himself took a break from His work of creation, as this Scripture says. And He expects us to take a break as well.

It's not lazy to relax every once in a while. Sundays are personally my favorite days to do this. After spending time in worship on Sundays, I like to kick back in my recliner with a stack of books and a latte. Then, when I return to my work, I'll have fully recovered.

Just as spending time with God helps us replenish spiritually, taking a break helps us replenish physically. Perhaps that's why God chose the Sabbath for the day of rest.

So don't feel guilty the next time you need to rest. If you don't have work that needs immediate attention, such as a homework assignment, then allow yourself time to kick your feet up and binge-watch your favorite TV show or play a game with your siblings.

Don't worry, the work will still be there when you return.

LET'S THINK ABOUT IT...

When do you give yourself a break?

LET'S PRAY ABOUT IT...

Lord, help me to know when I need to give myself a break. Amen.

TODAY'S DARE

If your schedule doesn't allow for a break, perhaps it's time to cut out an activity. Look over your calendar and talk with your parents about what commitment you might need to step down from.

A SHOT OF INSPIRATION

Rest time is not waste time. It is economy to gather fresh strength.
. . . In the long run, we shall do more by sometimes doing less.

Charles H. Spurgeon

Join the convo! Inspired by today's chat? Share what you learned! Snap a photo of this book (or the drink you're sipping on), and spark a discussion on social media by answering this question:

What's the difference between being lazy and taking a break?

Be sure to use the hashtag #CoffeeShopDevos!

In His Arms

Praise the Lord; praise God our savior!
For each day he carries us in his arms.

Psalm 68:19

LET'S CHAT ABOUT IT...

I've never enjoyed being independent. Maybe it's because I'm the baby of my family and grew up relying on others. Whether or not that's the case, I'd prefer to have someone by my side. Two is better than one, right?

However, today's society has often made me feel like this is a form of weakness. That I should be fine to be alone and rely on myself.

But you know what? The opposite is true: *Independence* can be a form of weakness. The assumption that we can handle and manage everything on our own—with no help from anyone—comes from a place of pride. And when we carry this independent attitude into our relationship with God, it can separate us from Him because we become determined to rely on ourselves rather than on Him.

Our Father *wants* us to depend on Him. We can't go through the day on our own, so He offers to carry us in His arms—the same way our parents carried us in their arms when we were little.

Now that I'm in my twenties, I've had to step out of my comfort zone and do things on my own. Otherwise, I wouldn't be able to travel across the country to speak and teach at writing conferences. But you know what? I'm still not independent. In fact, there's no way I could do this on my own.

Thankfully, I don't have to. When I feel weak and unequipped (to carry my heavy luggage), God equips me with His strength. When I'm nervous (about missing my flight), He stills my beating heart. When I'm shaking from fear (because of turbulence during a flight), He grasps my hand. When I don't know the way ahead of me (and have to navigate an unfamiliar airport), He guides me, step-by-step.

So don't worry: You'll never have to face *anything* by yourself. There is One who never leaves your side. One who carries you in His arms daily.

And there's nothing we can do apart from Him.

LET'S THINK ABOUT IT...

Are you independent or dependent, and is this carried into your relationship with God?

LET'S PRAY ABOUT IT...

Lord, I trust that you go with me and carry me in your arms daily. Amen.

TODAY'S DARE

Listen to "You'll Never Be Alone" by Capital Kings.

A SHOT OF INSPIRATION

Lean on your Beloved, because the soul who abandons themselves in the hands of Jesus in all they do, is carried in his arms.

Saint Clare

Join the convo! Inspired by today's chat? Share what you learned! Snap a photo of this book (or the drink you're sipping on), and spark a discussion on social media by answering this question:

When have you had to depend on God's help?

Be sure to use the hashtag #CoffeeShopDevos!

Train Derailed

Scripture to sip on

Think about the things of heaven, not the things of earth.

Colossians 3:2

LET'S CHAT ABOUT IT...

Have you ever sat down to pray, only to find yourself falling asleep? Or perhaps you've opened the Bible app on your phone, but somehow ended up checking your social media instead.

Been there. Done that. Distractions come in all shapes and sizes, and they especially pop out of nowhere during my quiet time.

Maybe you don't find yourself distracted, but you might procrastinate. Perhaps you intend to wake up an extra thirty minutes early for quiet time, but then hit the snooze button.

The enemy knows how valuable it is for us to further our walk with Christ. He'll do anything he can to prevent it from happening! If he's so intimidated by our time with God that he tempts us with distractions and excuses, then just think about how much we must accomplish during this time. This should motivate us even more to give Jesus our full attention.

Let's be determined not to derail from the track we're on. How can we do this?

By following this Scripture and thinking about things of heaven, not things of earth.

When we think about things of earth, our focus will easily be diverted and fly out the window. Yet when our focus is set on things of heaven, our eyes will remain on the path ahead. The things of earth that pass by the window won't be attractive enough to divert our focus.

So let's set our eyes on "things of heaven." This earth will always provide us with endless excuses and distractions—but when our eyes are set on Christ, we'll understand the importance of continuing on this path with Him.

Besides—a train derailed almost always results in disaster.

LET'S THINK ABOUT IT...

Do things of earth derail you from furthering your walk with God?

LET'S PRAY ABOUT IT...

Lord, help me to keep my eyes set on things of heaven, not things of earth. Amen.

TODAY'S DARE

Next time you're distracted during a quiet time, write down the distractions. Then, tell yourself that you'll get back to those things *after* you finish your quiet time.

A SHOT OF INSPIRATION

> Look straight ahead,
> and fix your eyes on what lies before you.
> Proverbs 4:25

Join the convo! Inspired by today's chat? Share what you learned! Snap a photo of this book (or the drink you're sipping on), and spark a discussion on social media by answering this question:

How do you eliminate distractions and excuses?

Be sure to use the hashtag #CoffeeShopDevos!

Spiritual Declutter

Scripture to sip on

Don't keep looking at my sins.
Remove the stain of my guilt.
Create in me a clean heart, O God.
Renew a loyal spirit within me.

Psalm 51:9–10

LET'S CHAT ABOUT IT...

Did you know it's proven that hanging on to clutter in our bedrooms can disrupt our sleep? So if we want to get a good night's rest, we need to clean up the miscellaneous clutter.

Likewise, when we fill ourselves with worldly clutter, our spiritual rest becomes disrupted.

We can't go many days without our minds being exposed to trash. This clutter comes in various ways: through TV commercials, negative news, trash talk from people at school, and even billboards we pass on the road.

If we don't take the time to renew our minds and our spirits through God's Word, we'll continue "hoarding" this trash. We won't receive the rest that comes from God's refreshing presence. We won't be able to think His thoughts when our minds are cluttered with the world's filth.

Let's not go another day without removing this clutter. Before going to bed at night, let's ask Jesus to remove the filth of our sin and renew our thinking. This cleansing cannot be attained from our own effort; it can only come through renewing ourselves in His Spirit. Then, we can approach each day with a clean slate and receive the spiritual rest we need.

How disgusting would it be to become a hoarder of nothing but filthy trash?

LET'S THINK ABOUT IT...

How often do you declutter through receiving God's mercy and renewing your mind in His Word?

LET'S PRAY ABOUT IT...

Lord, remind me to come to you when I need to renew my mind and spirit. Amen.

TODAY'S DARE

Take inventory of the filth you're exposed to daily. If there's anything you can avoid—such as reading a certain magazine—consider throwing it out.

A SHOT OF INSPIRATION

Don't copy the behavior and customs of this world, but let God transform you into a new person by changing the way you think. Then you will learn to know God's will for you, which is good and pleasing and perfect.

Romans 12:2

Join the convo! Inspired by today's chat? Share what you learned! Snap a photo of this book (or the drink you're sipping on), and spark a discussion on social media by answering this question:

Why do you think it's important to declutter from worldly filth by renewing ourselves in God's Word?

Be sure to use the hashtag #CoffeeShopDevos!

Like a Child

Then Jesus said, "Come to me, all of you who are weary and carry heavy burdens, and I will give you rest. Take my yoke upon you. Let me teach you, because I am humble and gentle at heart, and you will find rest for your souls. For my yoke is easy to bear, and the burden I give you is light."

Matthew 11:28–30

LET'S CHAT ABOUT IT...

Wasn't it nice, when you were a kid, to trust your parents for all of your needs? Sure, you're still probably dependent on them in some ways—but now that you're a teen, you've been entrusted with more responsibilities. Yet how great would it be to rely on someone else to take care of *everything*?

Even though we can't run away from our responsibilities, Jesus tells us our burden should be *light*. We don't have to carry around a heavy weight.

When parents prove to be trustworthy, their kids can trust in them. They trust they'll take care of their finances and safety. Our Father has also proven himself to be trustworthy. He's faithful to take care of His children. He won't abandon us. So why should we fret?

We can't rest when we're clinging to our worries. So let's release them at the feet of Jesus. Then, when the burden is lifted and no longer crushing us, we can be free to enjoy our lives—not because we don't have responsibilities, but we know that we don't have to manage them on our own. We trust in our Father's care and provision.

Just like a child.

LET'S THINK ABOUT IT...

How can you release your fears, worries, and anxieties and leave them at the feet of Jesus?

LET'S PRAY ABOUT IT...

Lord, I trust you to take care of every detail of my life. Amen.

TODAY'S DARE

Write a list of the worries you've had recently. Pray about them, then throw the piece of paper away. The act of doing this will be a symbolic act of placing your care into the hands of God.

A SHOT OF INSPIRATION

> The person who worries reveals his lack of trust in God and that he is trusting too much in self.
>
> Lee Roberson

Join the convo! Inspired by today's chat? Share what you learned! Snap a photo of this book (or the drink you're sipping on), and spark a discussion on social media by answering this question:

What's the difference between being responsible versus managing our responsibilities on our own, without asking for God's help?

Be sure to use the hashtag #CoffeeShopDevos!

Stress vs. Rest

Scripture to sip on

Commit everything you do to the Lord.
Trust him, and he will help you.

Psalm 37:5

LET'S CHAT ABOUT IT...

If you're an overachiever, like I am, you might overcommit yourself like I do. Right now, I'm preparing to teach at four writing conferences in two months, meet a writing deadline, manage a magazine, work for a literary agency, and start up an imprint at a small publishing company.

The pressure's getting to me.

Have you felt the kind of stress that comes from having too much work and not enough time to do it? Stress can leave us with migraine headaches, disrupt our sleep, cause our hair to fall out, and tie our stomach in knots.

So how can we respond to these stressors?

Here's what I've learned:

When I'm swamped, I need to take a moment to pause, breathe, and ask God for His supernatural help. This Scripture tells us to commit *everything* we do to the Lord. If we trust Him, He'll help us get the jobs done.

We shouldn't work from a place of unrest. God can give us the peace we need. This can then empower us to face pressure without being overwhelmed; thus, we're able to work with a clear mind.

With His help, we can face seemingly impossible situations—but *only* when we commit our work to Him. So rather than stress being our automatic reaction to a unending workload, let's allow ourselves time to rest, breathe in God's grace, then work in peace.

Now, if only God would maximize my time so I can meet these deadlines . . . ;)

LET'S THINK ABOUT IT...

What's your natural reaction to an abundance of work?

LET'S PRAY ABOUT IT...

Lord, I commit my work to you. I want rest to be my natural response rather than stress. Amen.

TODAY'S DARE

Some people squeeze stress balls to help them deal with stress. What can you do the next time you're tempted to stress?
Here are some ideas:

* Write Psalm 37:5 on an index card and place it in your book bag.
* Listen to soothing worship music.
* Go on a prayer walk.

A SHOT OF INSPIRATION

Anxiety happens when you think you have to figure everything out. Turn to God. He has a plan.

Unknown

Join the convo! Inspired by today's chat? Share what you learned! Snap a photo of this book (or the drink you're sipping on), and spark a discussion on social media by answering this question:

Have you witnessed God helping you manage impossible situations?

Be sure to use the hashtag #CoffeeShopDevos!

Give Your Brain a Break

Scripture to sip on

God is not a God of confusion but a God of peace.

1 Corinthians 14:33 NCV

LET'S CHAT ABOUT IT...

Do you tend to scrutinize everything? I do this at times. And although there's nothing wrong with analyzing Scripture, we have to be careful that we don't *think* our way out of our faith.

Sometimes, faith just doesn't make sense. But we're spiritual beings more so than natural beings. So even if something doesn't make sense in the natural, we can trust it's from God if it was revealed to us by His Word.

We became Christians by first believing Jesus Christ died for our sins so we could be saved. Believing this requires faith. The Bible says we're saved through faith (see Ephesians 2:8). We can't *think* our way into receiving salvation; it has to come through the renewing of our spirits.

In the same way, if we're not careful, we could analyze certain biblical topics so much that we enter into confusion. When this happens, let's remind ourselves of what this verse tells us: God is a God of peace, *not* confusion.

So the next time you're tempted to overanalyze, give yourself a break. Fill yourself with God's Word to build your faith. It's only then that we'll have the clarity to see from His perspective.

Besides, our brains deserve a break every now and then. Don't you think?

LET'S THINK ABOUT IT...

Do you have a tendency to be an overthinker?

LET'S PRAY ABOUT IT...

Lord, help me not to overanalyze. Thank you for the clarity that comes from giving my mind a break and relaxing in your peace. Amen.

TODAY'S DARE

Is there something you've been confused about recently? Bring your questions to God. Let Him fill you with His peace and clarity as you read His Word.

A SHOT OF INSPIRATION

I once asked the Lord why so many people are confused and He said to me, "Tell them to stop trying to figure everything out, and they will stop being confused." I have found it to be absolutely true. Reasoning and confusion go together.

Joyce Meyer

Join the convo! Inspired by today's chat? Share what you learned! Snap a photo of this book (or the drink you're sipping on), and spark a discussion on social media by answering this question:

Have you experienced the confusion that overthinking can cause?

Be sure to use the hashtag #CoffeeShopDevos!

Restored Strength

Scripture to sip on

Even youths will become weak and tired,
and young men will fall in exhaustion.
But those who trust in the Lord will find new strength.
They will soar high on wings like eagles.
They will run and not grow weary.
They will walk and not faint.

Isaiah 40:30–31

LET'S CHAT ABOUT IT...

When I was a teen, I preferred to stay at home most weekends rather than hang out with friends. Partly because I enjoyed being with my family, but also because I'm an introvert. I can't be around too many people for too long without needing alone time.

If you're an introvert, you probably understand what it feels like to have your energy zapped from socializing. Spending time alone is how we refuel.

Whatever our personality type, life can leave us drained at times. It can be tiring to feel like we have to constantly please people. Meet high expectations. Make As on tests.

This verse says, "Even youths will become weak and tired, and young men will fall in exhaustion." So how can we pick ourselves back up again?

It's through trusting the Lord that we can "soar high on wings like eagles." When life leaves us weary, we can trust He's on our side. He won't leave us to face our circumstances on our own.

How can we build this trust? By spending time with Him. Then, our muscles will become strengthened. Our energy will be restored. We'll receive the supernatural power we need to "run and not grow weary." It's through trusting God that we'll be restored and refueled, ready to conquer whatever comes our way.

Yes, even us introverts.

LET'S THINK ABOUT IT...

How often do you find yourself exhausted from life?

....

....

....

....

LET'S PRAY ABOUT IT...

Lord, whenever I grow weary and tired, remind me to place my trust in you. Amen.

TODAY'S DARE

Listen to "Eagle's Wings" by Hillsong.

A SHOT OF INSPIRATION

He fills my life with good things.
My youth is renewed like the eagle's!
Psalm 103:5

Join the convo! Inspired by today's chat? Share what you learned! Snap a photo of this book (or the drink you're sipping on), and spark a discussion on social media by answering this question:

How can Christians build their trust in God so they can "soar high on wings like eagles"?

Be sure to use the hashtag #CoffeeShopDevos!

The Safest Place

"Don't let your hearts be troubled. Trust in God, and trust also in me."

John 14:1

LET'S CHAT ABOUT IT...

My first experience driving was intimidating. To realize that I—a five-foot-tall fifteen-year-old—had control of a large piece of machinery was not a comforting thought. One mistake could lead to a fatal crash.

Are you facing an intimidating situation? Maybe it's not learning to drive, but perhaps you're preparing to leave home to attend college. Fear can be exhausting, yet we face threats daily.

Lightning could strike us. An earthquake could bury us within the earth. A wildfire could sweep away our home.

When we focus on intimidating possibilities, we become paralyzed, unable to move forward and enjoy our lives. Yet God knew this life would bring many reasons to fear. If we allow our hearts to be immersed in God's peace—which comes when we trust in Him—something miraculous happens: Fear shrinks.

I used to think I'd always be afraid behind the wheel of a car. But as I trusted God, He gave me the peace I needed. Peace *always* comes when we trust in the Lord.

Remember, as Christians, we're in the palm of His hand.

And whether we're on a boat, in a car, or on a plane—when we remain in the center of God's hand, then we're in the safest place we could be.

LET'S THINK ABOUT IT...

What fears are you facing? What would your life look like if you never conquered these fears?

_____

_____

_____

_____

LET'S PRAY ABOUT IT...

_Lord, help me build my trust in you so I can have the peace I
need to overcome fears. Amen._

TODAY'S DARE

Is there a specific fear that's held you back in the past? If so, take a
step today—even if it's a small one—toward trusting God and over-
coming it.

A SHOT OF INSPIRATION

Such love has no fear, because perfect love expels all fear. If we are
afraid, it is for fear of punishment, and this shows that we have
not fully experienced his perfect love.

1 John 4:18

Join the convo! Inspired by today's chat? Share what you learned!
Snap a photo of this book (or the drink you're sipping on), and spark
a discussion on social media by answering this question:

Have you overcome a certain fear?

Be sure to use the hashtag #CoffeeShopDevos!

Wasted Energy

The Lord is for me, so I will have no fear.
What can mere people do to me?

Psalm 118:6

LET'S CHAT ABOUT IT...

I don't like letting people down—whether it's a friend I don't have time to hang out with, an unanswered email in my inbox, or a family member who wants my attention. But every time I try to please *everyone* all the time, I still end up letting someone down . . . and my energy becomes drained. I'm only human. Why should I expect myself to make everyone happy? Not only is this impossible, but it's also a form of idolatry. When I live for other people's approval, then I put them on a pedestal rather than God.

Have you been known to be a people pleaser, too? It can be exhausting, right? Thankfully, God doesn't call us to do this. He wants us to fear *Him* rather than "mere people," as this Scripture puts it.

When we do this, a burden will lift from our shoulders. The energy we wasted attempting to be everything to everyone will be restored. We can instead direct this energy toward doing the work God has called us to do today.

We weren't created to make others happy. That's a need only God can fulfill. We can show love to others without striving to constantly please them.

The Lord is for us. So what can the opinion of mere people do to us?

LET'S THINK ABOUT IT...

Do you devote more energy to pleasing God or people?

348

LET'S PRAY ABOUT IT...

Lord, help me not to waste energy by striving to please others rather than you. Amen.

TODAY'S DARE

The next time you're tempted to strive for the approval of others, direct your focus to God. Ask how He would like you to handle the situation.

A SHOT OF INSPIRATION

What shall we say about such wonderful things as these? If God is for us, who can ever be against us?

Romans 8:31

Join the convo! Inspired by today's chat? Share what you learned! Snap a photo of this book (or the drink you're sipping on), and spark a discussion on social media by answering this question:

Where do we draw the line between loving others and doing everything we can to please them constantly?

Be sure to use the hashtag #CoffeeShopDevos!

Perfect Peace in a Restless World

Scripture to sip on

Cease striving and know that I am God.

Psalm 46:10 NASB

LET'S CHAT ABOUT IT...

I had sleep issues when I was in high school. Many times, I took melatonin, an over-the-counter medicine that helps you fall asleep and stay asleep. A few other things helped, such as creating a sleep playlist on my iPhone, having quiet time before bed, drinking bedtime tea—and reciting this Scripture to myself until God's peace eventually coaxed me into a deep sleep.

If you're human, then you probably have reasons to fear. Stress. Worry. But even though this world provides reasons for us to lose sleep, our Father provides the peace we need in the midst of chaos.

Some might try to attain perfect peace through other means, such as alcohol, drugs, yoga, or pills. Yet nothing can calm our anxious hearts the way the Holy Spirit does.

So release whatever it is that keeps you from rest. Then, receive the love He has for you—a love bigger and more powerful than the greatest threats of this world. *Nothing* compares to the perfect peace He offers.

No, not even melatonin.

LET'S THINK ABOUT IT...

Is anything keeping you from receiving rest?

LET'S PRAY ABOUT IT...

Lord, help me to turn to you the next time I become restless. Amen.

TODAY'S DARE

Listen to "Restless" by Audrey Assad.

A SHOT OF INSPIRATION

God, you have made us for yourself, and our hearts are restless till they find their rest in you.

Augustine

Join the conva! Inspired by today's chat? Share what you learned! Snap a photo of this book (or the drink you're sipping on), and spark a discussion on social media by answering this question:

Have you experienced restlessness that comes from seeking peace apart from God?

Be sure to use the hashtag #CoffeeShopDevos!

Free Service

"Look at the birds. They don't plant or harvest or store food in barns, for your heavenly Father feeds them. And aren't you far more valuable to him than they are?"

Matthew 6:26

LET'S CHAT ABOUT IT...

Going out to eat at a restaurant is pretty luxurious if you think about it. We can select any meal listed on the menu, and a chef will whip it up for us. A waiter stops by the table consistently to ask if we need anything. This is a common experience we are privileged to enjoy in the United States, but when you think about it, shouldn't this make us feel special? Cared for, even?

Of course, this type of service isn't free. But there is one type of service that *is* free, and it's even more luxurious than being cared for at a restaurant.

Even though God isn't our waiter, He watches over us at all times. We're continuously on His mind. And when we seek Him first, He sees to it that our needs are met. We're treated with care. Not because He needs to get something in return, but because that's just how much we mean to Him.

Let this truth—the fact that you and your needs are cared for—melt away your anxieties. You no longer have to look after yourself. Your Father's on the job.

And trust me: You'll never find a restaurant that offers better service than the care He provides!

LET'S THINK ABOUT IT...

What are ways that God has taken care of and provided for you?

_____

_____

_____

LET'S PRAY ABOUT IT...

Lord, thank you for loving me so much, even though I did nothing to deserve it. I trust my life into your care. Amen.

TODAY'S DARE

Make a list of five ways God has shown His care for you recently. You may want to keep a running list so you can keep track of His care on a daily basis.

A SHOT OF INSPIRATION

> Even if my father and mother abandon me,
> the Lord will hold me close.
>
> Psalm 27:10

Join the convo! Inspired by today's chat? Share what you learned! Snap a photo of this book (or the drink you're sipping on), and spark a discussion on social media by answering this question:

Share about a time when you were in need and God provided for you.

Be sure to use the hashtag #CoffeeShopDevos!

Flat White

Strength to Carry On

French Toast Flat White

On the days when I'm feeling sluggish and need to stay extra alert, flat whites are my go-to coffee drink. The concentrated espresso laced throughout this drink provides just the pick-me-up I need.

If you're like me, and you, too, enjoy a strong taste of coffee that isn't overshadowed by milk, this is the drink for you. The texture isn't as creamy as a latte, but the micro-foam creates a smooth velvet-like substance—yet another reason why they're my favorite! Plus, the French toast flavor this recipe creates makes this the must-have breakfast companion.

INGREDIENTS

- 2–3 espresso shots (or ½ cup strong coffee)
- 1 teaspoon maple extract
- 1 teaspoon vanilla extract
- 1/2 teaspoon ground cinnamon
- 1/8 teaspoon ground nutmeg
- 1 1/2 tablespoons honey
- 1/2 cup whole milk

INSTRUCTIONS

1. Brew strong espresso (or strong coffee).
2. Stir maple extract, vanilla extract, cinnamon, nutmeg, and honey into the espresso (or coffee).
3. Steam the milk. The frother should remain deep in the milk and not reach the surface of the milk. This should result in micro-bubbles throughout the milk rather than the typical dry foam on the surface.
4. Pour milk quickly into espresso (or coffee).
5. Optional garnish: cinnamon and nutmeg

Staying Hydrated

Scripture to sip on

"Anyone who believes in me may come and drink! For the Scriptures declare, 'Rivers of living water will flow from his heart.'"

John 7:38

LET'S CHAT ABOUT IT...

I almost collapsed from dehydration once when I was a kid. My family was hiking down Stone Mountain, Georgia, in the hot sun, and we ran out of water. I still remember the dryness of my mouth, feeling dizzy, and how envious I was every time I saw a hiker drinking from a bottle of water. Finally, when we reached the bottom of the mountain, I guzzled water to make up for what I'd lost.

Are you familiar with the desperation that comes from being dehydrated? The only thing you can think about is water. However, there are some people who, after being nearly dehydrated, choose to replenish with a soft drink rather than water. I've never understood this. The soft drink might taste good for the moment and rid the dryness in your mouth—but in reality, it won't last. The sugar pulls water from your cells, whereas water hydrates them. Eventually you'll become *even more* desperate.

Likewise, we can't last long without needing to quench our thirst for God. The mountains we climb require too much energy. We need to fuel ourselves with the living water, God's Word.

But when we're thirsty, let's not seek to satisfy this longing through things of this world that will only decrease our energy.

I now carry a water bottle with me at all times; that way, I never have to become desperate. Let's do the same with God's Word. Let's saturate ourselves in Scripture so rivers of living water will flow from our hearts, as this verse says.

I probably would've enjoyed my hike much more if I'd had water with me, don't you think?

LET'S THINK ABOUT IT...

How often do you fill yourself with living water?

....

....

....

....

LET'S PRAY ABOUT IT...

Lord, nothing in this life satisfies my thirst the way your living water does. Keep me thirsty for your Word so I never neglect to stay hydrated. Amen.

TODAY'S DARE

Try to commit some Scripture to memory. Here are some ideas:

- If you have a smartphone, download the free app called "Remember Me."
- Write Scriptures on index cards and read over them daily.
- Find Scripture on wall art that you can display in your bedroom.

A SHOT OF INSPIRATION

For the word of God is alive and powerful.
Hebrews 4:12

Join the convo! Inspired by today's chat? Share what you learned! Snap a photo of this book (or the drink you're sipping on), and spark a discussion on social media by answering this question:

Why is it important for Christians to stay hydrated with God's Word?

Be sure to use the hashtag #CoffeeShopDevos!

Meaning of Life

So we don't look at the troubles we can see now; rather, we fix our gaze on things that cannot be seen. For the things we see now will soon be gone, but the things we cannot see will last forever.

2 Corinthians 4:18

LET'S CHAT ABOUT IT...

I've always wondered what the final thoughts are for those who commit suicide. What led them to make such a devastating decision? Although I'm sure there are many causes, I believe an underlying factor is a lack of hope. They fall for the lie that they don't have a purpose to keep living.

They run out of strength to carry on.

When you think about it, this makes sense. Everything on earth is meaningless. This includes our riches, achievements, and popularity. None of these things brings true meaning to life. If we focus on the meaningless things of earth, then the enemy can weave his way into our thoughts and make us believe we have no reason to continue living.

That's why we must lift our gaze away from worldliness and filth and fix it on Christ. In order to endure, let's do as this verse says and focus on the unseen rather than the seen. Why? Because the troubles we see now will be gone tomorrow, but the unseen will last *forever*.

So let's find our purpose in our relationship with Christ. This world and everything in it will pass away in the blink of an eye. Yet as long as we're still here, and as long as we're living for God, we have a reason for being alive. And that's to fulfill our mission as believers—to love God and love others.

Only then, when our focus is set on the unseen, will we find the strength we need to endure this seen world.

LET'S THINK ABOUT IT...

Have you ever felt as though you don't have a purpose for your life?

_____

_____

_____

_____

LET'S PRAY ABOUT IT...

Lord, help me to focus on the unseen rather than the seen, because nothing of this earth can bring meaning to my life like you can. Amen.

TODAY'S DARE

Read through the book of Ecclesiastes with your friends and further this discussion on the meaning of life.

A SHOT OF INSPIRATION

The fact that our heart yearns for something earth can't supply is proof that heaven must be our home.

C. S. Lewis

Join the convo! Inspired by today's chat? Share what you learned! Snap a photo of this book (or the drink you're sipping on), and spark a discussion on social media by answering this question:

Where do you find strength to endure this life?

Be sure to use the hashtag #CoffeeShopDevos!

Out of the Boat and into the Spotlight

Scripture to sip on

Then Peter got down out of the boat, walked on the water and came toward Jesus. But when he saw the wind, he was afraid and, beginning to sink, cried out, "Lord, save me!" Immediately Jesus reached out his hand and caught him. "You of little faith," he said, "why did you doubt?"

Matthew 14:29–31 NIV

LET'S CHAT ABOUT IT...

Public speaking is terrifying for many introverts, including me. Yet, I felt God nudging me. Telling me to take a leap of faith.

I knew I had to do it. But I also knew I couldn't conquer the fear alone; rather, my strength would have to be drawn 100 percent from God. Did I feel ready? No. Did I feel qualified? Not at all. But when God calls us to step out, we can trust He'll catch us if we begin to fall.

When Peter stepped out of the boat and into the waves (see Matt. 14:28–32), can you imagine how crazy he looked? Why would anyone risk walking onto a rough sea, *while it was storming* nonetheless? He could've stayed in the boat. But Peter took a leap of faith—out of the familiar, and into the crashing waves.

"Stepping into the spotlight" seemed almost as crazy as stepping into the rough sea. But I knew God could enable me to walk on the treacherous sea and rise above the fear—only if I kept my eyes focused on Him rather than the seemingly impossible situation below.

As my first speaking event approached, supernatural peace rose within me. Now, any time I speak in front of a group, I get a rush of adrenaline rather than fear.

And as I begin to walk and keep my eyes on Jesus, what I once thought was rough sea transforms into quiet waters. But it's only because I took that first step out of my boat and into the spotlight.

LET'S THINK ABOUT IT...

Is a fear keeping you from experiencing all God has in store?

LET'S PRAY ABOUT IT...

Lord, give me the faith to step out of the safe and comfortable boat so I can rise above the precarious waters that taunt me. Amen.

TODAY'S DARE

Rely on God's strength to do one thing that terrifies you.

A SHOT OF INSPIRATION

Everything you want is on the other side of fear.
Jack Canfield

Join the convo! Inspired by today's chat? Share what you learned! Snap a photo of this book (or the drink you're sipping on), and spark a discussion on social media by answering this question:

What fear(s) has God helped you overcome?

Be sure to use the hashtag #CoffeeShopDevos!

One-Armed Strength

Each time he said, "My grace is all you need. My power works best in weakness." So now I am glad to boast about my weaknesses, so that the power of Christ can work through me.

2 Corinthians 12:9

LET'S CHAT ABOUT IT...

When I was seventeen, my friend and I saw the movie *Soul Surfer* in the theater. This movie features the true story of Bethany Hamilton, a teen surfer who survived a shark attack that left her with only one arm. I remember coming back from the theater completely touched by her story. This teen continued her surfing dream and has since become an inspiration for thousands of people.

Even though a shark didn't bite off my arm, I still have my own weaknesses. We all do. I admire Bethany for not being ashamed of having only one arm, and especially for not letting it hold her back from furthering her surfing dream.

When we expose our weaknesses and give them to God, He can fill us with His perfect strength. Our lack fits perfectly with His immeasurable power. Perhaps that's why He gives us weaknesses—so we can realize we are *nothing* apart from Him, and so we'll rely on Him rather than ourselves.

Since Bethany focused on the arm she *did* have rather than the one she didn't have, she was able to press on and overcome. Throughout the movie, she continued to remind herself that she could do all things through Christ (Philippians 4:13).

If we keep the right attitude and bring our shortcomings to God, then we, too, can persevere, even when it seems impossible.

Who knows, we may even serve as an inspiration for thousands of people, just like Bethany.

LET'S THINK ABOUT IT...

What weakness have you struggled to overcome?

....

....

....

....

LET'S PRAY ABOUT IT...

Lord, your strength is made perfect in my weaknesses, and only you can empower me to accomplish the impossible. Amen.

TODAY'S DARE

Watch the movie *Soul Surfer*.

A SHOT OF INSPIRATION

God will give us the strength to be able to handle things. I mean, you can try to do it on your own, and sometimes you can pull off some stuff, but in the long run, it's much easier with Him by our side.

Bethany Hamilton

Join the convo! Inspired by today's chat? Share what you learned! Snap a photo of this book (or the drink you're sipping on), and spark a discussion on social media by answering this question:

When have you had to rely on God's strength in your weakness?

Be sure to use the hashtag #CoffeeShopDevos!

Weighed Down

Then Jesus said, "Come to me, all of you who are weary and carry heavy burdens, and I will give you rest."

Matthew 11:28

LET'S CHAT ABOUT IT...

When I was in sixth grade, I refused to use my locker. Don't ask why. Maybe I was afraid I'd leave a textbook in there and miss a homework assignment. (Yes, I was a goody-goody.) Whatever the case, I soon discovered the back pain that resulted from carrying around too much weight.

What kind of weight are you carrying in your backpack? I'm not referring to the physical bag, of course. Perhaps you're weighed down from school stress or family issues. Can I remind you that we weren't created to carry all of that weight? If we keep going too long with a heavy backpack, we'll eventually have to see a chiropractor. (Perhaps that's why I have to go to mine every month!) Similarly, carrying the weight of our lives can lead to other complications—such as physical and mental health problems.

Let's not be afraid to use our "locker." Let's allow God to take the weight from us so we can be free to enjoy our lives to the fullest. But rather than putting only some of the weight in the locker and keeping the rest on our backs, we should give it *all* to Him. He can handle it.

The locker was created for that very reason—to keep us from being weighed down. It'd be senseless not to take advantage of it!

LET'S THINK ABOUT IT...

Do you attempt to carry the weight of your life rather than giving it to God?

LET'S PRAY ABOUT IT...

Lord, I don't want to carry around unnecessary burdens. I invite you to take this load so I can enjoy my life even more. Amen.

TODAY'S DARE

When life hands you more "weight," write down this concern on a piece of paper, then slip it into a mason jar. As you do, pretend you're releasing the burden to God so you can carry on. In a year, open the jar and read the papers. Reflect on how God lifted those weights as you gave them to Him.

A SHOT OF INSPIRATION

> Give your burdens to the Lord,
> and he will take care of you.
> He will not permit the godly to slip and fall.
>
> Psalm 55:22

Join the convo! Inspired by today's chat? Share what you learned! Snap a photo of this book (or the drink you're sipping on), and spark a discussion on social media by answering this question:

Have you experienced the "back pain" that results from carrying around excess life burdens?

Be sure to use the hashtag #CoffeeShopDevos!

Spiritually Caffeinated

Scripture to sip on

But you belong to God, my dear children. You have already won a victory over those people, because the Spirit who lives in you is greater than the spirit who lives in the world.

1 John 4:4

LET'S CHAT ABOUT IT...

Without coffee, I don't think I'd have the energy to do many things, such as these: Multi-task. Wake up early. Stay awake for a long drive through the night.

And without the help of the Holy Spirit, there are many things that would be impossible to do on my own, such as these: Face my fears. Take God-prompted risks. Do things that might not make sense in the natural.

Yet the more time I spend with God, the more I become filled with spiritual caffeine. I don't have to rely on myself, my own strength and abilities, to overcome difficult and terrifying situations.

Having too much caffeine might sometimes cause me to do crazy things; likewise, when I'm led by the Holy Spirit rather than my flesh, I can step out and do something God's called me to do—even if it seems crazy. How? By relying on the Spirit rather than myself. And according to this verse, the Spirit who lives in me is greater than *anything* in this world.

So the next time you're faced with a challenge, difficulty, or terrifying situation, spend time with God. Ask the Holy Spirit to empower you to overcome. Then step out in faith, and watch how He helps you win the victory.

And guess what? Even though it can be dangerous to have too much caffeine, we can never get too much of the Holy Spirit!

LET'S THINK ABOUT IT...

Do you rely on the Holy Spirit to help you overcome challenges?

LET'S PRAY ABOUT IT...

Lord, help me to be led by your Holy Spirit so I can do what you've called me to do, even if it's scary. You are greater than anything I face in this world, and through you I find victory. Amen.

TODAY'S DARE

Do at least one thing today that the Holy Spirit prompts you to do. As you step out, remember that you can find victory through Him.

A SHOT OF INSPIRATION

No, despite all these things, overwhelming victory is ours through Christ, who loved us.

Romans 8:37

Join the convo! Inspired by today's chat? Share what you learned! Snap a photo of this book (or the drink you're sipping on), and spark a discussion on social media by answering this question:

When has God helped you overcome a challenge and find victory?

Be sure to use the hashtag #CoffeeShopDevos!

Battle against the Enemy

Scripture to sip on

Put on all of God's armor so that you will be able to stand firm against all strategies of the devil. For we are not fighting against flesh-and-blood enemies, but against evil rulers and authorities of the unseen world, against mighty powers in this dark world, and against evil spirits in the heavenly places.

Ephesians 6:11–12

LET'S CHAT ABOUT IT...

Every good story needs an antagonist, or a villain. This is the person, place, or force that keeps the hero from achieving his ultimate goal. The antagonist throws obstacles along the hero's path in an attempt to make life even more difficult for them.

The reason this works in story structure, I believe, is because it's a model of the spiritual realm. "Good vs. evil" is a reflection of the gospel. Jesus is the hero of the story, and His children are on His side. The enemy is Satan and his demons. Their intention is to destroy us. Satan doesn't want us to be followers of Jesus. He doesn't want us to build the Kingdom, because the bigger the Kingdom gets, the smaller Satan's kingdom becomes.

But we can fight back with the Word. We can fight back by putting on God's armor and standing firm, as this Scripture says.

This battle will continue until Jesus returns—but we don't have to be afraid of the "powers in this dark world." As children of God, we know how this story ends: Jesus will arrive on His white horse, come to our rescue, and ride off into the sunset. So let's continue to fight back until the enemy is defeated.

Then we'll live happily ever after in eternity. :)

LET'S THINK ABOUT IT...

How can you fight back against the enemy's attempts to attack you?

LET'S PRAY ABOUT IT...

Lord, thank you for already defeating the enemy. Help me to fight back against his attacks. Amen.

TODAY'S DARE

Read about the armor of God in Ephesians 6:13–17.

A SHOT OF INSPIRATION

> Stay alert! Watch out for your great enemy, the devil. He prowls around like a roaring lion, looking for someone to devour. Stand firm against him, and be strong in your faith. Remember that your family of believers all over the world is going through the same kind of suffering you are.
>
> 1 Peter 5:8–9

Join the convo! Inspired by today's chat? Share what you learned! Snap a photo of this book (or the drink you're sipping on), and spark a discussion on social media by answering this question:

How can we remain firm in our faith and put on the armor of God?

Be sure to use the hashtag #CoffeeShopDevos!

Unused Treasure

Such things were written in the Scriptures long ago to teach us. And the Scriptures give us hope and encouragement as we wait patiently for God's promises to be fulfilled.

Romans 15:4

LET'S CHAT ABOUT IT...

Wouldn't it be crazy to have gold worth a million dollars, yet not take advantage of it? What if it remained on our nightstand day-by-day, collecting dust?

We might not have gold, but we *do* have God's Word—which is worth far more than gold.

Scripture is alive and powerful. It contains God's messages to His children. It's more than just a book of historical stories, poetry, prophecies, and parables. Sure, it was written thousands of years ago—but it was written for us *today*. Its truth is just as applicable to our lives today as it was to God's children in biblical times.

The Bible contains the greatest treasure. If that's the case, why do we often shrug it off as though it's just another book? Why do we allow it to remain on the bookshelf, collecting dust?

Let's take advantage of the fact that we have access to Scripture. As we study it, the Holy Spirit will give us wisdom—then we'll transform into the image of Christ as we apply its truth.

So dust off your Bible and treat it with the respect it deserves. Let's take hold of the Word to fight against the enemy and grow stronger in Christ.

Then we'll discover for ourselves how valuable the treasure inside truly is.

LET'S THINK ABOUT IT...

Do you treat Scripture with the respect it deserves?

_____

_____

_____

_____

LET'S PRAY ABOUT IT...

Lord, thank you that I have access to your Word. Give me wisdom so I can apply its truths to my life and grow in my walk with You. Amen.

TODAY'S DARE

Download a Bible app on your smartphone. That way, you'll have access to Scripture at your fingertips and can read it at any free moment you may have throughout the day.

A SHOT OF INSPIRATION

> The grass withers and the flowers fade,
> but the word of our God stands forever.
>
> Isaiah 40:8

Join the convo! Inspired by today's chat? Share what you learned! Snap a photo of this book (or the drink you're sipping on), and spark a discussion on social media by answering this question:

Have you experienced the transformation that comes through studying and applying the Word?

Be sure to use the hashtag #CoffeeShopDevos!

Waiting for Harvest

Scripture to sip on

So let's not get tired of doing what is good. At just the right time we will reap a harvest of blessing if we don't give up.

Galatians 6:9

LET'S CHAT ABOUT IT...

The writer's life is not for those who are impatient. It can take months, if not years, to write a book. And if the author doesn't already have a contract, then the writer can *only hope* it will one day see the light of publication.

I've always compared the writer's life to one who harvests crops. We have to dedicate an entire season to planting crops before we see those crops come to fruition.

Have you discovered the struggle that comes as you persevere in faith? It can be frustrating when the harvest doesn't come when we'd hoped. When we spend day after day in prayer over a situation, and yet the answer doesn't come when we thought it would.

When this happens, we have two choices. One: give up. Or two: keep going.

Sounds simple, right? If we give up, then it's guaranteed that the harvest won't come. But if we persevere through faith and patience, we'll eventually bear the harvest of our good work—but only in God's perfect timing.

If you've found yourself weary recently, don't give up. Find the strength you need in the promises of God's Word. He hears your prayers. And if you commit your work to Him, rest assured: Your work, time, and energy will never be used in vain.

Trust me when I say that the season of preparation will be worth the hard work when the book—I mean, the harvest—finally arrives!

LET'S THINK ABOUT IT...

What kind of harvest do you believe God for?

LET'S PRAY ABOUT IT...

Lord, thank you for being in control of the seasons of my life. Help me to be faithful to you, because I know my perseverance will reap a harvest in due time. Amen.

TODAY'S DARE

Keep a journal to record your daily progress as you persevere in faith. Then, when the harvest comes, you'll look back and be reminded of God's faithfulness and perfect timing.

A SHOT OF INSPIRATION

God's job is to unfold our future. Our job is to trust and glorify Him as He does.

Karen Ehman

Join the convo! Inspired by today's chat? Share what you learned! Snap a photo of this book (or the drink you're sipping on), and spark a discussion on social media by answering this question:

When have you had to persevere in faith and trust God for the harvest?

Be sure to use the hashtag #CoffeeShopDevos!

Clear Vision

For you are the fountain of life,
the light by which we see.

Psalm 36:9

LET'S CHAT ABOUT IT...

When I was fifteen, I was prescribed my first pair of glasses. It was amazing how my vision cleared up as soon as I slid them on. Before then, I had no idea how bad my near-sighted vision was! Sure, I knew some things were blurry—that's why I went to the eye doctor to begin with. But I saw details I couldn't see before. Putting on this new pair of glasses brought clarity to my vision, and I had no idea how I'd gone so long without them.

The same happens when we spend time with God and read Scripture. He gives us a new lens. And when we come away from our quiet time, we face circumstances with clarity. We realize that the perspective we once had was blurry and out of focus; but now, the details have been intensified, and we don't have to worry about making a wrong move due to blurred vision.

So when our future is unclear, and when we can't make sense of the circumstances around us, let's enter into God's presence. Then, after we close our eyes in prayer, we'll open them with a fresh vision.

A perfect pair of lenses prescribed by our Maker.

LET'S THINK ABOUT IT...

Do you enter into God's presence and read Scripture when you need a fresh perspective?

LET'S PRAY ABOUT IT...

Lord, *when my vision is blurred, remind me to enter into your presence so I can receive your fresh vision. Thank you for the clarity your perspective brings. Amen.*

TODAY'S DARE

Make it a habit to enter into God's presence every morning, before you do anything else. That way, you'll go throughout your day looking through His lens.

A SHOT OF INSPIRATION

The presence of God will not always fix your problems, but it will clarify your perspective.

Steven Furtick

Join the convo! Inspired by today's chat? Share what you learned! Snap a photo of this book (or the drink you're sipping on), and spark a discussion on social media by answering this question:

How has spending time in God's presence brought clarity to the world around you?

Be sure to use the hashtag #CoffeeShopDevos!

Eternally Fit

Physical training is good, but training for godliness is much better, promising benefits in this life and in the life to come.

1 Timothy 4:8

LET'S CHAT ABOUT IT...

After I quit cheerleading as a teenager, I soon realized how easy it was for me to get out of shape. So I started exercising on my own. But over the years, I've been through phases when I don't commit to working out as much as I should. And when I neglect exercise, I'm miserable.

Yet once I *do* become consistent with my workouts, something amazing happens: I have more energy. I can breathe better. I'm generally happier because of the endorphins released through exercise. And I look forward to my workouts rather than dread them.

It can be tempting to procrastinate doing any physical exercise. But the longer we do, the more sluggish and flabby we become.

Don't we sometimes do the same thing in our walk with Christ? There are times when we're *on fire* for Him. Then there are times when we run out of motivation and make excuses. Eventually we become spiritually sluggish and flabby.

The days I neglect spending time with Him are miserable—yet when I do take time for my regular spiritual exercise routine, something amazing happens:

I have more energy to face the day. I can more fully enjoy life. I have joy. And I look forward to my next my spiritual exercise.

So let's not view our time with God as something we *have* to do; let's instead view it as a privilege. Sure, we can take time for our physical exercise—but this Scripture says it profits little compared to the profit we receive from our spiritual exercise. This is the only kind that will last throughout eternity.

And the only kind that *doesn't* require a gym membership.

LET'S THINK ABOUT IT...

Do you spend time working out spiritually every day?

LET'S PRAY ABOUT IT...

Lord, help me not to neglect my quiet times with you. Thank you for giving me the strength and endurance I need as I exercise spiritually. Amen.

TODAY'S DARE

Keep a spiritual workout log! Make a record of how often you have a quiet time.

A SHOT OF INSPIRATION

> He gives power to the weak
> and strength to the powerless.
> Isaiah 40:29

Join the conva! Inspired by today's chat? Share what you learned! Snap a photo of this book (or the drink you're sipping on), and spark a discussion on social media by answering this question:

If you spend time with God regularly, what kind of difference have you noticed in your mood, behavior, and overall joy?

Be sure to use the hashtag #CoffeeShopDevos!

Becoming Like Babies

Then he said, "I tell you the truth, unless you turn from your sins and become like little children, you will never get into the Kingdom of Heaven."

Matthew 18:3

LET'S CHAT ABOUT IT...

This morning, my cousin and her eleven-month-old, Gabe, came over—and I was reminded again of how needy and dependent toddlers are.

Here are just a few things that happened . . .

Gabe put an earring in his mouth. Started to crawl up the stairs on his own. Knocked over and broke a large floor lamp. Each of these things happened within the split second, it seems, that our focus wasn't on him. If we were to ignore him entirely, there's no telling the kinds of messes he'd get himself into! Yet every time we tried to straighten him out, he cried.

As a toddler, Gabe doesn't understand why he isn't allowed to do those things—but as adults, we know the consequences that could result from swallowing an earring!

Many times, we also insist on doing things our way. We want to make our own decisions and handle our own problems.

But we're only human. Prone to follow our fleshly desires. God knows the kind of trouble we could get into—that's why He wants to keep us from it. Not because He's mean and wants to keep us from having fun, but because He loves us.

In this Scripture, we're told to become like children in order to enter the kingdom of heaven. This means we should be dependent on our Father. Trust Him. Stay humble enough to know we don't have everything figured out. Obey His wisdom, even if it doesn't make sense to our human brains. He knows what's best.

So the next time we're compelled to go off on our own and knock over a floor lamp, let's ask our Father's permission first—because as tempting as it looks, the damage that could result might not be worth the thrill.

LET'S THINK ABOUT IT...

How can you become more like a child in your walk with Christ?

LET'S PRAY ABOUT IT...

Lord, I'm helpless without you. Thank you for guiding me so I'm not led astray and don't get into trouble. Amen.

TODAY'S DARE

Read Matthew 18:1–10.

A SHOT OF INSPIRATION

Lord, I know that our lives don't really belong to us.
We can't control our own lives.

Jeremiah 10:23 NCV

Join the convo! Inspired by today's chat? Share what you learned! Snap a photo of this book (or the drink you're sipping on), and spark a discussion on social media by answering this question:

When has your obedience to God kept you from getting into trouble?

Be sure to use the hashtag #CoffeeShopDevos!

Good Christians

Scripture to sip on

For I can do everything through Christ, who gives me strength.

Philippians 4:13

LET'S CHAT ABOUT IT...

Have you heard someone referred to as a "good Christian"? Even though I'm guilty of using this phrase, there really is no such thing. Each of us was born into sin. Does a "good Christian" mean that person is highly religious, or that they're sinless (which is impossible)?

Thankfully, when we get to heaven, Jesus isn't going to look at our name in the Book of Life and say, "You were a *great* Christian." Because of His death on the cross, when we come to Christ in repentance, we attain mercy and favor. Our Christian walk shouldn't be defined by how "good" or "bad" we are; it's defined by what Jesus did on the cross for us two thousand years ago. He knows our weakness as humans. He knows we're prone to sin. That's why we must strengthen ourselves in His Word. No, this won't make us "good Christians"; however, it *will* help us resist temptation and be led by the Holy Spirit rather than by our flesh.

As a struggling perfectionist, this is a relief. I don't have to strive to be "good." I don't have to count how many times I sin. I don't have to read a certain number of chapters in my Bible in order to stay right in God's eyes. He already views me as redeemed. So rather than feeling condemned, I can repent, receive grace, and ask God for strength in my weakness.

Let's see how often we can rely on Christ every second of every day. *That's* what should define a "good Christian."

LET'S THINK ABOUT IT...

Do you put pressure on yourself to be a "good Christian"?

LET'S PRAY ABOUT IT...

Lord, thank you that I don't have to worry about being good or bad, because I have righteousness in you. Help me to rely on you every second of every day. Amen.

TODAY'S DARE

Feeling weak? Meditate on these Scriptures:

Philippians 4:13
2 Corinthians 12:9
Isaiah 40:31
Psalm 46:1
Ephesians 3:16
Isaiah 40:29

A SHOT OF INSPIRATION

"Is your faith strong?" a Christian man was asked a few hours before his death. "No, but my Jesus is."

Unknown

Join the convo! Inspired by today's chat? Share what you learned! Snap a photo of this book (or the drink you're sipping on), and spark a discussion on social media by answering this question:

Why could it be dangerous to judge ourselves based on how "good" or "bad" we are?

Be sure to use the hashtag #CoffeeShopDevos!

Watered-Down Brew

Like newborn babies, you must crave pure spiritual milk so that you will grow into a full experience of salvation. Cry out for this nourishment, now that you have had a taste of the Lord's kindness.

1 Peter 2:2–3

LET'S CHAT ABOUT IT...

I recently bought a Ninja Coffee Bar®. This coffee maker doesn't just make regular brew, but it also makes concentrated coffee—similar to espresso. This is my favorite feature. I much prefer strong coffee rather than watered-down brew.

There was a time when I was satisfied with regular brew. Yet now that I've had a taste of the strong stuff, I can't return to anything weaker.

Similarly, now that I've tasted how amazing life is since establishing a relationship with Christ, I can't settle for a "watered-down Christianity." I can't simply go to church once a week, say a prayer before meals, and get out my Bible only during Sunday's sermon.

My relationship with Christ gives me supernatural empowerment to face anything. If I returned to a watered-down version of Christianity, then I could expect a watered-down result.

I want to go all in. I want to embrace all God has for me, become who He's created me to be, and experience the depths of His love.

Jesus didn't pay such a huge sacrifice so I could say the prayer of salvation, attend church, and get into heaven. He paid this sacrifice so I could receive the abundant life that comes through knowing Him personally.

No, now that I've tasted how good specialty brew is, the watered-down wannabe coffee just won't do!

LET'S THINK ABOUT IT...

Have you experienced the benefits that come from living life on fire for Christ?

....

....

....

LET'S PRAY ABOUT IT...

Lord, I don't want to settle for anything less than a life on fire for you. Amen.

TODAY'S DARE

Make a list of things you can do to help build your relationship with Christ.

Here are ideas:

- Listen to more Christian/worship music so your mind can be set on things above (see Colossians 3:2).
- Start a new Bible-reading plan.
- Create a "prayer closet," or a private place you can go that'll cut out distractions as you talk with God.

A SHOT OF INSPIRATION

"Look! I stand at the door and knock. If you hear my voice and open the door, I will come in, and we will share a meal together as friends."

Revelation 3:20

Join the convo! Inspired by today's chat? Share what you learned! Snap a photo of this book (or the drink you're sipping on), and spark a discussion on social media by answering this question:

What does it look like to have a relationship with Christ?

Be sure to use the hashtag #CoffeeShopDevos!

Prison of Laziness

Scripture to sip on

Those too lazy to plow in the right season
will have no food at the harvest.

Proverbs 20:4

LET'S CHAT ABOUT IT...

When I was in high school, my sister introduced me to a popular TV show. I was only going to watch the first episode—but once it ended, I had to find out what happened next. Pretty soon, we watched every season.

I wonder how many hours I could've gained if I hadn't devoted so much time to that show.

It's not wrong to take a break and watch TV with your friends and family occasionally. In fact, I enjoyed watching that show with my sister. But we need to be careful that these occasional *breaks* don't transform into a lazy lifestyle.

You might be thinking, *I have time on my hands to be lazy. I'm a teenager.* There's so much you can do now to invest in your future! The habits you cultivate will likely carry on throughout your lifetime.

Lazy tendencies can carry into our Christian walk as well. We might make excuses to avoid having quiet time or going to church. We might not *feel* like fighting against the attacks of the enemy or resisting temptation. We might not carry out our work in God's kingdom or embrace new challenges.

Laziness creates a prison around us by keeping us from becoming stronger physically, mentally, and spiritually. When we reach eternity, we're not going to say, "If only I'd been more lazy!" No, we're going to say, "I wish I'd recognized the value of the short time I had on earth."

Let's allow the Spirit to guide our actions and replace our lazy habits with more productive habits. How?

It all starts with taking that first step from behind the prison bars of laziness, and into the light of His freedom.

LET'S THINK ABOUT IT...

What lazy habits should you cut out of your lifestyle?

LET'S PRAY ABOUT IT...

Lord, help me not to be lazy and instead have self-control. Show me how to wisely spend the short time I have on this earth. Amen.

TODAY'S DARE

Make a list of productive ways to spend your time.
Here are some ideas:

- Read a book that can further your walk with Christ. I recommend *This Changes Everything* by Jaquelle Crowe.
- Practice cultivating your gifts and talents.
- Exercise.

A SHOT OF INSPIRATION

A little extra sleep, a little more slumber,
a little folding of the hands to rest—
then poverty will pounce on you like a bandit;
scarcity will attack you like an armed robber.

Proverbs 24:33–34

Join the convo! Inspired by today's chat? Share what you learned! Snap a photo of this book (or the drink you're sipping on), and spark a discussion on social media by answering this question:

How can laziness weaken the body of Christ?

Be sure to use the hashtag #CoffeeShopDevos!

Born to Be Bold

Scripture to sip on

The wicked run away when no one is chasing them,
but the godly are as bold as lions.

Proverbs 28:1

LET'S CHAT ABOUT IT...

I wasn't competitive enough when I played basketball in elementary school. The coach would constantly tell us to *be aggressive*, but it didn't come naturally to me.

I have a tendency to carry the same habit with me today; however, as Christians, we aren't called to play it safe. Even those who are introverts, like me, will need to be aggressive.

We need to fight back against the powers of darkness. Stand up for our faith in Christ, even if we're persecuted. Make a bold stand against sin. Witness to unbelievers. Pray for those in need. Step out in faith and obedience.

We can find our boldness in Christ. He will help us become as "bold as lions," as this verse says.

In basketball, if you play it safe and comfortable, then guess what? The other team will steal the ball, make all the shots, and win the game. This kind of behavior isn't accepted in God's kingdom.

Jesus is coming soon. The enemy and his army are trying to keep people from accepting Jesus as their Savior. Satan wants to weaken our faith. If we choose to remain comfortable, we'll easily fall for his game plan without fighting back.

Let's take a stand. We have too much to lose if we don't rise up in boldness and fight back. And yes, I've learned it *is* possible to be bold in your walk with Christ even if you're reserved.

But I still haven't learned how to be aggressive in basketball.

LET'S THINK ABOUT IT...

Do you carry reserved habits into your walk with Christ?

....

....

....

....

LET'S PRAY ABOUT IT...

Lord, thank you for giving me a supernatural boldness. Help me to rise up to challenges that stretch my faith, even if it's uncomfortable, so your gospel is carried throughout this world. Amen.

TODAY'S DARE

Read Matthew 14:28–31. Where did Peter find the courage to walk on water? What happened when he took his eyes off of Christ?

A SHOT OF INSPIRATION

This is my command—be strong and courageous! Do not be afraid or discouraged. For the Lord your God is with you wherever you go.

Joshua 1:9

Join the conva! Inspired by today's chat? Share what you learned! Snap a photo of this book (or the drink you're sipping on), and spark a discussion on social media by answering this question:

How can it be dangerous for Christians to remain in their comfort zones?

Be sure to use the hashtag #CoffeeShopDevos!

Daily Vitamins

Scripture to sip on

The name of the Lord is a strong fortress;
the godly run to him and are safe.

Proverbs 18:10

LET'S CHAT ABOUT IT...

There are several vitamin supplements I take daily: Vitamin D, which protects my bones and teeth. Vitamin B, which helps me stay energized. Biotin, which helps me maintain healthy skin, hair, and nails. Fish oil, which keeps my brain and lungs healthy.

When my body absorbs these vitamins—whether through food or supplements—then I'm well nourished; without them, I may become weak and feeble, depressed and discouraged. I'm more prone to disease and sickness.

These supplements provide my body with what it needs to carry on. Similarly, in God's name—and in His Word—we find the nourishment to persevere throughout our lives. His various names, which are given to us in the Bible, remind us of who He is and all He provides . . .

In Jehovah-Rapha, we find healing. In Jehovah-Jireh, we find provision. In Jehovah-Rohi, we find a shepherd. In Jehovah-Shammah, we find a friend. In Jehovah-Shalom, we find peace. In Jehovah-Tsidkenu, we have righteousness. In Jehovah-M'Kaddesh, we find our sanctifier. In Jehovah-Nissi, we have a banner of victory.

God is our Father. Jesus is our Savior. The Holy Spirit is our helper. The Bible is our guide. In Him, we are delivered. Nourished. Sustained. Saved. Set free.

Therefore, why should we worry about lacking? As long as we cling to Him, we are well nourished and can face whatever comes our way.

Vitamins may lengthen our earthly lives—but only Jesus has the power to grant us eternal life with Him.

LET'S THINK ABOUT IT...

Are you lacking any of these spiritual vitamins?

LET'S PRAY ABOUT IT...

Lord, thank you that in your name—as well as your Word—I find everything I need to sustain me throughout this life. Amen.

TODAY'S DARE

Read the following Bible passages for further study on these various names of God:

Jehovah-Rapha: Exodus 15:26

Jehovah-Jireh: Genesis 22:14

Jehovah-Rohi: Psalm 23:1

Jehovah-Shammah:
Ezekiel 48:35

Jehovah-Shalom: Judges 6:24

Jehovah-Tsidkenu:
Jeremiah 33:16

Jehovah-M'Kaddesh:
Leviticus 20:8

Jehovah-Nissi: Exodus 17:15

A SHOT OF INSPIRATION

Lord, there is no one like you!
For you are great, and your name is full of power.
Jeremiah 10:6

Join the convo! Inspired by today's chat? Share what you learned! Snap a photo of this book (or the drink you're sipping on), and spark a discussion on social media by answering this question:

What do God's various names teach you about His character?

Be sure to use the hashtag #CoffeeShopDevos!

What's the Password?

Scripture to sip on

The Spirit and the bride say, "Come." Let anyone who hears this say, "Come." Let anyone who is thirsty come. Let anyone who desires drink freely from the water of life.

Revelation 22:17

LET'S CHAT ABOUT IT...

Even though I love working from coffee shops every now and then, I'd prefer to work from home instead. It often becomes frustrating to connect to the internet—whether it's because the Wi-Fi is slow, or because the password is different than it was the previous time I connected to it. (It's complicated to change the automatic password!)

But if you don't have the right password, then you're not welcome to access the internet.

I wonder how many Christians view church the same way. I wonder how many people have avoided attending because they felt like they didn't have the right password, as if church were a Christians-only club.

When Jesus was on earth, He didn't turn away *anyone*. Jesus came for all of us sinners, despite our history. He came to wash that away through His blood and give us a clean slate. The only passcode we'll need is His Spirit living inside of us when we enter eternity.

Actually, our access to Jesus isn't available only at church; He's with us anywhere. (Unlike Wi-Fi!) All He searches for is a heart that seeks Him.

Searching for a new start? Longing to know the One who gave His life so you could be welcomed into the kingdom? Come as you are: Thirsty. Weak. Desperate. Dirty. Because no matter how you might look to begin with, one thing's for sure: *No one* remains the same once they meet Jesus.

And His name is the only password that offers eternal salvation.

LET'S THINK ABOUT IT...

Have you ever had the misconception that you have to "clean up" in order to be accepted by Jesus (or the church)?

LET'S PRAY ABOUT IT...

Lord, thank you for welcoming me as I am. I believe you sent your Son to die for my sins so I can have a new life. I want to live my life for you. Amen.

TODAY'S DARE

Read Romans 5:6. Have you accepted Christ as your Savior? If not, confess you are a sinner and that you believe Jesus died for your sins, and receive the new life He offers you! Then, consider finding a Christian church to get plugged into.

A SHOT OF INSPIRATION

If you openly declare that Jesus is Lord and believe in your heart that God raised him from the dead, you will be saved.

Romans 10:9

Join the convo! Inspired by today's chat? Share what you learned! Snap a photo of this book (or the drink you're sipping on), and spark a discussion on social media by answering this question:

How has your life changed since knowing Jesus?

Be sure to use the hashtag #CoffeeShopDevos!

Tessa Emily Hall writes inspirational yet authentic books for teens to show others they're not alone—and because she remembers the teen life like it was yesterday (or a few years ago). In addition to being a frequent contributor to both online and print publications, including *Devozine*, MoreToBe.com, and *Guide* magazine, she published her first novel while still in her teens. She's the founder and editor-in-chief of PursueMagazine.net and enjoys mentoring other young writers. Connect with her online through social media (@tessaemilyhall) and her website at www.tessaemilyhall.com.

Made in the USA
Monee, IL
14 December 2020